The
Core Knowledge™
Series

Resource Books for Children
from Year 1 to Year 6

PRAISE FOR THE CORE KNOWLEDGE UK SERIES

'The Core Knowledge Sequence puts knowledge back into primary education. Rich in content, challenging and with clear progression and continuity, it offers an excellent framework to ensure that pupils leave primary school with solid foundations for future learning.'

– Peter Lawson, Head of Primary, Grindon Hall Christian School

'Our recent Core Knowledge lessons on the Arctic have provided our children with a wealth of understanding. The lessons give children the facts, then we are free to create an enjoyable and engaging learning experience. Core Knowledge fuels our pupils' desire to learn more about the world around them.'

– Emma Greaves, Reception Teacher, West London Free School Primary

'It is vital that children receive a solid body of knowledge when they are at primary school because it allows them to expand their comprehension and access a wider field of learning. The Core Knowledge approach does just that. I cannot recommend it enough.'

– Matthew Laban, Headteacher, Kingfisher Hall Primary Academy, London

'Creativity, the arts and design are crucial to the environment and life of every citizen. They should occupy a central place in the curriculum at both primary and secondary levels. The new series published by Civitas, giving examples of how the arts and creativity can play a part in the education of every child, is a real contribution to the teaching of these subjects in all our schools.'

– Sir Nicholas Serota, Director of Tate

'A strong foundation of knowledge gained in the earliest years of education is such an important asset for children, sparking their imagination and providing the cornerstone for their future learning. I welcome the aim of the Core Knowledge books to do just that and I am sure that they will be valued by many parents wishing to help their children to do well at school.'

– Munira Mirza, Deputy Mayor for Education and Culture of London

What Your Year 2 Child Needs to Know

PREPARING YOUR CHILD
FOR A LIFETIME OF LEARNING

Edited by E. D. HIRSCH, JR.

General Editor for the Civitas UK edition ROBERT WHELAN
Deputy Editor TANYA LUBICZ-NAWROCKA
Original illustrations for this edition by MARK BEECH

Published by

Civitas
55 Tufton Street
London SW1P 3QL

First edition published in the USA in 1991, revised 1997, as *What Your First Grader Needs to Know*

UK edition published August 2012

Independence: Civitas: Institute for the Study of Civil Society is a registered educational charity (No. 1085494) and a company limited by guarantee (No. 04023541). Civitas is financed from a variety of private sources to avoid over-reliance on any single or small group of donors.

ISBN: 978-1-906837-24-2

Book design and layout by Luke Jefford (www.lukejefford.com)

Printed in Great Britain by Berforts Group Ltd, Stevenage, SG1 2BH

Editor-in-Chief of the Core Knowledge Series: E. D. Hirsch, Jr.

Text Editor: John Holdren

Project Manager and Art Editor: Tricia Emlet

Writers: Curriculum Concepts, Inc. (Mathematics); Diane Darst (Visual Arts); John Holdren (Language and Literature, History and Geography, Music, Mathematics, Science); Susan Tyler Hitchcock (Science); Mary Beth Klee (History and Geography); Janet Smith (Music); Linda Williams (Reading, Writing and Your First Grader)

Artists and Photgraphers: Catherine Bricket, Leslie Evans, Jonathan Fuqua, Julie Grant, Steve Henry, Hannah Holdren, Philip Jones, Bob Kirchman, Gail Mcintosh, Nic Siler

Art and Photo Research, Art and Text Permissions: Martha Clay Sullivan, Jeanne Nicholson Siler

Research Assistant: Deborah Hyland

Acknowledgements: US edition

This series has depended on the help, advice, and encouragement of two thousand people. Some of those singled out here already know the depth of our gratitude; others may be surprised to find themselves thanked publicly for help they gave quietly and freely for the sake of the enterprise alone. To helpers named and unnamed we are deeply grateful.

Advisers on Multiculturalism: Minerva Allen, Barbara Carey, Frank de Varona, Mick Fedullo, Dorothy Fields, Elizabeth Fox-Genovese, Marcia Galli, Dan Garner, Henry Louis Gates, Cheryl Kulas, Joseph C. Miller, Gerry Raining Bird, Connie Rocha, Dorothy Small, Sharon Stewart-Peregoy, Sterling Stuckey, Marlene Walking Bear, Lucille Watahomigie, Ramona Wilson

Advisers on Elementary Education: Joseph Adelson, Isobel Beck, Paul Bell, Carl Bereiter, David Bjorklund, Constance Jones, Elizabeth LaFuze, J. P. Lutz, Sandra Scarr, Nancy Stein, Phyllis Wilkin

Advisers on Technical Subject Matter: Marilyn Jager Adams, Diane Alavi, Richard Anderson, Judith Birsh, Cheryl Cannard, Paul Gagnon, David Geary, Andrew Gleason, Blair Jones, Connie Juel, Eric Karell, Joseph Kerr, Mary Beth Klee, Michael Lynch, Joseph C. Miller, Jean Osborne, Margaret Redd, Nancy Royal, Mark Rush, Janet Smith, Ralph Smith, Nancy Strother, Nancy Summers, James Trefil, Nancy Wayne, Linda Williams, Lois Williams

Conferees, March 1990: Nola Bacci, Joan Baratz-Snowden, Thomasyne Beverley, Thomas Blackton, Angela Burkhalter, Monty Caldwell, Thomas M. Carroll, Laura Chapman,

Carol Anne Collins, Lou Corsaro, Henry Cotton, Anne Coughlin, Arletta Dimberg, Debra P. Douglas, Patricia Edwards, Janet Elenbogen, Mick Fedullo, Michele Fomalont, Mamon Gibson, Jean Haines, Barbara Hayes, Stephen Herzog, Helen Kelley, Brenda King, John King, Elizabeth LaFuze, Diana Lam, Nancy Lambert, Doris Langaster, Richard LaPointe, Lloyd Leverton, Madeline Long, Allen Luster, Joseph McGeehan, Janet McLin, Gloria McPhee, Marcia Mallard, William J. Maloney, Judith Matz, John Morabito, Robert Morrill, Roberta Morse, Karen Nathan, Dawn Nichols, Valeta Paige, Mary Perrin, Joseph Piazza, Jeanne Price, Marilyn Rauth, Judith Raybern, Mary Reese, Richard Rice, Wallace Saval, John Saxon, Jan Schwab, Ted Sharp, Diana Smith, Richard Smith, Trevanian Smith, Carol Stevens, Nancy Summers, Michael Terry, Robert Todd, Elois Veltman, Sharon Walker, Mary Ann Ward, Penny Williams, Charles Whiten, Clarke Worthington, Jane York

Schools: Special thanks to Three Oaks Elementary for piloting the original Core Knowledge Sequence in 1990. And thanks to the schools that have offered their advice and suggestions for improving the Core Knowledge Sequence, including (in alphabetical order): Academy Charter School (CO); Coleman Elementary (TX); Coral Reef Elementary (FL); Coronado Village Elementary (TX); Crooksville Elementary (OH); Crossroads Academy (NH); Gesher Jewish Day School (VA); Hawthorne Elementary (TX); Highland Heights Elementary (IN); Joella Good Elementary (FL); Mohegan School-CS 67 (NY); The Morse School (MA); Nichols Hills Elementary (OK); Ridge View Elementary (WA); R. N. Harris Elementary (NC); Southside Elementary (FL); Three Oaks Elementary (FL); Washington Core Knowledge School (CO). And to the many other schools teaching Core Knowledge – too many to name here, and some of whom we have yet to discover – our heartfelt thanks for 'sharing the knowledge'!

Benefactors: The Brown Foundation, The Challenge Foundation, Mrs. E. D. Hirsch, Sr., The Walton Family Foundation.

Our grateful acknowledgment to these persons does not imply that we have taken their (sometimes conflicting) advice in every case, or that each of them endorses all aspects of this project. Responsibility for final decisions must rest with the editors alone. Suggestions for improvements are very welcome, and we wish to thank in advance those who send advice for revising and improving this series.

Acknowledgements: UK edition

General Editor of the UK edition: Robert Whelan
Deputy Editor of the UK edition: Tanya Lubicz-Nawrocka
Contributing Editor and editor of the Mathematics chapter for the UK edition: Nick Cowen

Editor and author of the Visual Arts chapter for the UK edition: Jo Saxton
Author of British and European Geography and British History: Andrew Phemister
Editor of the Music chapter for the UK edition: Nigel Williams
Design and typesetting of the UK edition: Luke Jefford
Original illustrations for the UK edition: Mark Beech
Maps and owl illustrations for the UK edition: Mark Otton

Compiling the UK edition of a book that has already become an established classic in the USA has been both a privilege and a challenge. Our first thanks must go to E.D. Hirsch, Jr., Linda Bevilacqua and the team at the Core Knowledge Foundation for sharing with us the fruits of their labours over so many years. We fully share their view that all children deserve access to a first-class education, and we hope that the Civitas edition of the Core Knowledge texts will do as much for children in the UK as the US edition has done for thousands of children in America and elsewhere.

Many people have helped us. We are especially grateful for the assistance given to the project by Jo Saxton in Visual Arts; Alex Standish in Geography; Andrew Phemister in British and European History and Geography; Sean Lang, Margaret Lenton and Chris Gray in History; Nigel Williams and Chris Cull in Music; Peter Clarke in Mathematics; and Matthew Robinson in Language and Literature. Marilyn Brocklehurst of the Norfolk Children's Book Centre shared her passion for children's books and helped us to find titles for the recommended resources.

Thanks are due to all those who have provided us with material. We are grateful to Gail McIntosh and Steve Henry for permission to reproduce their original illustrations from the US edition; to Paul Collicutt for adding the dimension of colour to illustrations that were originally black and white; to Desmond Shawe-Taylor, Surveyor of the Queen's Pictures; to the David Hockney Trust for 'The Road To York Through Sledmere'; to Mike Townesend for the classic illustrations from *Pinocchio* by his grandfather Charles Folkard; to Nick Butterworth for the illustration to 'Pussycat, Pussycat'; and to Peter Firmin, Dan Postgate and all at The Dragons' Friendly Society for Oliver Postgate's text and Peter Firmin's illustrations from 'King of the Nogs'.

Thanks to our colleagues past and present at Civitas, especially Catherine Green and Janet Russell for help with the text, Annaliese Briggs for help with the UK Sequence, Aoife O'Donnell for her adaptations of fairy stories from original sources, Nigel Williams for work on Science, Emily Clarke for Music and David Merlin-Jones for History. Special thanks are due to Anastasia de Waal, Head of Family and Education at Civitas, for her help and guidance.

A Note to Teachers

Throughout the book, we have addressed the suggested activities and explanations to 'parents', since you as teachers know your students and will have ideas about how to use the content of this book in relation to the lessons and activities you plan. To discuss using Core Knowledge UK materials in your school, please contact Civitas at 55 Tufton Street, London SW1P 3QL, 020 7799 6677.

Email: coreknowledge@civitas.org.uk

Website: www.coreknowledge.org.uk

About the Editor

E.D. Hirsch, Jr. is a professor at the University of Virginia and the author of *The Schools We Need* and the bestselling *Cultural Literacy* and *The Dictionary of Cultural Literacy*. He and his wife, Polly, live in Charlottesville, Virginia, where they raised their three children.

E. D. Hirsch, Jr. receives no renumeration for editing the series nor any other renumeration from the Core Knowledge Foundation.

Contents

Language and Literature

History and Geography

Visual Arts

Music

Mathematics

Science

Foreword to the UK Edition of the Core Knowledge Series

This is the second in a series of books for parents who want to help their children do well at school. It describes what every child should aim to have learnt by the end of the school year. It is not a description of everything that could be known but rather a guide to the knowledge that children will need to advance to the next stage of their education. Nor is it primarily a textbook, although it could be used as such – along with other teaching resources – if schools wish.

The Core Knowledge series gives parents the tools to judge how effectively their children are being taught. And it provides teachers with clear aims that can be shared with parents, thereby enlisting them in the common cause of getting the best from every child.

Why publish a British version of a book originally designed for American children? For the last 50 years in both Britain and America there has been no consensus about how and what children should be taught. Sometimes knowledge was dismissed as mere 'rote learning', which was contrasted unfavourably with 'critical thinking skills'. Others argued that education should be 'child centred' not 'subject centred'. Professor Hirsch, who inspired the Core Knowledge series, was among the first to see that the retreat from knowledge was misguided. Above all, he showed that to compare 'knowledge' with 'thinking skills' was to make a false contrast. They are not mutually exclusive alternatives. Thinking skills can be 'knowledge-rich' or 'knowledge-lite'. The purpose of a good education is to teach children how to think clearly – to see through dubious reasoning, to avoid being conned, to learn how to question their own assumptions, to discover how to be objective or to argue a case with clarity. Knowledge does not get in the way of reasoning: it's what we reason with.

The Core Knowledge approach has six main strengths.

- It helps parents to bring out the best in their children. It provides a guide to what young people should be learning and helps parents decide on the school best suited to their child.

- It helps teachers. By providing clear expectations that are shared with parents, teachers are better able to benefit every child. Schools are always at their best when parents and teachers work together.

- It helps children to learn on their own initiative. The books are written in language suitable for each year group, so that children can read alone or with their parents.

- It provides more equal opportunities for everyone. Some children do not receive effective support at home, perhaps because some of us did not ourselves get the best education. A good school can do much to make up for lost ground and the Core Knowledge curriculum is designed for this very task. The books describe what every child can learn if given the chance. What's more, many parents find that they learn as much as their children!

- It encourages social cohesion. Britain today has more cultures, ethnic groups and religions than 50 years ago. If we all share in a common stock of knowledge, social solidarity based on mutual respect for our legitimate differences is more likely.

- It strengthens democracy. A free and democratic society depends on the mass of people being well-informed. We often say that modern societies are 'knowledge based'. It's true. People who do not share in the knowledge that is regularly used by television news programmes or in our newspapers are at risk of being misled.

We are keen to work with teachers who share our ideals and who hope to play a leading part in developing this new curriculum in Britain. In co-operation with teachers, we will be evolving model lesson plans and resource guides, and if any teachers would like their school to be one of the pioneers, please contact Civitas at coreknowledge@civitas.org.uk

David G. Green
Director of Civitas

Introduction to the UK Edition of the Core Knowledge Curriculum for Year 2

The concerns which led Professor Hirsch and others to set up the Core Knowledge Foundation in the USA in 1986 are shared by many in Britain. Civitas has acquired direct experience of the problem through its network of supplementary schools. Beginning with a group of Bengali children in the East End of London in 2005, Civitas now runs 20 supplementary schools for over 600 children in different parts of the country. The children attend once a week, either on Saturdays or after school, for help with English and maths. The children are, for the most part, attending full-time schools in areas with higher-than-average indicators of social deprivation, where academic outcomes are not the best in the country. Some children join supplementary schools at the age of seven, eight or even older, unable to read properly and unable to handle simple addition and subtraction. Our approach in the Civitas schools has been to employ dedicated teachers with high expectations and a commitment to providing solid learning foundations. Children are assessed annually and it has become quite usual to see them make two or three years of progress in their reading and maths ages over the course of one calendar year.

The concepts that Professor Hirsch mentions in his General Introduction such as 'critical thinking' and 'learning to learn' have been just as prevalent in the UK's schools, where the curriculum has become less knowledge-based and more focused on attaining 'skills', as if the two things can be separated. The acquisition of skills requires knowledge, and a knowledge-poor curriculum is one that condemns pupils – especially children from less advantaged backgrounds – to remain outside the mainstream of attainment and fulfilment. The Core Knowledge Foundation believes that all children should be able to unlock the library of the world's literature; to comprehend the world around them; to know where they stand (literally) on the globe; and to realise the heritage that the history of their country has bestowed on them.

Making a reality of this ideal has been the outstanding achievement of the Core Knowledge Foundation in the hundreds of schools across the USA where its curriculum is being taught, and it is why we so admire the work of Professor Hirsch and his colleagues at the Core Knowledge Foundation.

As Professor Hirsch explains in his General Introduction, the project operates within the overarching framework of the Core Knowledge Sequence, produced by dozens of educators over a gestational period of several years. To bring this sequence into the classroom or the home, the Sequence is fleshed out by a book for each year group. We at Civitas were honoured and delighted to be entrusted by the Core Knowledge Foundation with the task of adapting the books for teachers, parents and pupils in the UK. This has entailed some changes to reflect differences between our cultures, for example using British musical nomenclature in the Music chapter and changing imperial weights and measures to metric in Science, but for the most part the US text has been left intact – because knowledge is universal! We have revised recommended resource lists to include books and other materials readily available in the UK.

Since the publication of the Year 1 volume, we have put the Core Knowledge Sequence UK online at http://www.coreknowledge.org.uk/sequence.php. This will enable parents and teachers to understand how the grammar of each subject is unrolled over six years of primary school education. The UK Sequence follows the US Sequence very closely, with a few obvious changes. Maths has been slightly revised to reflect the demands of the National Curriculum; the works of art illustrated in the Visual Arts chapters can almost all be found in British museums and galleries; and British history and geography replace American. (American history and geography will be covered under World History and Geography.)

We share the view of the Core Knowledge Foundation that knowledge is best conveyed through subjects, and so we have followed their division of each book into chapters covering Language and Literature, History and Geography, Visual Arts, Music, Mathematics and Science. We will be producing volumes for each year group up to Year 6, and these will tie in with the UK version of the Core Knowledge Sequence.

In the USA children start full-time education in most states at Kindergarten when they are five rising six, whereas in the UK children of that age would be starting in Year 1. The first book in the Core Knowledge UK series, *What Your Year 1 Child Needs to Know*, was therefore based on the US volume *What Your Kindergartner Needs to Know*. This book, *What Your Year 2 Child Needs to Know*, is based on the US title *What Your First Grader Needs to Know*. There will be further year-books to cover the primary school age-range up to and including Year 6.

Robert Whelan
General Editor, Civitas Core Knowledge Project

General Introduction to the Core Knowledge Series

I. WHAT IS YOUR CHILD LEARNING IN SCHOOL?

A parent of identical twins sent me a letter in which she expressed concern that her children, who are in the same grade in the same school, are being taught completely different things. How can this be? Because they are in different classrooms; because the teachers in these classrooms have only the vaguest guidelines to follow; in short, because the school, like many in the United States, lacks a definite, specific curriculum.

Many parents would be surprised if they were to examine the curriculum of their child's elementary school. Ask to see your school's curriculum. Does it spell out, in clear and concrete terms, a core of specific content and skills all children at a particular grade level are expected to learn by the end of the school year?

Many curricula speak in general terms of vaguely defined skills, processes and attitudes, often in an abstract, pseudo-technical language that calls, for example, for children to 'analyse patterns and data', or 'investigate the structure and dynamics of living systems', or 'work cooperatively in a group'. Such vagueness evades the central question: what is your child learning in school? It places unreasonable demands upon teachers, and often results in years of schooling marred by repetitions and gaps. Yet another unit on dinosaurs or 'pioneer days'. *Charlotte's Web* for the third time. 'You've never heard of the Bill of Rights?' 'You've never been taught how to add two fractions with unlike denominators?'

When identical twins in two classrooms of the same school have few academic experiences in common, that is cause for concern. When teachers in that school do not know what children in other classrooms are learning on the same grade level, much less in earlier and later grades, they cannot reliably predict that children will come prepared with a shared core of knowledge and skills. For an elementary school to be successful, teachers need a common vision of what they want their students to know and be able to do. They need to have *clear, specific learning goals*, as well as the sense of mutual accountability that comes from shared commitment to helping all children achieve those goals. Lacking both specific goals and mutual accountability, too many schools exist in a state of curricular incoherence, one result of which is that they fall far short of developing the full potential of our children. To address this problem, I started the non-profit Core Knowledge Foundation in 1986. This book and its companion volumes in the Core

Knowledge Series are designed to give parents, teachers – and through them, children – a guide to clearly defined learning goals in the form of a carefully sequenced body of knowledge, based upon the specific content guidelines developed by the Core Knowledge Foundation (see below, 'The Consensus Behind the Core Knowledge Sequence').

Core Knowledge is an attempt to define, in a coherent and sequential way, a body of widely used knowledge taken for granted by competent writers and speakers in the United States. Because this knowledge is taken for granted rather than being explained when it is used, it forms a necessary foundation for the higher-order reading, writing and thinking skills that children need for academic and vocational success. The universal attainment of such knowledge should be a central aim of curricula in our elementary schools, just as it is currently the aim in all world-class educational systems.

For reasons explained in the next section, making sure that all young children in the United States possess a core of shared knowledge is a necessary step in developing a first-rate educational system.

II. WHY CORE KNOWLEDGE IS NEEDED

Learning builds on learning: children (and adults) gain new knowledge only by building on what they already know. It is essential to begin building solid foundations of knowledge in the early grades when children are most receptive because, for the vast majority of children, academic deficiencies from the first six grades can *permanently* impair the success of later learning. Poor performance of American students in middle and high school can be traced to shortcomings inherited from elementary schools that have not imparted to children the knowledge and skills they need for further learning.

All of the highest-achieving and most egalitarian elementary school systems in the world (such as those in Sweden, France and Japan) teach their children a specific core of knowledge in each of the first six grades, thus enabling all children to enter each new grade with a secure foundation for further learning. It is time American schools did so as well, for the following reasons:

(1) Commonly shared knowledge makes schooling more effective.

We know that the one-on-one tutorial is the most effective form of schooling, in part because a parent or teacher can provide tailor-made instruction for the individual child. But in a non-tutorial situation – in, for example, a typical classroom with twenty-five or more students – the instructor cannot effectively impart new knowledge to all the students unless each one shares the background knowledge that the lesson is being built upon.

Consider this scenario: in third grade, Ms. Franklin is about to begin a unit on early explorers – Columbus, Magellan and others. In her class she has some students who were in Mr. Washington's second-grade class last year and some students who were in Ms. Johnson's second-grade class. She also has a few students who have moved in from other towns. As Ms. Franklin begins the unit on explorers, she asks the children to look at a globe and use their fingers to trace a route across the Atlantic Ocean from Europe to North America. The students who had Mr. Washington look blankly at her: they didn't learn that last year. The students who had Ms. Johnson, however, eagerly point to the proper places on the globe, while two of the students who came from other towns pipe up and say, 'Columbus and Magellan again? We did that last year.'

When all the students in a class *do* share the relevant background knowledge, a classroom can begin to approach the effectiveness of a tutorial. Even when some children in a class do not have elements of the knowledge they were supposed to acquire in previous grades, the existence of a specifically defined core makes it possible for the teacher or parent to identify and fill the gaps, thus giving all students a chance to fulfil their potential in later grades.

(2) Commonly shared knowledge makes schooling more fair and democratic.

When all the children who enter a grade can be assumed to share some of the same building blocks of knowledge, and when the teacher knows exactly what those building blocks are, then all the students are empowered to learn. In our current system, children from disadvantaged backgrounds too often suffer from unmerited low expectations that translate into watered-down curricula. But if we specify the core of knowledge that all children should share, then we can guarantee equal access to that knowledge and compensate for the academic advantages some students are offered at home. In a Core Knowledge school, *all* children enjoy the benefits of important, challenging knowledge that will provide the foundation for successful later learning.

(3) Commonly shared knowledge helps create cooperation and solidarity in our schools and nation.

Diversity is a hallmark and strength of our nation. American classrooms are usually made up of students from a variety of cultural backgrounds, and those different cultures should be honoured by all students. At the same time, education should create a school-based culture that is common and welcoming to all because it includes knowledge of many cultures and gives all students, no matter what their background, a common foundation for understanding our cultural diversity.

In the next section, I will describe the steps taken by the Core Knowledge Foundation to develop a model of the commonly shared knowledge our children need (which forms the basis for this series of books).

III. THE CONSENSUS BEHIND THE CORE KNOWLEDGE SEQUENCE

The content in this and other volumes in the Core Knowledge Series is based on a document called the *Core Knowledge Sequence*, a grade-by-grade sequence of specific content guidelines in history, geography, mathematics, science, language arts and fine arts. The *Sequence* is not meant to outline the whole of the school curriculum; rather, it offers specific guidelines to knowledge that can reasonably be expected to make up about *half* of any school's curriculum, thus leaving ample room for local requirements and emphases. Teaching a common core of knowledge, such as that articulated in the Core Knowledge Sequence, is compatible with a variety of instructional methods and additional subject matters.

The *Core Knowledge Sequence* is the result of a long process of research and consensus building undertaken by the Core Knowledge Foundation. Here is how we achieved the consensus behind the *Core Knowledge Sequence*.

First we analysed the many reports issued by state departments of education and by professional organisations – such as the National Council of Teachers of Mathematics and the American Association for the Advancement of Science – that recommend general outcomes for elementary and secondary education. We also tabulated the knowledge and skills through grade six specified in the successful educational systems of several other countries, including France, Japan, Sweden and West Germany.

In addition, we formed an advisory board on multiculturalism that proposed a specific knowledge of diverse cultural traditions that American children should all share as part of their school-based common culture. We sent the resulting materials to three independent groups of teachers, scholars and scientists around the country, asking them to create a master list of the knowledge children should have by the end of grade six. About 150 teachers (including college professors, scientists and administrators) were involved in this initial step.

These items were amalgamated into a master plan, and further groups of teachers and specialists were asked to agree on a grade-by-grade sequence of the items. That sequence was then sent to some one hundred educators and specialists who participated in a national conference that was called to hammer out a working agreement on an appropriate core of knowledge for the first six grades.

This important meeting took place in March 1990. The conferees were elementary school teachers, curriculum specialists, scientists, science writers, officers of national organisations, representatives of ethnic groups, district superintendents and school principals from across the country. A total of twenty-four working groups decided on revisions in the *Core Knowledge Sequence*. The resulting provisional *Sequence* was further fine-tuned during a year of implementation at a pioneering school, Three Oaks Elementary in Lee County, Florida.

In only a few years, many more schools – urban and rural, rich and poor, public and private – joined in the effort to teach Core Knowledge. Based largely on suggestions from these schools, the *Core Knowledge Sequence* was revised in 1995: separate guidelines were added for kindergarten, and a few topics in other grades were added, omitted, or moved from one grade to another, in order to create an even more coherent sequence for learning. Revised editions of the books in the Core Knowledge Series reflect the revisions in the *Sequence*. Based on the principle of learning from experience, the Core Knowledge Foundation continues to work with schools and advisors to 'fine-tune' the Sequence, and is also conducting research that will lead to the publication of guidelines for grades seven and eight, as well as for preschool. (*The Core Knowledge Sequence UK* can be downloaded from the Civitas Core Knowledge website www.coreknowledge.org.uk/sequence.php)

IV. THE NATURE OF THIS SERIES

The books in this series are designed to give a convenient and engaging introduction to the knowledge specified in the *Core Knowledge Sequence*. These are resource books, addressed primarily to parents, but which we hope will be useful tools for both parents and teachers. These books are not intended to replace the local curriculum or school textbooks, but rather to serve as aids to help children gain some of the important knowledge they will need to make progress in school and be effective in society.

Although we have made these books as accessible and useful as we can, parents and teachers should understand that they are not the only means by which the *Core Knowledge Sequence* can be imparted. The books represent a single version of the possibilities inherent in the *Sequence*, and a first step in the Core Knowledge reform effort. We hope that publishers will be stimulated to offer educational software, games, alternative books and other imaginative vehicles based on the *Core Knowledge Sequence*.

These books are not textbooks or workbooks, though when appropriate they do suggest a variety of activities you can do with your child. In these books, we address your child directly, and occasionally ask questions for him or her to think about. The earliest books in the series are intended to be read aloud to children. Even as children become able to read the books on their own, we encourage parents to help their children read more actively by reading along with them and talking about what they are reading. You and your child can read the sections of this book in any order, depending on your child's interests or depending on the topics your child is studying in school, which this book may complement or reinforce. You can skip from section to section and re-read as much as your child likes.

We encourage you to think of this book as a guidebook that opens the way to many paths you and your child can explore. These paths may lead to the library, to many other good books and, if possible, to plays, museums, concerts and other opportunities for knowledge and enrichment. In short, this guidebook recommends places to visit and describes what is important in those places, but only you and your child can make the actual visit, travel the streets and climb the steps.

V. WHAT YOU CAN DO TO HELP IMPROVE EDUCATION

The first step for parents and teachers who are committed to reform is to be sceptical about oversimplified slogans like 'critical thinking' and 'learning to learn'. Such slogans are everywhere and, unfortunately for our schools, their partial insights have been elevated to the level of universal truths. For example: 'What students learn is not important; rather, we must teach students to learn *how* to learn.' 'The child, not the academic subject, is the true focus of education.' 'Do not impose knowledge on children before they are developmentally ready to receive it.' 'Do not bog children down in mere facts, but rather, teach critical-thinking skills.' Who has not heard these sentiments, so admirable and humane, and – up to a point – so true? But these positive sentiments in favour of 'thinking skills' and 'higher understanding' have been turned into negative sentiments against the teaching of important knowledge. Those who have entered the teaching profession over the past forty years have been taught to scorn important knowledge as 'mere facts', and to see the imparting of this knowledge as somehow injurious to children. Thus it has come about that many educators, armed with partially true slogans, have seemingly taken leave of common sense.

Many parents and teachers have come to the conclusion that elementary education must strike a better balance between the development of the 'whole child' and the more limited but fundamental duty of the school to ensure that all children master a core of knowledge and skills essential to their competence as learners in later grades. But these parents and teachers cannot act on their convictions without access to an agreed upon, concrete sequence of knowledge. Our main motivation in developing the *Core Knowledge Sequence* and this book series has been to give parents and teachers something concrete to work with.

It has been encouraging to see how many teachers, since the first volume in this series was published, have responded to the Core Knowledge reform effort.

Parents and teachers are urged to join in a grassroots effort to strengthen our elementary schools. The place to start is in your own school and district. Insist that your school clearly state the core of *specific* knowledge and skills that each child in a grade must learn. Whether your school's core corresponds exactly to the Core Knowledge model is less important than the existence of some core – which, we hope, will be as solid, coherent, and challenging as the *Core Knowledge Sequence* has proven to be. Inform members of your community about the need for such a specific curriculum, and help make sure that the people who are elected or appointed to your local school board are independent minded people who will insist that our children have the benefit of a solid, specific, world class curriculum in each grade.

Share the knowledge!

E. D. Hirsch, Jr.
Charlottesville, Virginia

Language and Literature

Reading, Writing and Your Year 2 Child

> **PARENTS:** Before we present a selection of poems and stories for your child, we want to address you directly. This section, 'Reading, Writing and Your Year 2 Child', is intended to help you understand how children are – or should be – taught to read and write in a good Year 2 classroom, and to suggest a few ways that you can help at home. The first section below, 'Teaching Children to Read: The Need for a Balanced Approach', summarises a discussion presented in *What Your Year 1 Child Needs to Know*. If you have already read this, then you may wish to skip ahead to page 3 and begin with the section 'Goals for Reading and Writing: From Year 1 to Year 2'.

Teaching Children to Read:
The Need for a Balanced Approach

Everyone agrees that children should learn to read. But not everyone agrees how to achieve that goal. Many studies have demonstrated,[1] however, that while fashions come and go in education, pulling schools toward one extreme or another, there is a reasonable middle ground that is best for children.

This middle ground balances two approaches that some educators mistakenly see as mutually exclusive. The first approach emphasises the systematic teaching of the 'nuts and bolts' of written language: phonics and decoding skills (turning written letters into spoken sounds), spelling, handwriting, punctuation, grammar, vocabulary, sentence structure, paragraph form, and other rules and conventions. The second approach emphasises the need for children to be nourished on a rich diet of poetry, fiction and non-fiction. It focuses attention on the meanings and messages conveyed by written words and insists that children be given frequent opportunities to use language in creative and expressive ways.

---

[1] See, for example, Marilyn Jager Adams, *Beginning to Read: Thinking and Learning About Print* (Cambridge: MIT Press, 1990). For a discussion of the debate in the UK see Melanie Phillips, *All Must Have Prizes* (Little, Brown and Company, 1996).

Schools need to embrace both of these approaches. In particular, at the time of writing, many primary schools need to pay much more attention to the 'nuts and bolts': they need to take steps to balance a worthwhile emphasis on literature and creative expression with an equally necessary emphasis on the basic how-to skills of reading and writing.

Learning to Read and Write

To learn to read is to learn to understand and use our language, specifically our written language. Learning to read is not like learning to speak. While speech seems to come naturally, reading is a very different story. It is not enough just to see or hear others reading. Learning to read takes effort and instruction, because reading is not a natural process. Our written language is not

a natural thing — it is an artificial code. There is no natural reason why when you see this mark — A — that you should hear in your mind a sound that rhymes with 'day'. But you do, because you have learned the code. A few children seem to figure out this code for themselves, but most children need organised, systematic, direct instruction in how to decode the words on the page, that is, to turn the written symbols, the letters, into the speech sounds they represent.

The key to helping children unlock the code of our written language is to help them understand the relationships between individual letters, and combinations of letters, and the sounds they make. True, sometimes these relationships seem odd: consider, for example, the different sounds of the letters 'ough' in 'though' and 'enough'. Despite these occasional oddities, there is a logic to the written English alphabet: its basic symbols, the letters, represent the basic speech sounds, or phonemes, of our spoken language. The relationships between letters and sounds exhibit many regular patterns, as in, for example, 'cat', 'hat', 'sat', 'mat', 'fat' and 'rat'.

So, part of learning to read means learning the predictable letter-sound patterns in written words. Learning these letter-sound patterns enables a child who confronts a page of print to decode the written words into the sounds of spoken language that they represent. The other side of the coin here is learning the basic skills of writing, which enable a child who faces a blank page to encode the sounds of spoken language by putting on paper the corresponding written letters to form words, and by following other conventions of writing (such as capitalisation and punctuation) that allow us to get across our meanings, even when the person to whom we are communicating is not present before us.

All this talk about decoding and encoding may sound very mechanical and a little intimidating. It should be kept in mind that instruction in decoding and encoding is all in the service of meaning and understanding. If children are to communicate their ideas, thoughts, and desires in writing, as well as to understand what others are saying in print – whether it's a traffic sign, a film poster, a letter from a relative, or a story by A.A. Milne or Dr. Seuss – then they need to have the tools to encode and decode written English.

Goals for Reading and Writing:
From Year 1 to Year 2

In *What Your Year 1 Child Needs to Know*, we stated that a reasonable goal for instruction in Year 1 is to have all children beginning to read and write on their own by the end of the year. By this we meant that Year 1 pupils should:

● become comfortably familiar with the letters of the alphabet so that they can readily recognise and name the letters;

● develop a deliberate and conscious awareness of some of the sounds of oral language, and begin to make explicit connections between spoken sounds and printed letters;

● print both uppercase and lowercase letters with some proficiency, and write using some phonetic spelling (that is, spelling based on what they have learned so far about how words sound, for example, 'bot' for 'boat');

● be comfortable reading simple words they can sound out, as well as a few common 'sight words', words that occur very often in writing but do not conform to the usual letter-sound patterns, such as 'the', 'as', 'of', etc.

A reasonable goal for Year 2 is for children to become independent readers and writers — which, of course, doesn't mean that they ought to be able to read any book in the library or write a polished, perfectly spelt essay. By the end of the year, however, it is reasonable to expect that, with only limited assistance, Year 2 children will read books appropriate to beginning readers and express themselves comfortably and legibly in writing.

What Does a Good Year 2 Programme Do?

A good Year 2 programme can help children become independent readers and writers by taking a balanced approach that emphasises both meaning and decoding. In a good Year 2 class, children will be provided many opportunities to communicate and express themselves in speech and writing. As the year advances, they will be presented with appropriate 'beginner books' and other print materials to read, with some assistance as needed, but with the goal of reading independently. They will continue to listen to interesting poetry, fiction and non-fiction, and will be asked to talk about these pieces of literature and respond to them in thoughtful ways. Such literature gives children insight into a world of meaning expressed in words that they may not be able to read entirely on their own, but that they understand when the words are read aloud and discussed with an adult.

But for children to learn to read, it's not enough just to have good books read aloud to them. Listening to books does help children acquire a sense of what makes up a story, and motivates them to want to read. But it will not teach them how to read the words on the page. For that, children need repeated practice in working with letters and sounds in order to develop a good initial understanding of how language works. This does not mean mindless drill; rather, it means providing repeated and varied opportunities for children to work and play with letters and sounds.

There are many ways for a primary school to put together a good Year 2 programme in reading and writing, and many good materials for schools to use. Whatever the local approach or materials, any good Year 2 programme will do much of the following:

● A good Year 2 programme helps children develop their oral language, including speaking and listening. Children continue to hear good literature – both fiction and non-fiction – and read aloud, often with the written text displayed so they can 'follow along'. They are asked to talk about books that have been read to them, to ask and answer questions, and sometimes to retell or summarise the story.

● A good Year 2 programme continues the practice begun in Year 1 of explicitly and systematically developing children's phonemic awareness, that is, the understanding that the sounds of a word can be thought of as a string of smaller, individual sounds. Children participate in a variety of listening and speaking activities designed to help them recognise and compare sounds that make up words. For example, they may be asked to listen to a word, such as 'take', then to 'say it again but start with mmm' ('make'); 'say it again but start with rrr' ('rake'). Or, pupils may be asked which word has the short 'a' sound as in 'apple': 'mat' or 'mate'? Which word has the long 'o' sound as in 'hope': 'mop' or 'mope'? In Year 2, in addition to developing phonemic awareness through listening and speaking activities, children should consistently practise associating specific sounds with particular written letters and combinations of letters. They should be given regular opportunities to 'sound out', read, and write words that correspond to the letter-sound patterns they have been taught. Parents take note: some schools discourage children from sounding out words and urge them instead to 'guess' the words based on 'clues' from pictures or what's going on in the story. This is a serious mistake. Children need to learn a systematic, reliable way to figure out words they don't know, and this can come only from giving them explicit instruction in the code of our written language. It is important that this instruction be systematically organised to make explicit the letter-sound patterns and present them in a way that builds logically and sequentially, not in a haphazard or occasional fashion. Phonics instruction is most effective when it is regular, if not daily, with one skill building on another and with plenty of practice and review.

● As children master individual letter-sound patterns and become able to sound out words, a good programme provides phonetically controlled reading materials. These are simple stories written in a controlled vocabulary that corresponds to the letter-sound patterns that a child has been taught in preparation for reading the story. For example, after being taught how a silent 'e' at the end of a word can make a vowel long, a child might read a story about how 'Jake made a cake'. While such stories are of course not great literature, they are very helpful in teaching children to read, especially in providing the early and tremendously satisfying experience of being able 'to read it all by myself'. In preparation for reading these stories, children also need to add to their stock of sight words, such as 'of', 'was', 'do' and 'the'.

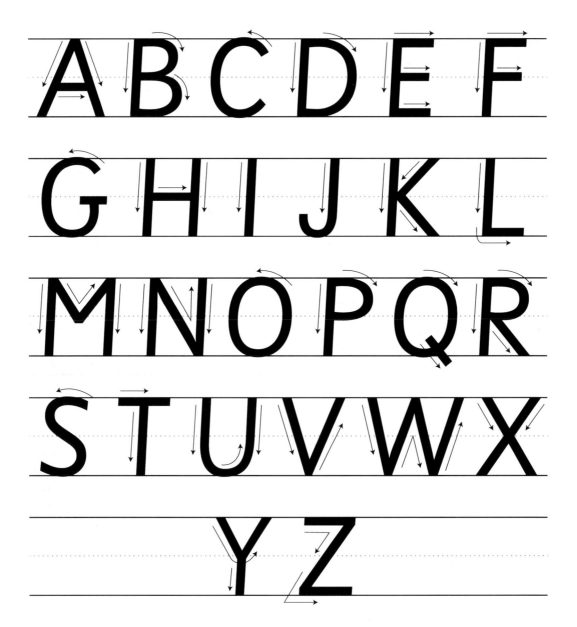

Handwriting chart: upper case (capital) letters

● Once children have demonstrated some success with phonetically controlled reading materials, they should be introduced to and asked to read, with occasional assistance, stories that are not phonetically controlled but are written for beginning readers, such as Arnold Lobel's Frog and Toad books or Rose Impey's *Titchy Witch* books. (See below, pages 12–13, for more titles of books for beginning readers.)

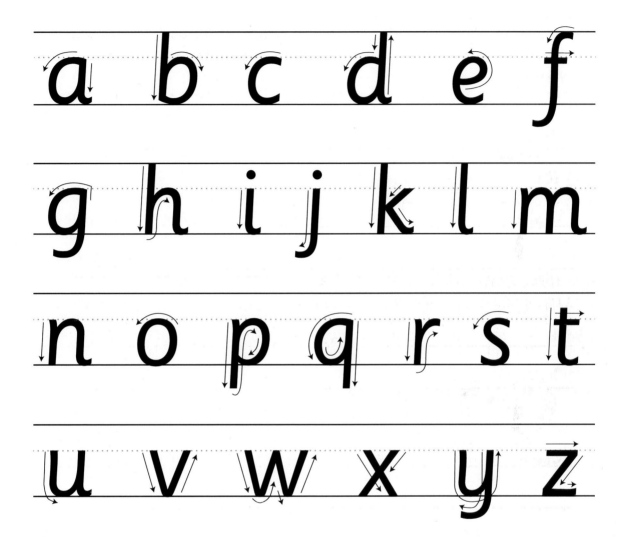

Handwriting chart: lower case (small) letters

- A good Year 2 programme provides regular handwriting practice through which children refine letter size and legibility, and learn to make appropriate use of the space on a page to present written information. (See charts, page 6 and above.)

- A good programme introduces a few conventions and rules of capitalisation, punctuation and spelling. (You can reinforce some basic rules by reading aloud the information in the box on page 9, and by gently reminding your child of these rules when she writes.)

● A good Year 2 programme provides a classroom environment in which children are surrounded by written language that is meaningful to them, such as posters with the children's names and birthdays, name labels on desks or lockers, and word labels on objects in the classroom ('door', 'blackboard' or 'smartboard', 'map', etc.). A good programme recognises that reading and writing reinforce each other, and it provides children with many opportunities to practise writing. Learning to read may be coordinated with learning to spell and write through regular dictation exercises in which the teacher calls out words that the children have practised reading and asks the children to spell them (that is, correctly write the words, or sometimes short sentences, on paper). Other writing is more for purposes of communication or creativity, such as writing letters, descriptions, short stories, poems, captions to pictures and the like. Year 2 pupils will often want to say more than they can write correctly, so in some cases the children should be encouraged to use phonetic spelling, that is, 'to spell it the way they think it sounds' (so that a child may write, for example, 'bot' for 'boat'). This occasional practice of phonetic spelling is beneficial for Year 2 children because it engages them in thinking actively about the sounds of words and how they are represented, and can make them more interested in writing and more willing to put their thoughts on paper. Of course, children need regular practice with conventional, correct spellings as well.

That, in brief, describes some of what a good Year 2 programme will do to help children achieve the goal of becoming independent readers and writers. Some pupils will surpass this goal; others may come close but not quite achieve it. But every child should receive appropriate instruction, materials and support, and they should be guided and encouraged to do his or her best to meet the goal. If a child is having difficulty, a school should not rationalise his difficulty by saying that the child is 'not developmentally ready'. You do not wait for readiness to happen. Rather, the child who is less ready should be given even more support, encouragement and practice in the areas posing difficulty.

What about the children who surpass the goals for Year 2? Children who surpass the goals should of course not be held back. There will always be, as proud parents are delighted to report, a few Year 2, and even Year 1, pupils who are 'reading everything they can get their hands on', even books like *Fantastic Mr. Fox* and *Charlotte's Web*. These few children who are reading dramatically beyond their year level should be encouraged, and their appetite for books should be fed with appropriately challenging material. At the same time, they can still benefit from explicit, systematic instruction in letter-sound correspondences, because such instruction gives them conscious knowledge of the conventions of written English, which is one of the tools they will need as they confront more challenging tasks in reading and writing.

A Few Rules for Writing

Year 2 pupils should practise using the following rules, though they should not be expected to use them with 100 per cent accuracy in all their writings. As part of their practice and review, children should sometimes be asked in school to apply what they have learned by proofreading and correcting selected samples of their written work.

● **Capital letters:** use a capital letter at the beginning of a sentence and at the beginning of names, such as: William the Conqueror was Duke of Normandy. When you refer to yourself, capitalise 'I'.

● **End punctuation:** when you write a sentence, use a punctuation mark to show where the sentence stops.

> Use a little dot called a 'full stop' to end most sentences.
>
> If you're asking a question, use a question mark.
>
> To show excitement, use an exclamation mark, as in 'I scored a goal!'

● **Contractions:** we sometimes combine two words into one short word called a contraction. To show that letters have been left out in a contraction, use the punctuation mark called an apostrophe. For example:

I am = I'm   do not = don't   it is = it's

● **Making words plural:** 'Plural' means 'more than one'. 'Singular' means 'just one'. You can put an 's' at the end of many words and change them from singular to plural. For example:

Singular	Plural
leg	legs
horse	horses
book	books

What Parents Can Do to Help

As parents, you can help your Year 2 child become a more independent reader and writer. Here are a few suggestions:

● Without question, the single most important and helpful thing you can do is to set aside fifteen or twenty minutes regularly, daily if possible, to read aloud to your child. See pages 15–17 in this book for suggested activities.

● In addition to reading aloud good literature to your Year 2 child, you can help him make the transition to independent reading through shared reading sessions in which he reads with you. See Suggested Resources, listed below, for some phonetically controlled readers and popular beginner books. While these books are only several pages long and may look very simple to you, they will be challenging for many Year 2 children, so we suggest you start by shared reading in which you take turns reading. How much your child reads will depend on the difficulty of the book and the progress he has made. You may want to begin by reading most of the book and asking him to read a familiar refrain or only a final rhyming word at the end of a line. Later, he might read aloud the even-numbered pages to you, and you read aloud the odd-numbered pages to him. The idea is to make your child's portion manageable, not overwhelming. Of course, if your child is reading confidently and accurately, offer praise and encouragement and let him keep going! As your child reads, have him point with his finger to each word. This will help focus his attention, keep his place and reinforce the idea that each spoken word corresponds to a written word. (You should run your finger under the words when you read, too.)

● As you read with your child, make special note of any difficulties. If she misreads a word, come back to it after she finishes the sentence. If it is a word she should be able to decode based on the letter-sound patterns she has been taught before reading the book, then use a pencil tip to point under each letter as she sounds out the word. If she hesitates, do it with her. If she misreads a sight word ('the', 'an', 'of', etc.), point to it, say the correct word, and ask her to repeat it.

● Designate a special notebook or exercise book as your child's writing notebook, and encourage him to write in it once or twice a week (in school, your child should be writing more frequently). In this notebook he can write down, for example, a funny joke, a few sentences about a favourite book or TV show or sports activity, something interesting he has learned in school, captions for pictures that he draws or cuts out of old magazines or even his own story or poem. If he likes, he can draw pictures to go along with his writing. Many children need to feel that they have something to say in order to make the effort to write it down, so talk with your child about what he might write: the more he thinks aloud, the more willing he will be to put words on paper. If while writing he seems unsure about the spelling of a word and

asks for your help, first ask him to 'sound out' the word and try to write it the way it sounds, but if this proves too frustrating, then provide the correct spelling. When he has finished writing, ask him to read aloud what he has written. Praise and encourage! Show an interest in the content of what he has written by asking questions and engaging him in conversation about the topic. Once you've affirmed your interest in what he has written, then you can ask him to take a closer look at how he has said it, and help him correct errors of spelling and punctuation. At first, do not try to correct every error. Instead, focus on the most familiar words and the most basic rules, such as ending a statement with a full stop. In helping him make corrections, the point is not to dwell on what's wrong but to show him that 'this is how that word is spelt' or 'this is how we begin a sentence, with a capital letter, remember?'

- Take advantage of unplanned moments to engage in spontaneous language games. Tell jokes. Ask riddles. Try tongue twisters. While driving in the car or waiting for the bus, you can play rhyming games and memory games, recite favourite poems and point to different signs and talk about what they mean. While shopping at the supermarket, ask your child to cross items off the shopping list, or to try reading the names on a few labels.

- You can send an important message about the value you place on reading and writing by talking with your child about the schoolwork she brings home. Set aside time to look at her papers with her. Be supportive; praise her effort and do not dwell on errors. (In school, the teacher should be observing your child's progress and working to correct any consistent pattern of errors.)

General Resources

The resources recommended here are meant to complement, not substitute for, the reading programmes and associated materials that schools use to teach reading and writing. Our suggestions are directed to parents, though some teachers may find these additional resources helpful as well, especially if their school has adopted a philosophy or set of materials that neglects the systematic early teaching of decoding skills and the conventions of written language.

The following list is intended to help you get started in locating a few of the many good resources available. There are many phonics materials available from many sources. In recommending a few here, we do not mean to exclude others. Here we suggest materials that are time-tested and/or readily available, generally at a reasonable cost, and usable by those without special training in the teaching of reading and writing.

Besides the books suggested below, other useful supplies are generally available from early learning centres and from online suppliers:

● magnetic letters and letter-sound flash cards

● letter-picture cards (cards with simple pictures and a corresponding letter, for example, the letter 'a' with a picture of an apple).

● Word-picture cards or workbooks to practise handwriting

● word games, puzzles and activity books

● computer programmes, children's online games or apps for teaching letter-sound patterns, words and early reading and writing skills – see the end of this chapter for suggestions.

Books for Teaching Phonics

● *Big Cat Phonics* series published by Harper Collins (2006) is an excellent introduction to phonics-based texts. Even though they are part of a reading programme the books are well written, varied and beautifully illustrated.

● *Sounds Fun* by Liz Baldwin (Learning Development Aids 2011) is a collection of phonics games to play in spare moments, which will help children to develop their understanding of the building blocks of reading.

- *The Butterfly Book* by Irina Tyk (Civitas 2007) is an excellent guide to reading by synthetic phonics. Short stories about Ponti Panda provide the child with the opportunity to try out newly acquired phonics decoding skills. This book has been used successfully with hundreds of children in Civitas Schools.

- *Step by Step Reading: A 50 Step Guide to Teach Reading with Synthetic Phonics* by Mona McNee (Galore Park) 2007 is, like *The Butterfly Book*, a complete, one-book guide to learning to read by synthetic phonics. It is ideal for use by parents at home. Games and activities can be downloaded from the publisher's website.

Beginning Reader Books

It is important to offer lots of beginning reader texts which allow your child to join in a story and ultimately take over the decoding. Stories such as *Class Two at the Zoo* and *Class Three all at Sea* written by Julia Jarman (Hodder) 2009 are good examples. *Burger Boy* by Alan Durant (Andersen) 2006 is a tongue-in-cheek version of the gingerbread boy, and *Charlie Cook's Favourite Book* written by Julia Donaldson (Macmillan) 2006 celebrates the diversity of favourite stories. *The Feather* by Dot Cleeve (Tamarind) 2003 and *But Martin!* by June Counsel (Random House) 2005 are delightful and Nick Butterworth's *The Whisperer* (Harper Collins) 2005 is a good first introduction to Romeo and Juliet.

As children become confident they can be encouraged by a simple series to build confidence:

- The Elephant and Piggie books by Mo Willems, published by Walker Books, encourage children to appreciate the fun of reading independently. These simple texts are very silly but hugely enjoyable.

- The series of Titchy Witch stories are good fun. The Animal Crackers series provide short sentences and simple grammatical construction yet offer a rich vocabulary. Titles include *Open Wide Wilbur, A Birthday for Bluebell* and *Precious Potter. The Ark Adventures* are a little more demanding. These three series are all published by Orchard.

- Walker's Starter series are beautifully written with a wide variety of stories at a simple level. Scholastic's Lighthouse Keeper stories written by Ronda and David Armitage have good, clear print and entertaining illustrations.

- You might share the reading of Egmont's more complex Blue Banana series. The Dilly the Dinosaur series is also a firm favourite.

Literature: Introduction

There is one simple practice that can make a world of difference for your Year 2 child. Read aloud to your child often, daily if possible. Reading aloud opens the doors to a world of meaning that most children are curious to explore but in Year 2 are still beginning to enter on their own. In reading aloud, you can offer your child a rich and varied selection of literature, including poetry, fiction and non-fiction.

For your Year 2 child, we offer a selection of poetry, including some traditional rhymes, Mother Goose classics and familiar tongue twisters. We also include some poems by favourite modern and contemporary writers. All of these selections should be considered a starting point. We encourage you to read many more poems with your child, to delight in the play of language and occasionally to help your child memorise a personal favourite.

The stories presented here are written in language more complex than most Year 2 children will be able to read on their own, though they can readily be understood and enjoyed when the words are read aloud with expression, and talked about with an adult. These stories are meant to complement, not replace, the stories with controlled vocabularies and syntax that children should be given as part of their instruction in learning to read. (See 'Reading, Writing, and Your Year 2 Child', page 1.)

In this book, we present many familiar and traditional tales that have stood the test of time. Some of the selections from other lands may not be familiar to British readers, but by including them here we hope to make them so.[2] Among the stories, you will find favourite folktales from many lands and cultures. We have paired two stories – 'Issun Boshi: One-Inch Boy' and 'Tom Thumb'— to help children see that people in different lands tell similar stories. We also include some modern classics of children's literature such as *The King of the Nogs* and a selection from *The House at Pooh Corner*.

Some of the stories in this Year 2 volume build upon the selection of fairy tales by the Brothers Grimm and others presented in *What Your Year 1 Child Needs to Know*. For children, such fairy tales can delight and instruct, and they provide ways of dealing with darker human emotions like jealousy, greed and fear. As G. K. Chesterton observed, fairy tales 'are not responsible for producing in children fear, or any of the shapes of fear... The baby has known the dragon intimately ever since he had an imagination. What the fairy tale provides for him is a St. George to kill the dragon.' And as the celebrated writer of children's tales, Wanda Gag, wrote in 1937: 'A fairy story is not just a fluffy puff of nothing... nor is it merely a tenuous bit of make believe... Its roots are real and solid, reaching far back into man's past... and into the lives and customs of many people and

---

[2] For a description of the process that led to the selection of poems and stories included in this book, see 'The Consensus Behind the Core Knowledge Sequence,' page xxi.

countries.' Whatever the geographical origin of the traditional tales we tell here – Africa, Europe, Asia, America – the stories have universal messages and lasting appeal across cultures and generations.

Consider this selection of stories a starting point for further exploration. Beyond stories and poems, you can share appropriate works of non-fiction with your child. Many Year 2 children enjoy, for example, illustrated books that explain what things are and how they work, books about animals and how they live and biographies of famous people.

Your local library has a treasury of good books, and guidance on wonderful books to share with young children can be found in the excellent *Ultimate First Book Guide* edited by Leonie Flynn, Daniel Hahn and Susan Reuben (A and C Black). The Federation of Children's Book Groups produces a very good journal three times a year called *Carousel*, obtainable from fcbg.org.uk.

Read-Aloud Activities

Try to set aside a regular time for reading aloud, a time free from other obligations or distractions (including the television!). When you read aloud, don't feel embarrassed about hamming it up a bit. Be expressive; try giving different characters different voices.

If your child is not used to hearing stories read aloud, you may want to begin by reading some poems or some of the shorter selections in this book. If your child starts to squirm as you read longer stories, take a break from reading and get your child involved: have him look at a picture, or ask him some questions, or ask him to tell you what he thinks about what has happened so far, or have him draw a picture to go with the part of the story you've read.

When you read aloud, most of the time your child will be involved in the simple pleasure of listening. At other times, you can involve your child in some additional activities to encourage comprehension and interest. Remember, these activities are not tests. Use them with a gentle touch: relax, and have fun together.

- Let your child look through the book before you read it. Let her skim the pages and look at pictures.

- Direct your child's attention to the book's title page. Point to the author's name and read it as written, for example 'Written by Beatrix Potter'. If the book is illustrated, also read the illustrator's name, for example, 'Illustrated by Quentin Blake'. Discuss what the words 'author' and 'illustrator' mean. As you read more and more books, talk with your child about her favourite authors or illustrators. Look in your local library for more works by your child's favourite authors and illustrators.

- Sometimes let your child pick the books for reading aloud. If your child has picked a book or books from the library, she may soon learn the lesson that 'you can't judge a book by its cover'. If you begin a book that she has chosen and she expresses dislike or lack of interest, don't force her to finish hearing it. Just put the book aside with the understanding that 'maybe we'll like this better later'.

- As you read, sometimes run your finger below the words as you say them. This will help confirm your child's sense of the left-to-right direction of print. In re-reading a selection, you can direct your child's attention to individual words as you say them aloud. You can also ask your child to try to read occasional words and phrases, especially ones with which he is likely to have some success.

- After reading a story, discuss the sequence of events. 'Can you tell me what happened first?' 'What did he do next?' You can draw three or four simple pictures representing scenes in the story, then ask your child to arrange the pictures in the proper sequence as she retells the story.

- After reading a poem or a story or a segment of a longer book, help your child recall details by asking questions. Keep in mind the five Ws: Who? What?

When? Where? Why? For example, after reading 'The Boy at the Dyke', ask, 'Where did Peter live?' 'Whom did Peter go to visit?' 'Why did he go there?' 'What happened on the way home?' 'Why couldn't he leave the dyke?' 'When did somebody find him?' (Maintain a playful, conversational tone; this is not a test!)

- In talking about stories, occasionally use words that are common in the discussion of literature, such as 'character', 'hero', and 'heroine'. For example, you might ask, 'Who is your favourite character in The House at Pooh Corner?' Not all stories have heroes or heroines, but you can bring up the terms when appropriate, for example by asking: 'Isn't it surprising that the hero of "Issun Boshi" is no bigger than your thumb (at least for most of the story)?' Or: 'That was a brave thing for Gretel to do. She's a real heroine, isn't she?'

- Engage your child in a discussion of the story by asking questions that go beyond recall of details and take her into interpretation. For example, after reading 'It Could Always Be Worse', ask: 'Why do you think the story has that title? What do you think it means?'

- Help your child memorise a favourite poem.

- Act out a story or scenes from a story. Your child doesn't need to memorise a set script; she can use her own language to express a character's thoughts. A few simple props can help: paper bags for masks, old shirts for costumes, a broomstick

Poetry
Traditional Rhymes

If Wishes Were Horses

If wishes were horses, beggars would ride.

If turnips were watches, I would wear one by my side,

And if 'ifs' and 'ands' were pots and pans,

There'd be no work for tinkers!

The Queen of Hearts

The Queen of Hearts
She made some tarts,
All on a summer's day.
The Knave of Hearts
He stole the tarts,
And took them clean away.
The King of Hearts
Called for the tarts,
And beat the Knave full sore.
The Knave of Hearts
Brought back the tarts,
And vowed he'd steal no more.

Three Wise Men of Gotham

Three wise men of Gotham
Went to sea in a bowl;
If the bowl had been stronger
My song had been longer.

Solomon Grundy

Solomon Grundy,
Born on a Monday,
Christened on Tuesday,
Married on Wednesday,
Took ill on Thursday,
Worse on Friday,
Died on Saturday,
Buried on Sunday:
This is the end
Of Solomon Grundy.

Thirty Days Hath September

Thirty days hath September,
April, June and November.
All the rest have thirty-one,
Except for February alone,
And that has twenty-eight days clear,
And twenty-nine in each leap year.

Tongue Twisters

Red lorry, yellow lorry. Red lorry, yellow lorry.
Red lorry, yellow lorry. Red lorry, yellow lorry.

Peter Piper picked a peck of pickled peppers;
A peck of pickled peppers Peter Piper picked.
If Peter Piper picked a peck of pickled peppers,
Where's the peck of pickled peppers Peter Piper picked?

Swan swam over the sea;
Swim, swan, swim.
Swan swam back again;
Well swum, swan.

How much wood would a woodchuck chuck
If a woodchuck could chuck wood?
He would chuck as much wood as a woodchuck could chuck
If a woodchuck would chuck wood.

Moses supposes his toeses are roses,
But Moses supposes erroneously;
For nobody's toeses are posies of roses,
As Moses supposes his toeses to be.

She sells seashells by the seashore.
The shells she sells are surely seashells.
So if she sells shells on the seashore,
I'm sure she sells seashore shells.

Riddle Rhymes (For answers, turn this page upside down.)

Riddle me, riddle me, what is that
Over the head, and under the hat?

(*Hair*)

A hill full, a hole full,
Yet you cannot catch a bowl full.

(*Fog, mist or smoke*)

Higher than a house, higher than a tree,
Oh, whatever can it be?

(*A Star*)

Thirty white horses upon a red hill,
Now they tramp, now they champ,
now they stand still.

(*Teeth*)

More Poems for Year 2

The Swing

by Robert Louis Stevenson

How do you like to go up in a swing,
Up in the air so blue?
Oh, I do think it the pleasantest thing
Ever a child can do!

Up in the air and over the wall,
Till I can see so wide,
Rivers and trees and cattle and all
Over the countryside –

Till I look down on the garden green,
Down on the roof so brown –
Up in the air I go flying again,
Up in the air and down!

A Good Play

by Robert Louis Stevenson

We built a ship upon the stairs
All made of the back-bedroom chairs,
And filled it full of sofa pillows
To go a-sailing on the billows.

We took a saw and several nails,
And water in the nursery pails;
And Tom said, 'Let us also take
An apple and a slice of cake';
Which was enough for Tom and me
To go a-sailing on, till tea.

We sailed along for days and days,
And had the very best of plays;
But Tom fell out and hurt his knee,
So there was no one left but me.

The Frog

by Hilaire Belloc

Be kind and tender to the Frog,
And do not call him names,
As 'Slimy skin', or 'Polly-wog',
Or likewise 'Ugly James',
Or 'Gape-a-grin', or 'Toad-gone-
wrong',
Or 'Billy Bandy-knees':
The Frog is justly sensitive
To epithets like these.
No animal will more repay
A treatment kind and fair;
At least so lonely people say
Who keep a frog (and, by the way,
They are extremely rare).

Hope

by Langston Hughes

Sometimes when I'm lonely,
Don't know why,
Keep thinkin' I won't be lonely
By and by.

The Pasture

by Robert Frost

I'm going out to clean the pasture spring;
I'll only stop to rake the leaves away
(And wait to watch the water clear, I may):
I shan't be gone long. — You come too.

I'm going out to fetch the little calf
That's standing by the mother. It's so young
It totters when she licks it with her tongue.
I shan't be gone long. — You come too.

The Owl and the Pussycat

by Edward Lear

The Owl and the Pussycat went to sea

In a beautiful pea-green boat,

They took some honey, and plenty
of money,

Wrapped up in a five-pound note.

The Owl looked up to the stars above,

And sang to a small guitar,

'O lovely Pussy! O Pussy, my love,

What a beautiful Pussy you are,

You are,

You are!

What a beautiful Pussy you are!'

Pussy said to the Owl, 'You elegant fowl!

How charmingly sweet you sing!

O let us be married! Too long we
have tarried:

But what shall we do for a ring?'

They sailed away, for a year and a day,

To the land where the Bong-tree grows

And there in a wood a Piggy-wig stood

With a ring at the end of his nose,

His nose,

His nose,

With a ring at the end of his nose.

'Dear Pig, are you willing to sell
for one shilling your ring?'

Said the Piggy, 'I will.'

So they took it away, and were married
next day

By the Turkey who lives on the hill.

They dined on mince, and slices
of quince,

Which they ate with a runcible spoon;

And hand in hand, on the edge of
the sand,

They danced by the light of the moon,

The moon,

The moon,

They danced by the light of the moon.

Jumbo Jet
by Spike Milligan

I saw a little elephant standing in my garden,
I said 'You don't belong in here', he said 'I beg you pardon?'
I said 'This place is England, what are you doing here?'
He said 'Ah, then I must be lost' and then 'Oh dear, oh dear'.

'I should be back in Africa, on Saranghetti's Plain',
'Pray, where is the nearest station where I can catch a train?'
He caught the bus to Finchley and then to Mincing lane,
And over the Embankment, where he got lost, again.

The police they put him in a cell, but it was far too small,
So they tied him to a lamp post and he slept against the wall.
But as the policemen lay sleeping by the twinkling light of dawn,
The lamp post and the wall were there, but the elephant was gone!

So if you see an elephant, in a Jumbo Jet,
You can be sure that Africa's the place he's trying to get!

'Pussycat, Pussycat, Where Have You Been?'

'Pussycat pussycat,
where have you been?'

'I've been up to London
to visit the Queen.'

'Pussycat, pussycat,
what did you there?'

'I frightened a little
mouse under her chair.'

I Know All the Sounds That the Animals Make

by Jack Prelutsky

I know all the sounds that the animals make,
and make them all day from the moment I wake,
I roar like a mouse and I purr like a moose,
I hoot like a duck and I moo like a goose.
I squeak like a cat and I quack like a frog,
I oink like a bear and I honk like a hog,
I croak like a cow and I bark like a bee,
no wonder the animals marvel at me.

Rope Rhyme

by Eloise Greenfield

Get set, ready now, jump right in

Bounce and kick and giggle and spin

Listen to the rope when it hits the ground

Listen to that clappedy-slappedy sound

Jump right up when it tells you to

Come back down, whatever you do

Count to a hundred, count by ten

Start to count all over again

That's what jumping is all about

Get set, ready now,

Jump right

out!

Ring a Ring o' Roses

Ring a ring o' roses,

A pocket full o' posies.

A-tishoo! A-tishoo!

We all fall down.

Scissors

by Allan Ahlberg

Nobody leave the room.
Everyone listen to me.
We had ten pairs of scissors
At half-past two,
And now there's only three.

Seven pairs of scissors,
Disappeared from sight.
Not one of you leaves
Till we find them.
We can stop here all night!

Sci... s don't lose themselves,
... t away, or explode.

Scissors have not got
Legs of their own
To go running off up the road.

We really need those scissors,
That's what makes me mad.
If it was seven pairs
Of children we'd lost,
It wouldn't be so bad.

I don't want to hear excuses.
Don't anyone speak.
Just ransack this room
Till we find them,
Or we'll stop here… all week!

Cats Sleep Anywhere

by Eleanor Farjeon

Cats sleep anywhere,
any table,
any chair.
Top of piano,
window-ledge,
in the middle,
on the edge.
Open drawer,
empty shoe,
anybody's lap will do.
Fitted in a cardboard box,
in the cupboard
with your frocks.
Anywhere!
They don't care!
Cats sleep anywhere.

The Purple Cow

by Gelett Burgess

I never saw a Purple Cow,
I never hope to see one;
But I can tell you, anyhow,
I'd rather see than be one.

My Shadow

by Robert Louis Stevenson

I have a little shadow that goes in and out with me,

And what can be the use of him is more than I can see.

He is very, very like me from the heels up to the head;

And I see him jump before me, when I jump into my bed.

The funniest thing about him is the way he likes to grow

Not at all like proper children, which is always very slow;

For he sometimes shoots up taller like an india-rubber ball,

And he sometimes gets so little that there's none of him at all.

He hasn't got a notion of how children ought to play,

And can only make a fool of me in every sort of way.

He stays so close beside me, he's a coward you can see;

I'd think shame to stick to nursie as that shadow sticks to me!

One morning, very early, before the sun was up,

I rose and found the shining dew on every buttercup;

But my lazy little shadow, like an arrant sleepy-head,

Had stayed at home behind me and was fast asleep in bed.

Table Manners

by Gelett Burgess

The Goops they lick their fingers,

And the Goops they lick their knives;

They spill their broth on the tablecloth –

Oh, they lead disgusting lives!

The Goops they talk while eating,

And loud and fast they chew;

And that is why I'm glad that I

Am not a Goop – are you?

Aesop's Fables

A fable is a special kind of story that teaches a lesson. People have been telling some fables over and over for hundreds of years. It is said that many of these fables were told by a man named Aesop [EE-sop], who lived in Greece a very, very long time ago.

Aesop knew bad behaviour when he saw it, and he wanted people to be better. But he knew that we don't like to be told when we're bad. That is why many of his fables have animals in them. The animals sometimes talk and act like people. In fact, the animals behave just as well and just as badly as people do. That's because, even when a fable is about animals, it is really about people. Through these stories about animals, Aesop teaches us how we should act as people.

At the end of the fable, Aesop often tells us a lesson we should learn. The lesson is called the moral of the story.

Here are six of Aesop's fables, most with animals in them. The moral of the story is stated at the end of each fable. As you read the fables, try saying what you think the lesson might be before you read the moral.

The Boy Who Cried Wolf

Once there was a shepherd boy who looked after his little flock of sheep on a hillside, just below a dark forest. He was bored, as there was no one near to talk to, so he decided to play a trick on the villagers below. 'Help me!' he cried out in a loud voice. 'There is a wolf prowling around my flock!'

The villagers came running to help him drive the wolf away, but when they found there was no wolf they were cross. 'Don't cry wolf when there isn't one!' they said to him, and returned to the village, grumbling.

The next day the shepherd boy was still bored and thought he would play the prank again. 'Wolf!' he cried, 'there's a big, bad wolf up here!'

Once again, the villagers came running. They were very cross indeed when they found it was another trick. 'Don't keep crying wolf like that,' they told him, 'or one day you will regret it.'

The next day a wolf really did appear. 'Help! Help!' he cried, 'Please help me to drive the wolf away.'

The villagers heard him, but this time they said: 'He won't catch us again with that old trick!'

And so the wolf ate all the sheep.

MORAL: If you often lie, people won't believe you even when you are telling the truth.

The Fox and the Grapes

On a very hot day in the summer, a fox was wandering along the road when he saw a vine curled around a tree-trunk, and a big bunch of juicy grapes dangling from it. 'Well, well,' he thought to himself, 'wouldn't those grapes be just the thing to quench my thirst on this hot day?'

But the grapes were too high up for him to reach. Even when he got up on his hind legs, he couldn't quite get them. So he decided to jump. He jumped as high as he could, but he couldn't get near them. He took a run and jumped even higher. Still no luck. He jumped again and again, until he was so hot, he had to give up.

'Oh well,' he said as he walked away, 'I don't really care. They are probably sour anyway.'

MORAL: When people cannot get what they want, they sometimes tell themselves that what they want is no good anyway.

'Sour grapes' has become a common saying. People say 'It's just sour grapes' to refer to griping or unkind remarks someone makes about something he or she can't have. For example:

Jim turned to his teacher, Mr. Walker, and asked, 'Why did Mark say our class play isn't going to be any good?' 'Oh, that's just sour grapes,' said Mr. Walker. 'Mark wanted to be the star, but he's playing a smaller part. But once he sees how much fun it is, he'll change his mind.'

The Dog in the Manger

There was once a dog who liked to get away from the heat of the day and sleep in the barn. His favourite place to take a nap was on the hay in the manger, which is a trough the animals eat from. How cool and soft it felt against his coat. He would have such nice dreams, asleep in the manger.

One evening, an ox came in from the fields, feeling tired after a hard day's work. 'Excuse me,' said the ox to the dog, 'would you mind moving so that I can eat some of my hay?'

The dog woke up with a start, and he was always bad tempered when he was woken up suddenly. He started barking at the ox. 'Please,' said the ox, 'you have been sleeping all day, and I have been working. Can I get to my hay?'

Now the dog didn't want the hay himself, because dogs don't eat it, but nevertheless he would not move for the ox, and just kept on barking. Eventually the poor ox gave up and went away feeling tired and hungry.

MORAL: Don't be selfish when you have no need of things yourself. Don't be a dog in the manger.

The Maid and the Milk Pail

Peggy, the milkmaid, was going to market. There she planned to sell the fresh, sweet milk in the pail that she had learned to carry balanced on her head. As she went along, she began thinking about what she would do with the money she would get for the milk. 'I'll buy some chickens from Farmer Brown,' she thought, 'and they will lay eggs each morning. When those eggs hatch, I'll have more chickens. Then I'll sell some of the chickens and some of the eggs, and that will get me enough money to buy the blue dress I've been longing for, and some blue ribbons to match. I'll look so lovely that all the boys will want to dance with me at the fair, and all the girls will be jealous. But I don't care, I shall toss my head at them, like this!'

She tossed back her head. The pail flew off, and the milk spilled all over the road. So Peggy had to return home and tell her mother what had happened. 'Ah, my child,' said her mother, 'don't count your chickens before they're hatched.'

MORAL: Don't count your chickens before they're hatched. Have you heard this saying before? It means: Do not count on getting everything you want, at having everything turn out exactly as you plan, because you may be disappointed.

The Wolf in Sheep's Clothing

Night after night, a wolf prowled around a flock of sheep looking for one to eat, but the shepherd and his dog always chased the wolf away. But one day the wolf found the skin of a sheep that had been thrown aside. He pulled the skin carefully over him so that none of his fur showed under the white fleece. Then he strolled among the flock. A lamb, thinking that the wolf was its mother, followed him into the woods – and there the wolf made a meal of the lamb!

So for many days the wolf was able to get a sheep whenever he pleased. But one day the shepherd decided to cook lamb for his own dinner. He chose the biggest, fattest sheep he could find and killed it on the spot. Guess who it was – the wolf!

TWO MORALS:

(1) **Beware of a wolf in sheep's clothing: things are not always what they appear to be.**

(2) **If you pretend to be what you are not, you might get caught.**

People sometimes use the phrase 'A wolf in sheep's clothing' to describe someone who appears to be harmless or friendly but who is really dangerous or untrustworthy. For example: 'I can't believe Ronnie took my idea for his art poster. He said he just wanted to know what I was working on, so I told him, but then he did it himself. What a wolf in sheep's clothing!'

The Goose That Laid the Golden Eggs

Once a farmer went to the nest of his goose and found there an egg, all yellow and shiny. When he picked it up, it was heavy as a rock. He was about to throw it away because he thought that someone was playing a trick on him. But on second thoughts, he took it home, and there he discovered to his delight that it was an egg of pure gold!

He sold the egg for a handsome sum of money. Every morning the goose laid another golden egg, and the farmer soon became rich by selling the eggs.

As he grew rich, he grew greedy. 'Why should I have to wait to get only one egg a day?' he thought. 'I will cut open the goose and take all the eggs out of her at once.'

And so he killed the goose and cut her open, only to find – nothing!

MORAL: He who wants more often loses all. When you want something, be patient. If you are greedy, you might lose what you already have.

Stories

All Stories Are Anansi's
(A tale from West Africa)

PARENTS: Anansi [ah-NAHN-see], the spider, is a popular figure in the folklore of parts of West Africa (the stories later came with slaves to the Caribbean islands). Like Brer Rabbit in America (see below, page 43), Anansi is a 'trickster' figure – clever, cunning, sometimes mischievous – who uses his wits to make up for what he lacks in size and strength.

This story tells how Anansi became the 'owner' of all stories.

In the beginning, all tales and stories belonged to Nyame [NYAH-meh], the Sky God. But Kwaku Anansi, the spider, yearned to be the owner of all the stories known in the world, and he went to Nyame and offered to buy them.

The Sky God said: 'I am willing to sell the stories, but the price is high. Many people have come to me offering to buy, but the price was too high for them. Rich and powerful families have not been able to pay. Do you think you can do it?'

Anansi replied to the Sky God: 'I can do it. What is the price?'

'My price is three things,' the Sky God said. 'I must first have Mmoboro [mmmoh-BOH-roh], the hornets. I must then have Onini [oh-NEE-nee], the great python. I must then have Osebo [oh-SAY-boh], the leopard. For these things I will sell you the right to tell all stories.'

Anansi said: 'I will bring them.'

He went home and made his plans. He first cut a gourd from a vine and made a small hole in it. He took a large calabash [like a bowl], and filled it with water. He went to the tree where the hornets lived. He poured some of the water over himself, so that he was dripping. He threw some water over the hornets, so that they too were dripping. Then he put the calabash on his head, as though to protect himself from a storm, and called out to the hornets: 'Are you foolish people? Why do you stay in the rain that is falling?'

The hornets answered: 'Where shall we go?'

'Go here, in this dry gourd,' Anansi told them.

The hornets thanked him and flew into the gourd through the small hole. When the last of them had entered, Anansi plugged the hole with a ball of grass, saying: 'Oh, yes, but you are really foolish people!'

He took his gourd full of hornets to Nyame, the Sky God. The Sky God accepted them. He said: 'There are two more things.'

Anansi returned to the forest and cut a long bamboo pole and some strong vines. Then he walked toward the house of Onini, the python, talking to himself. He seemed to be talking about an argument with his wife. Anansi said: 'My wife is wrong. I say he is longer and stronger. My wife says he is shorter and weaker. I give him more respect. She gives him less respect. Is she right or am I right? I am right, he is longer. I am right, he is stronger.'

When Onini, the python, heard Anansi talking to himself, he said: 'Why are you arguing this way with yourself?'

The spider replied: 'Ah, I have had a dispute with my wife. She says you are shorter and weaker than this bamboo pole. I say you are longer and stronger.'

Onini said: 'It's useless and silly to argue when you can find out the truth. Bring the pole and we will measure.'

So Anansi laid the pole on the ground, and the python came and stretched himself out beside it.

'You seem a little short,' Anansi said.

The python stretched further.

'A little more,' Anansi said.

'I can stretch no more,' Onini said.

'When you stretch at one end, you get shorter at the other end,' Anansi said. 'Let me tie you at the front so you don't slip.'

He tied Onini's head to the pole. Then he went to the other end and tied the tail to the pole. He wrapped the vine all around Onini, until the python couldn't move.

'Onini,' Anansi said, 'it turns out that my wife was right and I was wrong. You are shorter than the pole and weaker. My opinion wasn't as good as my wife's. But you were even more foolish than I, and you are now my prisoner.'

Anansi carried the python to Nyame, the Sky God, who said: 'There is one thing more.'

Osebo, the leopard, was next. Anansi went into the forest and dug a deep pit where the leopard liked to walk. He covered it with small branches and leaves and put dust on it, so that it was impossible to tell where the pit was. Anansi went away and hid. When Osebo came prowling in the black of night, he stepped into the trap Anansi had prepared and fell to the bottom. Anansi heard the sound of the leopard falling, and he said: 'Ah, Osebo, you are half-foolish!'

When morning came, Anansi went to the pit and saw the leopard there. 'Osebo,' he asked, 'what are you doing in this hole?'

'I have fallen into a trap,' Osebo said. 'Help me out.'

'I would gladly help you,' Anansi said. 'But I'm sure that if I bring you out, I will have no thanks for it. You will get hungry, and later on you will be wanting to eat me and my children.'

'I promise it won't happen,' Osebo said.

'Very well. Since you promise it, I will take you out,' Anansi said.

He bent a tall green tree toward the ground, so that its top was over the pit, and he tied it that way. Then he tied a rope to the top of the tree and dropped the other end of it into the pit.

'Tie this to your tail,' he said.

Osebo tied the rope to his tail.

'Is it well tied?' Anansi asked.

'Yes, it is well tied,' the leopard said.

'In that case,' Anansi said, 'you are not merely half-foolish, you are all foolish.'

And he took his knife and cut the other rope, the one that held the tree bowed to the ground. The tree straightened up with a snap, pulling Osebo out of the hole. He hung in the air head downward, twisting and turning. As he twisted and turned, he got so dizzy that Anansi had no trouble tying the leopard's feet with vines. Anansi took the dizzy leopard, all tied up, to Nyame, the Sky God, saying: 'Here is the third thing. Now I have paid the price.'

Nyame said to him: 'Kwaku Anansi, great warriors and chiefs have tried, but they have been unable to do it. You have done it. Therefore, I will give you the stories. From this day onward, all stories belong to you. Whenever a man tells a story, he must acknowledge that it is Anansi's tale.'

And that is why, in parts of Africa, the people love to tell, and love to hear, the stories they call 'spider stories'. And now, you have heard one too.

Anansi stories are widely studied in primary schools. Check your local library for more stories about him, or try *Anancy and Mr Dry-Bone* by Fiona French (Frances Lincoln, 1991).

The Boy at the Dyke

PARENTS: If you have access to a world map or globe, help your child locate Holland (also called the Netherlands).

Many years ago, there lived a boy who did a brave deed. His name was Peter, and he lived in Holland, a country by the sea.

In Holland, the sea presses in on the land so much that the people built big walls of earth and stone to hold back the waters. Every little child in Holland was taught that these big walls, called dykes, must be watched at every moment. No water must be allowed to come through the dykes. Even a hole no larger than your little finger was a very dangerous thing.

One afternoon in the early fall, when Peter was seven years old, his mother called to him. 'Come, Peter,' she said. 'I want you to go across the dyke and take these cakes to your friend the blind man. If you go quickly, you will be home again before dark.'

Peter was happy to go, because his friend the blind man lived alone and was always glad to have a visitor. When he got to the blind man's home, Peter stayed awhile to tell him of his walk along the dyke. He told about the bright sun and the flowers and the ships far out at sea. Then Peter remembered that his mother wanted him to return home before dark. So he said goodbye and set out for home.

As he walked along, he noticed how the water beat against the side of the dyke. There had been much rain, and the water was higher than before. Peter remembered how his father always spoke of the 'angry waters'.

'I suppose Father thinks they are angry,' thought Peter, 'because we have been keeping them out for so long. Well, I am glad these dykes are so strong. If they gave way, what would become of us? All these fields would be covered with water. Then what would happen to the flowers, and the animals and the people?'

Suddenly Peter noticed that the sun was setting. Darkness was settling on the land. 'Mother will be watching for me,' he said. 'I must hurry.' But just then he heard a noise. It was the sound of trickling water. He stopped, looked down, and saw a small hole in the dyke, through which a tiny stream was flowing.

A leak in the dyke! Peter understood the danger at once. If water ran through a little hole, it would soon make a larger one, then the waters could break through and the land would be flooded!

Peter saw what he must do. He climbed down the side of the dyke and thrust his finger in the tiny hole. The water stopped! 'The angry waters will stay back now,' said Peter. 'I can keep them back with my finger. Holland will not be drowned while I am here.' But then he thought, 'How long can I stay here?' Already it was dark and cold. Peter called out, 'Help! Is anyone there? Help!' But no one heard him. No one came to help.

It grew darker and colder still. Peter's arm began to grow stiff and numb. 'Will no one come?' he thought. Then he shouted again for help. And when no one came, he cried out, 'Mother! Mother!'

Many times since sunset, his mother had looked out at the dyke and expected to see her little boy. She was worried, but then she thought that perhaps Peter was spending the night with his blind friend, as he had done before. 'Well,' she thought, 'when he gets home in the morning, I will have to scold him for staying away from home without permission.'

Poor Peter! He would rather have been home than anywhere else in the world, but he could not move from the dyke. He tried to whistle to keep himself company, but he couldn't because his teeth chattered with cold. He thought of his brother and sister in their warm beds, and of his father and mother. 'I must not let them be drowned,' he thought. 'I must stay here until someone comes.'

The moon and stars looked down on the shivering child. His head was bent and his eyes were closed, but he was not asleep. Now and then he rubbed the hand that was holding back the angry waters.

Morning came. A man walking along the dyke heard a sound, something like a groan. He bent down and saw the child below. He called out, 'What's the matter, boy? Are you hurt? Why are you sitting there?'

In a voice faint and weak, the boy said, 'I am keeping the water from coming in. Please, tell them to come quickly.' The man ran to get help. People came with shovels to fix the dyke, and they carried Peter, the little hero, home to his parents.

'Tis many a year since then; but still,
When the sea roars like a flood,
The children are taught
what a child can do
Who is brave and true and good.
For all the mothers and fathers
Take their children by the hand
And tell them of brave little Peter
Whose courage saved the land.

Brer Rabbit and the Tar Baby

PARENTS: The Brer Rabbit stories are African American folktales collected and retold in the late nineteenth century by the American writer Joel Chandler Harris. Harris wrote the tales in the speech of a character he called Uncle Remus, an old black man who tells stories to a young boy on a Southern plantation. The Tar Baby is one of the most famous Brer Rabbit stories, showing how Brer Rabbit is able to use his ingenuity to defeat Brer Fox's endless attempts to catch and eat him. It is written here in a modernised version.

'Did Brer Fox never catch Brer Rabbit, Uncle Remus?' asked the little boy.

'He come mighty near it, child, you be sure, Brer Fox did,' said Uncle Remus. 'And that was when he made a Tar Baby.'

'What's a Tar Baby?' asked the boy. And this is the story Uncle Remus told him.

One day Brer Fox woke up feeling grumpy.

'I've had just about enough of that pesky Brer Rabbit,' he said to himself. 'Over and over again he gets up to his tricks, running rings round me and making me look a fool. Every time I think I've got him, he comes up with some smart plan and he gets clean away. But I've got a plan of my own, and this time I'm going to get the better of Brer Rabbit.'

So Brer Fox went to work with his plan to catch Brer Rabbit and teach him a lesson. First of all, he took some tar and some turpentine, made it into a thick, gooey paste and shaped it into something like a doll, but bigger. He dressed it up in real clothes, with a hat and everything, until it looked just like a real human baby, but it was a Tar Baby, too sticky to touch.

Brer Fox sat the Tar Baby down, right in the middle of the road. Then that crafty old Fox hid himself in the bushes beside the road, to see what was going to happen.

He didn't have to wait too long, because, by-and-by, who should appear but Brer Rabbit, hoppin' along down the road, hippity-hoppity, just as happy with himself as can be. Brer Fox lay low. Then Brer Rabbit saw the Tar Baby. Was he surprised! He got up on his hind legs and looked at it. Brer Fox was still lying low.

'Mornin,' said Brer Rabbit to the Tar Baby. 'Nice weather we're havin' this mornin'.'

The Tar Baby said nothing at all. Brer Fox was still lying low.

'How you feelin' this fine mornin'?' Brer Rabbit asked the Tar Baby.

Brer Fox winked his eye and tried to lie even lower in the ground. The Tar Baby still said nothing.

'You deaf or something?' asked Brer Rabbit, beginning to feel irritated. ''cause if you are, I can always shout louder.'

Brer Fox still lay low. The Tar Baby sat quite still and said nothing. Brer Rabbit began to get the feeling he was being ignored, and he didn't like that one little bit.

'Why don't you say something? Cat got your tongue?' he asked, getting really angry. 'Or are you just too stuck-up to talk to the likes of me, Mr High-and-Mighty?'

Brer Fox wanted to laugh but he daren't, in case he gave himself away. He had to bury his face in his paws to muffle it.

'I'm going to teach you some manners if it's the last thing I do,' said Brer Rabbit, getting very angry indeed. 'Now take off your hat and say "Good morning", like respectable folks do.'

Still Brer Fox lay low, and still the Tar Baby said nothing.

'OK, have it your own way, but don't say I didn't warn you,' said Brer Rabbit, drawing back his paw to make a fist, which he planted on the Tar Baby's arm, as hard as he could. His fist stuck fast in the tar.

'I'm warning you, you'd better let me go,' Brer Rabbit shouted at the Tar Baby, 'or you're going to get another one of those.'

With that, he made his other paw into a fist and punched the Tar Baby in the other arm. His second fist stuck in the tar. Was he angry! And you know, when people are angry they don't always think straight. They sometimes do really stupid things to make a bad situation worse. So Brer Rabbit, with both of his fists stuck in the tar, used his head to butt the Tar Baby in the stomach. And guess what? He soon had his head and both paws stuck in the tar. Then he used his feet to push himself away from the Tar Baby, but his feet sank into the tar as well. He was well and truly stuck, and the harder he struggled, the deeper he got stuck.

All this time, Brer Fox had been lying low, watching and waiting. Now his moment had come. He came out from where he was hiding and sauntered over to Brer Rabbit, looking as innocent as could be.

'My, my, Brer Rabbit,' he said, 'you sure look like you're in a spot of bother. Truth to tell, you look really stuck-up!'

And with that, he couldn't keep up his innocent look any more. Brer Fox started to laugh, and once he'd started, he couldn't stop. He laughed until the tears rolled through the fur on his cheeks. He laughed until he couldn't stand up. He rolled around in the dirt, laughing and clutching his sides until he couldn't laugh any more.

At last, he was so tired out with laughing that he just lay on the ground, staring at Brer Rabbit and the Tar Baby. Brer Rabbit didn't like it when Brer Fox was laughing at him. But he liked it a whole lot less when Brer Fox went silent, because he didn't know what was coming next. He thought it might be something bad.

'Brer Fox,' he said, wanting to break the silence, 'could you be really kind and pull me out of this thing that I'm stuck to?'

'I could,' said Brer Fox. 'I could pull you off that there Tar Baby, that I made to trap you with, just as easy as anything. But what do you think I'm going to do then?'

'Let me go?' asked Brer Rabbit.

Well, that just set Brer Fox off laughing again. He roared and gasped and rolled around in the dirt of the road, with tears running through the fur on his foxy cheeks.

'Let you go? Oh yes indeedy, it's very likely I'm going to let you go, after all the time you've been bouncing around these parts, behaving like you own it, and making me look the fool with all your smart little rabbity pranks. You think you're so clever don't you, Brer Rabbit? A real Mr Smarty-Pants. Thought I'd never catch you. And now I have. So no, Brer Rabbit, I'm not going to let you go. But I'm going to do something better than that. I'm going to ask you to dinner.'

'Well that is real neighbourly of you, Brer Fox,' said Brer Rabit, feeling relieved. 'I would be glad to eat dinner with you. Maybe the two of us can turn over a new leaf and be friends from now on.'

'Eat dinner with you? Who says I'm going to eat dinner with you?'

'Why you did, Brer Fox, you said you wanted to eat dinner with me.'

'No no, little rabbit, your long ears must be deceiving you,' said Brer Fox with a nasty grin on his face. 'I didn't say I want to eat dinner with you. I want to eat you for my dinner! Same difference!'

At this Brer Rabbit began to shake. He knew Brer Fox wanted to have his own back for all the tricks Brer Rabbit had played on him. So he started to cry.

'Oh Brer Fox, if you want to eat me for your dinner, there's nothing I can do to stop you, but I beg you, just don't throw me in that there briar patch.'

'Do you know what I feel like, Brer Rabbit? I feel like nothing tastes so good as barbecued rabbit. So I'm going to build a fire and roast you.'

'Oh yes, please, Brer Fox, build the fire as big as you like and roast me just as slowly as you like, just don't throw me in that there briar patch.'

'On the other hand,' said Brer Fox, 'this is a mighty hot day to be building a fire. Maybe I'll hang you instead.'

'Yes, yes, Brer Fox, hang me as high as you please, only just don't throw me in that there briar patch.'

'On the other hand,' said Brer Fox, 'I don't have any rope. Maybe I'll have to drown you.'

'Drown me just as deep as you please, Brer Fox, just don't throw me in that there briar patch.'

'On the other hand,' said Brer Fox, 'there's no pond nearby. So what am I going to do with you, Brer Rabbit, 'cos you sure as anything is going to be my dinner.'

'Anything, anything at all, Brer Fox, just don't throw me in that there briar patch.'

Now, Brer Fox was an evil and sly old fox. He really wanted to hurt Brer Rabbit as much as he could. So he took him by the back legs, pulled him off the Tar Baby, and threw him, just as hard as he could, right smack bang into the middle of the briar patch.

There was a flurry as Brer Rabbit disappeared into the middle of the thorn bushes. Then nothing. Silence. Brer Fox had been hoping to hear Brer Rabbit scream. He expected to see the thorn bushes waving this way and that as Brer Rabbit struggled to get free of them. But nothing.

Then, by and by, old Brer Fox heard someone calling his name from high up on the hill. He raised his old grey paw to shade his eyes from the midday sun, and he was just about able to see Brer Rabbit. That crafty Brer Rabbit was sitting on a log, cool as you please, eating a carrot.

'Howdy, Brer Fox,' he called down from the hill top. 'Thanks for putting me into the briar patch. Home from home for me, is that briar patch. Born and bred in it. I know the briar patch like I know the back of my paw.'

And he laughed his high-pitched rabbit laugh. He laughed and laughed as he hopped away over the top of the hill, leaving Brer Fox staring after him, and not laughing at all.

The Frog Prince
(A tale from the Brothers Grimm)

In olden times, when wishing was still of some use, there lived a king whose daughters were all beautiful, but the youngest was so beautiful that the sun itself, which has seen so many wonders, was astonished whenever it shone on her face.

Close by the King's castle lay a great dark forest, and under an old lime tree in the forest was a wishing well. When the day was very warm, the King's child went out into the forest and sat down by the side of the cool well. There she would play with her favourite plaything, a golden ball, tossing it up high and catching it in her little hands.

Now it so happened that on one occasion the princess's golden ball did not fall into the little hand which she was holding up for it, but onto the ground beyond, and it rolled straight into the well. The King's daughter followed it with her eyes, but it vanished, and the well was so deep that the bottom could not be seen. She began to cry, louder and louder, and could not be comforted. And as she sat there crying someone said to her, 'What is the matter, little princess? You're crying so that even a stone would pity you.' She looked round to the side from whence the voice came, and saw a frog stretching forth its thick, ugly head from the water. 'Oh, it's you old water-splasher,' she said, 'I am weeping for my golden ball, which has fallen into the well.'

Did the princess heed the advice about frogs from the poem 'The Frog'?

'Be quiet, and do not weep,' answered the frog, 'I can help you, but what will you give me if I bring your plaything to the surface again?'

'Whatever you want, dear frog,' she said, 'My clothes, my pearls and jewels, and even the golden crown that I am wearing.'

The frog answered, 'I do not care for your clothes, your pearls and jewels, or even your golden crown, but if you will love me and let me be your friend and playmate, and sit by me at your little table, and eat off your little golden plate, and drink out of your little cup and sleep in your little bed — if you will promise me this, I will go down into the deep well and bring you your golden ball.'

'Oh yes,' said she, 'I promise you anything if you will but bring me my ball back again.' However, she secretly thought, 'How the silly frog does talk! He lives in the water with the other frogs and croaks, and can be no companion to any human being!'

But as soon as he heard her promise, the frog put his head into the water and sank down, and in a short while came swimming up again with the ball in his mouth, and threw it on the grass. The King's daughter was delighted to see her pretty plaything once more, and she picked it up and ran away with it.

'Wait, wait,' said the frog. 'Take me with you. I can't run as fast as you.' But what good did it do him to scream his 'Croak! Croak!' after her, as loudly as he could? She did not listen to it, but ran home and soon forgot the poor frog, who was forced to go back into his well again.

The next day when she had seated herself at the dinner table with the King and all the courtiers, and was eating from her little golden plate, something came creeping splish splash, splish splash, up the marble staircase, and when it had got to the top, it knocked at the door and cried: 'Youngest daughter of the King, open the door for me.'

She ran to see who was outside, but when she opened the door, there sat the frog in front of it looking very slimy and wet. She quickly slammed the door and sat down to dinner again, and was quite frightened. The King saw plainly that her heart was beating violently, and said: 'My child, what are you so afraid of? Is there perhaps a giant outside who wants to carry you away?'

'Ah, no,' she replied. 'It is not a giant but a disgusting frog.'

'What does a frog want with you?'

'Ah, dear father, yesterday as I was in the forest sitting by the well and playing, my golden ball fell into the water. Because I cried so, the frog brought it out again for me, and because he so insisted, I promised him he should be my companion, but I never thought he would be able to come out of his water! He wants to be my playmate, and sit by me at my little table, and eat off my little golden plate, and drink out of my little cup and sleep in my little bed with me, and I can't bear it. Now he is outside there, and wants to come in.'

In the meantime the frog knocked a second time and cried,

'Princess, keep your promises:
Open wide the door.
Else will other princesses
Be believed no more.'

At that the King said: 'If we make promises, daughter, we must keep them, so you had better open the door and let him in.' The youngest princess went and opened the door, and the frog hopped in and followed her – splish splash, splish splash – to her chair. There he sat and cried, 'Lift me up beside you.' She hesitated – the frog was so cold and slimy! At last the King commanded her to do it.

Once the frog was on the chair, he wanted to be on the table, and when he was on the table he said: 'Now, push your little golden plate nearer to me so that we can eat together.' She did this, but it was easy to see that she did not do it willingly. The frog enjoyed what he ate, but almost every mouthful the princess took choked her. At last the frog said: 'I have eaten and now I am tired. Carry me into your little room and make your little silken bed ready, and we will both lie down and go to sleep.'

The King's daughter began to cry, for she was afraid of the cold frog that she did not like to touch, and who was now to sleep in her pretty, clean little bed. But the King grew angry and said: 'This good frog helped you when you were in trouble. Now it is not fair of you to scorn him.' So she took hold of the frog with two fingers, carried him upstairs, and put him in the corner of the bedroom.

But when she was in bed, the frog crept to her and said: 'I am tired and the floor is hard. I want to sleep in your nice bed, so lift me up and mind your words at the wishing well.' Although the princess hated the thought of the frog in her bed, she thought of her father's words. She gingerly picked the frog up and put him at the foot of her bed. The frog slept soundly there throughout the night but the princess tossed and turned – she could not sleep at all. In the morning, the frog sprung out of the bed and went out – splish splash, splish splash – to the wishing well for a swim.

In the evening, the frog returned. The princess was not pleased to see him but let him in again. After dinner, she let the frog come to her room and she put him at the end of her bed. 'Will you give me a kiss goodnight, dear princess?' asked the frog. The youngest princess couldn't bear the thought of kissing the frog, but she reluctantly did so. All of a sudden there was no longer a frog before her but a handsome prince with beautiful, kind eyes. He told her, 'Appearances are deceptive and I was not what I appeared to be. I was bewitched by a wicked old witch who turned me into a frog. She put a spell on me that no one but you could break. Oh how long I have waited to get you to kiss me and break the spell!'

Then they went to sleep, and next morning, when the sun awoke them, a carriage came driving up with eight white horses, which had white ostrich feathers on their heads and were harnessed with golden chains. The handsome prince and the youngest daughter of the king travelled to the land that the prince was born to rule, where they were married and lived happily ever after.

Hansel and Gretel
(A tale from the Brothers Grimm)

Once upon a time, by a great forest, lived a poor woodcutter with his wife and his two children. The boy was called Hansel and the girl Gretel. They had little food, and once, when a great famine fell on the land, the woodcutter could no longer provide even a daily meal for his family.

He was so worried that he could not sleep and lay tossing and turning. He groaned and said to his wife: 'What is to going to happen to us? How are we to feed our poor children, when we no longer have enough even for ourselves?'

'I'll tell you what,' answered the woman, who was the children's stepmother and was not fond of them, 'early tomorrow morning we will take the children out into the forest to where it is thickest. There we will light a fire for them, and give each of them one more piece of bread, and then we will go to our work and leave them alone. They will not find the way home again, and we shall be rid of them.'

'No!' said the man, 'I will not do that. How can I bear to leave my children alone in the forest? The wild animals would soon come and tear them to pieces.'

'Oh! You fool!' she said, 'Then we must all four die of hunger, you may as well get four coffins ready!' She left him no peace until he consented.

'But I feel very sorry for the poor children, all the same,' said the man.

The two children had been so hungry that they also had not been able to sleep, and they had heard what their stepmother had said to their father. Gretel started crying and said to Hansel, 'Now all is over with us.'

'Be quiet, Gretel,' said Hansel, 'don't worry, I will soon find a way to help us.' And when their father and stepmother had fallen asleep, Hansel got up, put on his little coat, opened the door below and crept outside.

The moon shone brightly, and the white pebbles which lay in front of the house glittered like real silver pennies. Hansel stooped and stuffed the little pocket of his coat with as many as he could fit in it. Then he went back and said to Gretel: 'Sleep well, little sister, for I have a plan!' and he lay down again in his bed.

When day dawned, but before the sun had risen, the stepmother came and awoke the two children, saying: 'Get up, you lazy children. We are going into the forest to fetch wood.' She gave each a little piece of bread, and said: 'There is something for your dinner, but do not eat it up before then, for you will get nothing else.'

Gretel took the bread under her apron, as Hansel had the pebbles in his pocket. Then they all set out together on the way to the forest.

When they had walked a short time, Hansel stood still and peeped back at the house, and did so again and again. His father said, 'Hansel, pay attention! Keep up! Do not forget how to use your legs.'

'Ah, father,' said Hansel, 'I am looking at my little white cat, which is sitting up on the roof, and wants to say goodbye to me.'

The wife said, 'Fool, that is not your little cat, that is the morning sun which is shining on the chimneys.'

Hansel, however, had not been looking back at the cat, but had been constantly throwing one of the white pebble-stones out of his pocket on the road.

When they had reached the middle of the forest, the father said: 'Now, children, pile up some wood, and I will light a fire so you won't get cold.'

Hansel and Gretel gathered brushwood together, as high as a little hill. The brushwood was lighted, and when the flames were burning very high, the woman said: 'Now, children, lay yourselves down by the fire and rest, we will go into the forest and cut some wood. When we have finished, we will come back and fetch you away.'

Hansel and Gretel sat by the fire, and when noon came, each ate a little piece of bread. As they could hear the strokes of an axe, they believed that their father was near. It was not the axe, however, but a branch which he had fastened to a withered tree which the wind was blowing backwards and forwards. And as they had been sitting such a long time, their eyes closed with tiredness, and they fell fast asleep.

When at last they awoke, it was already dark night. It was scary for the children all alone out in the dark and spooky forest. Gretel said, 'How are we to get out of the forest now?'

But Hansel comforted her and said: 'Just wait a little, until the moon has risen, and then we will soon find the way.' And when the full moon had risen, Hansel took his little sister by the hand, followed the pebbles which shone like silver coins and showed them the way.

They walked the whole night long, and by day-break, they came once more to their father's house. They knocked at the door, and when the woman opened it and saw that it was Hansel and Gretel, she said: 'You naughty children, why have you slept so long in the forest? We thought you were never coming back at all.'

The father, however, rejoiced, for it had cut him to the heart to leave them behind alone.

Not long afterwards, there was once more a shortage of food throughout the land, and the children heard their stepmother saying at night to their father: 'Everything is eaten again, we have only half a loaf of bread left, and that is the end. The children must go. We will take them further into the wood, so that they will not find their way out again. There is no other means of saving ourselves.'

The man's heart was heavy, and he thought: 'It would be better for you to share the last mouthful with your children.' The woman, however, would listen to nothing that he had to say, but only scolded him. As he had said 'yes' the first time, he had to do so a second time also.

The children, however, were still awake and had heard the conversation. When their parents were asleep, Hansel again got up, and wanted to go out and pick up pebbles as he had done before, but the woman had locked the door and Hansel could not get out. Nevertheless he comforted his little sister, and said: 'Do not cry, Gretel, go to sleep quietly and everything will be alright.'

Early in the morning the woman came in and took the children out of their beds. Their piece of bread was given to them, but it was smaller than the time before. On the way into the forest Hansel crumbled his bread in his pocket, and often stood still and threw a morsel on the ground.

'Hansel, why do you stop and look round?' said the father. 'Come on!'

'I am looking back at my little pigeon which is sitting on the roof, and wants to say goodbye to me,' answered Hansel.

'Fool,' said the woman, 'that is not your little pigeon, that is the morning sun that is shining on the chimney.'

Hansel, however, little by little, threw all the crumbs on the path. The woman led the children still deeper into the forest, where they had never in their lives been before.

Then a great fire was again made, and the mother said: 'Just sit there, you naughty children, and when you are tired you may sleep a little. We are going into the forest to cut wood, and in the evening when we are done, we will come and fetch you away.'

When it was noon, Gretel shared her piece of bread with Hansel, who had scattered his on the way. Then they fell asleep and evening passed, but no one came to the poor children.

They did not awake until it was dark night, and Hansel comforted his little sister and said: 'Just wait, Gretel, until the moon rises, and then we shall see the crumbs of bread which I have thrown about, for they will show us our way home again.'

When the moon came they set out, but they found no crumbs, for the many thousands of birds that fly about in the woods and fields had eaten them all. Hansel said to Gretel: 'We shall soon find the way.'

But they did not find it. They walked the whole night and all the next day too from morning until evening, but they did not get out of the forest, and were very hungry, for they had nothing to eat but a few berries, which grew on the ground. And when they were so tired that their legs would carry them no further, they lay down beneath a tree and fell asleep.

It was now two days since they had left their father's house. They began to walk again, but they always came deeper into the forest, and if help did not come soon, they would surely die of hunger. When it was midday, they saw a beautiful snow-white bird sitting on a branch, which sang so delightfully that they stood still and listened to it. And when its song was over, it spread its wings and flew away before them, and they followed it until they reached a little house, on the roof of which it landed. And when they approached the little house, they saw that it was built of gingerbread and covered with cakes, and that the windows were of clear sugar.

'Let's get to work,' said Hansel, 'and have a good meal! I will eat a bit of the roof, and you Gretel, can eat some of the window. It will taste sweet.'

Hansel reached up above, and broke off a little of the roof to try how it tasted, and Gretel leant against the window and nibbled at the panes. Then a shrill voice cried from inside the house:

> *'Nibble, nibble, like a mouse,*
> *Who is nibbling at my house?'*

The children answered,

> *'It is only the air heaving a sigh,*
> *It is only the wind gently passing by.'*

And they went on eating because they were so hungry. Hansel, who liked the taste of the roof, tore down a great piece of it, and Gretel pushed out the whole of one round windowpane, sat down and enjoyed herself.

Suddenly the door opened, and a woman as old as the hills, who supported herself on crutches, came creeping out. Hansel and Gretel were so terribly frightened that they dropped what they had in their hands.

The old woman, however, nodded her head, and said: 'Oh, you dear children, who has brought you here? Do come in, and stay with me. No harm shall happen to you.'

She took them both by the hand, and led them into her little house. Then good food was set before them, milk and pancakes with sugar, apples and nuts. Afterwards two pretty little beds were covered with clean white linen, and Hansel and Gretel lay down in them, and they felt as though they were in heaven.

Now, the old woman had only pretended to be so kind. She was in reality a wicked witch, who lay in wait for children, and had only built the little house of gingerbread in order to lure them. When a child fell into her power, she killed, cooked and ate the poor child! Witches have red eyes and cannot see far, but they have a great sense of smell, like animals, and are aware when human beings draw near.

Early in the morning before the children were awake, she was already up, and when she saw both of them sleeping and looking so pretty, with their rosy cheeks, she muttered to herself: 'That will be a delicious mouthful!'

Then she seized Hansel with her shrivelled hand, carried him into a little stable, and locked him in behind a door with bars in it. Scream as he might, it would not help him. Then the wicked old woman went to Gretel, shook her till she awoke, and cried: 'Get up, lazy thing. Fetch some water and cook something good for your brother. He is in the stable outside, and is to be made fat. When he is fat, I will eat him.'

Gretel began to weep bitterly, but it was all in vain, for she was forced to do what the wicked witch commanded. And now the best food was cooked for poor Hansel, but Gretel got nothing but egg shells. Every morning the woman crept to the little stable, and cried: 'Hansel, stretch out your finger that I may feel if you will soon be fat.'

Hansel, however, stretched out to her a little bone he had found on the floor of the stable, and the old woman, who had bad eyesight, could not see it, and thought it was Hansel's finger, and was astonished that there was no way of fattening him.

When four weeks had gone by, and Hansel still remained thin, she was seized with impatience and would not wait any longer.

'Now, then, Gretel,' she cried to the girl, 'wake yourself, and bring some water. Whether Hansel be fat or thin, tomorrow I will kill him and cook him.'

Ah, how the poor little sister did cry when she had to fetch the water, oh how the tears did flow down her cheeks.

'We will bake first,' said the old woman, 'I have already heated the oven, and kneaded the dough.' She pushed poor Gretel out to the oven, from which flames of fire were already darting. 'Put your head in,' said the witch, 'and see if it is properly heated, so that we can put the bread in.' But Gretel saw what she had in mind: the wicked witch intended to push her into the oven and bake her in it, and then she would eat her, too.

So Gretel said: 'I do not know how I am to do it. Where am I to look in?'

'Silly goose,' said the old woman, 'Just open the large door and stick your head in. I can do it myself.' And the witch thrust her head into the oven.

Then Gretel quickly gave her a massive push that drove the witch far into the oven, and she shut the iron door and fastened the bolt. Then the witch began to howl quite horribly, but Gretel ran away like lightning to Hansel, opened his little stable door, and cried: 'Hansel, we are saved! The old witch is dead.'

Then Hansel sprang like a bird from its cage. How they rejoiced and embraced and danced. As they had no longer any need to fear her, they went into the witch's house, and in every corner there stood chests full of pearls and jewels.

'These are far better than pebbles,' said Hansel, and thrust into his pockets as many as he could fit in.

Gretel said: 'Let me have some too!' and filled her apron with the precious stones.

'But now we must be off,' said Hansel, 'so that we may get out of the witch's forest.'

When they had walked for two hours, they came to a great stretch of water.

'We cannot cross,' said Hansel, 'there aren't any stepping stones or even a bridge.'

'Nor is there a ferry,' answered Gretel, 'but a white duck is swimming there. If I ask her, she will help us over.' Then she cried,

'Little duck, little duck, can you see,

Hansel and Gretel are waiting for thee.

There's neither a stone nor a bridge in sight,

take us across on your back so white.'

The white duck came to them, and Hansel seated himself on its back, and told his sister to sit by him.

'No,' replied Gretel, 'that will be too heavy for the little duck. She shall take us across, one after the other.'

The good little duck did so, and when they were once safely across and had walked for a short time, the forest seemed to be more and more familiar to them, and at length they saw from afar their father's house. Then they began to run, rushed into the house, and threw themselves round their father's neck. He had not known one happy hour since he had left the children in the forest. His evil wife had died. Gretel emptied her apron until pearls and precious stones ran about the room, and Hansel threw one handful after another out of his pocket to add to them. Then all their troubles were over and they lived together in perfect happiness.

In Which Tigger Comes to the Forest and Has Breakfast

(A selection from *The House at Pooh Corner* by A. A. Milne)

> **PARENTS:** If your children have not yet met the bear named Winnie-the-Pooh and his friends in the Hundred Acre Wood, you might first want to read to them from the book called *Winnie-the-Pooh* by A. A. Milne (a chapter from which is included in *What Your Year 1 Child Needs to Know*).

Winnie-the-Pooh woke up suddenly in the middle of the night and listened. Then he got out of bed, and lit his candle, and stumped across the room to see if anybody was trying to get into his honey-cupboard, and they weren't, so he stumped back again, blew out his candle, and got into bed. Then he heard the noise again.

'Is that you, Piglet?' he said.

But it wasn't.

'Come in, Christopher Robin,' he said.

But Christopher Robin didn't.

'Tell me about it tomorrow, Eeyore,' said Pooh sleepily.

But the noise went on.

'*Worraworraworraworraworra,*' said Whatever-it-was, and Pooh found that he wasn't asleep after all.

'What can it be?' he thought. 'There are lots of noises in the Forest, but this is a different one. It isn't a growl, and it isn't a purr, and it isn't a bark, and it isn't a noise-you-make-before-beginning-a-piece-of-poetry, but it's a noise of some kind, made by a strange animal. And he's making it outside my door. So I shall get up and ask him not to do it.'

He got out of bed and opened his front door. 'Hallo!' said Pooh, in case there was anything outside.

'Hallo!' said Whatever-it-was.

'Oh!' said Pooh. 'Hallo!'

'Hallo!'

'Oh, there you are!' said Pooh. 'Hallo!'

Pooh would like Jack Prelutsky's poem 'I Know All the Sounds That the Animals Make' on page 26, don't you think?

'Hallo!' said the Strange Animal, wondering how long this was going on.

Pooh was just going to say 'Hallo!' for the fourth time when he thought that he wouldn't so he said: 'Who is it?' instead.

'Me,' said a voice.

'Oh!' said Pooh. 'Well, come here.'

So Whatever-it-was came here, and in the light of the candle he and Pooh looked at each other. 'I'm Pooh,' said Pooh.

'I'm Tigger,' said Tigger.

'Oh!' said Pooh, for he had never seen an animal like this before. 'Does Christopher Robin know about you?'

'Of course he does,' said Tigger.

'Well,' said Pooh, 'it's the middle of the night, which is a good time for going to sleep. And tomorrow morning we'll have some honey for breakfast. Do Tiggers like honey?'

'They like everything,' said Tigger cheerfully.

'Then if they like going to sleep on the floor, I'll go back to bed,' said Pooh, 'and we'll do things in the morning. Good night.' And he got back into bed and went fast asleep. When he awoke in the morning, the first thing he saw was Tigger, sitting in front of the glass and looking at himself.

'Hallo!' said Pooh.

'Hallo!' said Tigger. 'I've found somebody just like me. I thought I was the only one of them.'

Pooh got out of bed, and began to explain what a looking-glass was, but just as he was getting to the interesting part, Tigger said:

'Excuse me a moment, but there's something climbing up your table,' and with one loud *Worraworraworraworraworra* he jumped at the end of the tablecloth, pulled it to the ground, wrapped himself up in it three times, rolled to the other end of the room, and, after a terrible struggle, got his head into the daylight again, and said cheerfully: 'Have I won?'

'That's my tablecloth,' said Pooh, as he began to unwind Tigger.

'I wondered what it was,' said Tigger.

'It goes on the table and you put things on it.'

'Then why did it try to bite me when I wasn't looking?'

'I don't think it did,' said Pooh.

'It tried,' said Tigger, 'but I was too quick for it.' Pooh put the cloth back on the table, and he put a large honey-pot on the cloth, and they sat down, Tigger took a large mouthful of honey ... and he looked up at the ceiling with his head on one side, and made exploring noises with his tongue and considering noises, and what-have-we-got-here noises ... and then he said in a very decided voice: 'Tiggers don't like honey.'

'Oh!' said Pooh, and tried to make it sound Sad and Regretful. 'I thought they liked everything.'

'Everything except honey,' said Tigger. Pooh felt rather pleased about this, and said that, as soon as he had finished his own breakfast, he would take Tigger round to Piglet's house, and Tigger could try some of Piglet's haycorns.

'Thank you, Pooh,' said Tigger, 'because haycorns is really what Tiggers like best.' So after breakfast they went round to see Piglet, and Pooh explained as they went that Piglet was a Very Small Animal who didn't like bouncing, and asked Tigger not to be too Bouncy just at first. And Tigger, who had been hiding behind trees and jumping out on Pooh's shadow when it wasn't looking, said that Tiggers were only bouncy before breakfast, and that as soon as they had had a few haycorns they became Quiet and Refined. So by and by they knocked at the door of Piglet's house.

'Hallo, Pooh,' said Piglet.

'Hallo, Piglet. This is Tigger.'

'Oh, is it?' said Piglet, and he edged round to the other side of the table. 'I thought Tiggers were smaller than that.'

'Not the big ones,' said Tigger.

'They like haycorns,' said Pooh, 'so that's what we've come for, because poor Tigger hasn't had any breakfast yet.'

Piglet pushed the bowl of haycorns towards Tigger, and said: 'Help yourself,' and then he got close up to Pooh and felt much braver, and said, 'So you're Tigger? Well, well!' in a careless sort of voice. But Tigger said nothing because his mouth was full of haycorns...

After a long munching noise he said:

'Ee-eers o i a-ors.'

And when Pooh and Piglet said 'What?' he said 'Skoos ee,' and went outside for a moment. When he came back he said firmly: 'Tiggers don't like haycorns.'

'But you said they liked everything except honey,' said Pooh.

'Everything except honey and haycorns,' explained Tigger. When he heard this Pooh said, 'Oh, I see!' and Piglet, who was rather glad that Tiggers didn't like haycorns, said, 'What about thistles?'

'Thistles,' said Tigger, 'is what Tiggers like best.'

'Then let's go along and see Eeyore,' said Piglet.

So the three of them went; and after they had walked and walked and walked, they came to the part of the Forest where Eeyore was. 'Hallo, Eeyore!' said Pooh. 'This is Tigger.'

'What is?' said Eeyore.

'This,' explained Pooh and Piglet together, and Tigger smiled his happiest smile and said nothing.

Eeyore walked all round Tigger one way, and then turned and walked all round him the other way. 'What did you say it was?' he asked.

'Tigger.'

'Ah!' said Eeyore.

'He's just come,' explained Piglet.

'Ah!' said Eeyore again. He thought for a long time and then said: 'When is he going?'

Pooh explained to Eeyore that Tigger was a great friend of Christopher Robin's, who had come to stay in the Forest, and Piglet explained to Tigger that he mustn't mind what Eeyore said because he was always gloomy; and Eeyore explained to Piglet that, on the contrary, he was feeling particularly cheerful this morning; and Tigger explained to anybody who was listening that he hadn't had any breakfast yet.

'I knew there was something,' said Pooh. 'Tiggers always eat thistles, so that was why we came to see you, Eeyore.'

'Don't mention it, Pooh.'

'Oh, Eeyore, I didn't mean that I didn't want to see you — '

'Quite — quite. But your new stripy friend — naturally, he wants his breakfast. What did you say his name was?'

'Tigger.'

'Then come this way, Tigger.' Eeyore led the way to the most thistly-looking patch of thistles that ever was, and waved a hoof at it. 'A little patch I was keeping for my birthday,' he said; 'but, after all, what are birthdays? Here today and gone tomorrow. Help yourself, Tigger.'

Tigger thanked him and looked a little anxiously at Pooh. 'Are these really thistles?' he whispered. 'Yes,' said Pooh.

'What Tiggers like best?'

'That's right,' said Pooh.

'I see,' said Tigger. So he took a large mouthful, and he gave a large crunch. 'Ow!' said Tigger. He sat down and put his paw in his mouth.

'What's the matter?' asked Pooh.

'*Hot!*' mumbled Tigger.

'Your friend,' said Eeyore, 'appears to have bitten on a bee.'

Pooh's friend stopped shaking his head to get the prickles out, and explained that Tiggers didn't like thistles.

'Then why bend a perfectly good one?' asked Eeyore.

'But you said,' began Pooh – 'you *said* that Tiggers liked everything except honey and haycorns.'

'*And* thistles,' said Tigger, who was now running round in circles with his tongue hanging out. Pooh looked at him sadly.

'What are we going to do?' he asked Piglet. Piglet knew the answer to that, and he said at once that they must go and see Christopher Robin.

'You'll find him with Kanga,' said Eeyore. He came close to Pooh, and said in a loud whisper: '*Could* you ask your friend to do his exercises somewhere else? I shall be having lunch directly, and don't want it bounced on just before I begin. A trifling matter, and fussy of me, but we all have our little ways.'

Pooh nodded solemnly and called to Tigger. 'Come along and we'll go and see Kanga. She's sure to have lots of breakfast for you.'

Tigger finished his last circle and came up to Pooh and Piglet.

'Hot!' he explained with a large and friendly smile. 'Come on!' and he rushed off.

Pooh and Piglet walked slowly after him. And, as they walked, Piglet said nothing, because he couldn't think of anything, and Pooh said nothing, because he was thinking of a poem. And when he had thought of it he began:

> *What shall we do about poor little Tigger?*
> *If he never eats nothing he'll never get bigger.*
> *He doesn't like honey and haycorns and thistles*
> *Because of the taste and because of the bristles.*
> *And all the good things which an animal likes*
> *Have the wrong sort of swallow or too many spikes.*

'He's quite big enough anyhow,' said Piglet.

'He isn't really very big.'

'Well, he *seems* so.'

Pooh was thoughtful when he heard this, and then he murmured to himself:

> *But whatever his weight in pounds, shillings, and ounces,*
> *He always seems bigger because of his bounces.*

'And that's the whole poem,' he said. 'Do you like it, Piglet?'

'All except the shillings,' said Piglet. 'I don't think they ought to be there.'

'They wanted to come in after the pounds,' explained Pooh, 'so I let them. It is the best way to write poetry, letting things come.'

We'll learn more about what certain animals eat on page 289.

'Oh, I didn't know,' said Piglet.

Tigger had been bouncing in front of them all this time, turning round every now and then to ask, 'Is this the way?' – and now at last they came in sight of Kanga's house, and there was Christopher Robin. Tigger rushed up to him.

'Oh, there you are, Tigger!' said Christopher Robin. 'I knew you'd be somewhere.'

'I've been finding things in the Forest,' said Tigger importantly. 'I've found a pooh and a piglet and an eeyore, but I can't find any breakfast.' Pooh and Piglet came up and hugged Christopher Robin, and explained what had been happening.

'Don't you know what Tiggers like?' asked Pooh.

'I expect if I thought very hard I should,' said Christopher Robin, 'but I thought Tigger knew.'

'I do,' said Tigger. 'Everything there is in the world except honey and haycorns and – what were those hot things called?'

'Thistles.'

'Yes, and those.'

'Oh, well then, Kanga can give you some breakfast.'

So they went into Kanga's house, and when Roo had said, 'Hallo, Pooh' and 'Hallo, Piglet' once, and 'Hallo, Tigger' twice, because he had never said it before and it sounded funny, they told Kanga what they wanted, and Kanga said very kindly, 'Well, look in my cupboard, Tigger dear, and see what you'd like.' Because she knew at once that, however big Tigger seemed to be, he wanted as much kindness as Roo.

'Shall I look, too?' said Pooh, who was beginning to feel a little eleven o'clockish. And he found a small tin of condensed milk, and something seemed to tell him that Tiggers didn't like this, so he took it into a corner by itself, and went with it to see that nobody interrupted it.

But the more Tigger put his nose into this and his paw into that, the more things he found which Tiggers didn't like. And when he found everything in the cupboard, and couldn't eat any of it, he said to Kanga, 'What happens now?'

But Kanga and Christopher Robin and Piglet were all standing round Roo, watching him have his Extract of Malt. And Roo was saying, 'Must I?' and Kanga was saying 'Now, Roo dear, you remember what you promised.'

'What is it?' whispered Tigger to Piglet.

'His Strengthening Medicine,' said Piglet. 'He hates it.'

So Tigger came closer, and he leant over the back of Roo's chair, and suddenly he put out his tongue, and took one large golollop, and, with a sudden jump of surprise, Kanga said,

'Oh!' and then clutched at the spoon again just as it was disappearing, and pulled it safely back out of Tigger's mouth. But the Extract of Malt had gone.

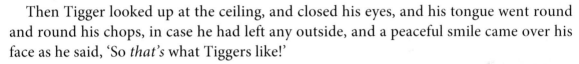

'Tigger *dear!*' said Kanga.

'He's taken my medicine, he's taken my medicine, he's taken my medicine!' sang Roo happily, thinking it was a tremendous joke.

Then Tigger looked up at the ceiling, and closed his eyes, and his tongue went round and round his chops, in case he had left any outside, and a peaceful smile came over his face as he said, 'So *that's* what Tiggers like!'

Which explains why he always lived at Kanga's house afterwards, and had Extract of Malt for breakfast, dinner and tea. And sometimes, when Kanga thought he wanted strengthening, he had a spoonful or two of Roo's breakfast after meals as medicine.

'But *I* think,' said Piglet to Pooh, 'that he's been strengthened quite enough.'

Issun Boshi: One-Inch Boy

PARENTS: 'Issun Boshi' [IH-soon BOH-she] is a folktale from Japan. If you have access to a world map or globe, help your child locate Japan. Like the next story in this book, 'Tom Thumb', this story is about the adventures of a very little person.

Long ago in a village in Japan, there lived an old man and his wife who more than anything wanted a child. They hoped and they wished and they prayed. 'May we be blessed with a child,' they said, 'even if it is no larger than a fingertip.'

And then their prayers were answered. A fine baby boy was born to the old couple. They called him Issun Boshi, which means 'One-Inch Boy', for he was no taller than his father's thumb.

Issun Boshi grew up strong, smart and helpful, though he grew no bigger. When twelve years had passed, Issun Boshi came to his parents and said: 'Father and Mother, please give me your permission to go to the capital city, for I wish to see the world, and learn many things, and make a name for myself.'

His parents were very worried, but they knew their boy was smart and strong, so they agreed to let him go. They made for him a tiny sword out of a sewing needle. They also gave him a rice bowl and some chopsticks.

In the rice bowl he floated down the river, using one of the chopsticks as a paddle. In a few days he arrived at the city of Kyoto. 'My, what a busy city this is!' he thought. 'So many feet and legs!' He walked carefully through the streets, dodging feet and cart wheels. He kept walking until he came to a beautiful house, the largest in the city. At the foot of the steps sat a pair of shiny black wooden shoes. They belonged to the owner of the house, who was the wealthiest lord in the city.

The door of the great house opened. Out walked a man who slipped on the shiny black shoes. Issun Boshi called out: 'Hello! Hello there!' The man looked around and, seeing no one, began to go back in. But Issun Boshi called out: 'Down here, I'm down here, near your shoes! Please be careful you don't step on me.' The man, who was the lord of the house, leaned down and was very surprised when he saw Issun Boshi. Issun Boshi bowed and politely introduced himself. 'My name,' he said, 'is Issun Boshi. I am new here and I would like to work for you.'

The lord picked up Issun Boshi in the palm of his hand. In a friendly voice he asked: 'But what can a little fellow like you do?'

A fly was buzzing around and bothering the lord, so Issun Boshi drew out a sewing needle that he used as a sword. With a quick swit-swat, down went the fly. Then Issun Boshi did an energetic little dance on the lord's hand.

'You are quite an amazing little fellow,' laughed the lord. 'Come, you may work for me and live in my house.'

And so Issun Boshi went to live in the big beautiful house. He made friends with everyone there, especially the princess, the lord's lovely daughter. It seemed that he was always at her side, helping her in whatever way he could, whether by holding down the paper when she wrote a letter or simply by riding on her shoulder and keeping her company while she walked through the beautiful gardens around the house.

In the spring, Issun Boshi travelled with the princess and her companions to the cherry blossom festival. On their way home they began to hear strange noises behind them on the narrow road. They could see nothing in the shadows, when suddenly a huge monster leaped into their path. Everyone screamed and ran – everyone except Issun Boshi and the princess.

'Who are you, and what do you want?' cried Issun Boshi.

'I am an oni [OH-nee],' growled the monster. An oni! Everyone feared the oni, who were fierce and terrible creatures, like demons or goblins. But Issun Boshi stepped forward and shouted: 'Get out of the way, you demon! I am here to guard the princess, and if you try anything, you will regret it!'

'Ha! We'll see about that!' growled the oni. Then he snatched up Issun Boshi, popped him into his mouth and, gulp, swallowed him whole. Down, down Issun Boshi slid until he landed, slap, in the oni's stomach.

'This big oaf should be more careful about what he eats,' said Issun Boshi. He pulled out his sewing-needle sword and began to jab it as hard as he could into the walls of the oni's stomach.

'Ow! Ooh! Agh!' shouted the oni. Then he gave a loud 'Burp!' and out popped Issun Boshi. In pain, the oni ran away whining and crying.

Issun Boshi ran over to the princess. She was bending down and picking up something from the ground. With great excitement she said, 'Look, Issun Boshi, the oni was so scared that he dropped this magic hammer. If you make a wish on it, it will come true.'

Issun Boshi bowed to the princess and said: 'My lady, I would ask that you make a wish.' 'No, Issun Boshi,' said the princess. 'You won this because of your bravery. You should be the first one to wish on it!'

So Issun Boshi took the hammer and said: 'I already have my greatest wish, which is to serve you. But if I could have another wish, I would wish to be as tall as other men.'

Then he gave the hammer to the princess, who made a silent wish on it herself. Then and there, Issun Boshi began to grow taller until beside the princess stood a handsome young man.

That night, when the princess told her father how brave Issun Boshi had been, and how he had risked his life to save her, the lord was so happy that he gave permission for Issun Boshi to marry the princess. And so, you see, the princess's wish came true, too.

Issun Boshi's brave deeds were celebrated throughout the land. He and the princess lived happily together, along with Issun Boshi's proud and happy parents, whom Issun Boshi had brought to the lord's house to be part of the family.

Tom Thumb

> **PARENTS:** People in many lands tell different stories about the little fellow called Tom Thumb. This version is from Germany, as collected by the Brothers Grimm. You might find it interesting to read this story to your child along with the previous story, a folktale from Japan called 'Issun Boshi' (One-Inch-Boy). At the end of this story, you'll find suggestions for reading other similar stories from different lands.

A poor woodman sat in his cottage one night, smoking his pipe by the fireside, while his wife sat by his side spinning. 'How lonely it is, wife,' said he, as he let out a long sigh, 'for you and me to sit here by ourselves, without any children to play about and amuse us, while other people seem so happy and merry with their children!'

'What you say is very true,' said the wife, sighing, and turning round her spinning wheel; 'how happy should I be if I had but one child! Even if he were no bigger than my thumb, I should be very happy.'

Now, odd as you may think it, it came to pass that this good woman's wish was fulfilled, just in the very way she had wished it; for, not long afterwards, she had a little boy, who was quite healthy and strong, but who was not much bigger than a thumb. So the man and the woman said: 'Well, we cannot say we have not got what we wished for, and, little as he is, we will love him dearly.' And they called him Tom Thumb.

They gave him plenty of food, yet for all they could do he never grew bigger, but kept just the same size as he had been when he was born. Still, his eyes were sharp and sparkling, and he soon showed himself to be a clever little fellow, who always knew well what he was about.

One day, as the woodman was getting ready to go into the wood to cut trees for fuel, he said: 'I wish I had someone to bring the cart after me, for it would be much quicker.'

'Oh, father,' cried Tom, 'I will take care of that. The cart shall be in the wood by the time you want it.'

Then the woodman laughed and said: 'How can that be? You cannot even reach up to the horse's bridle.'

'Never mind that, father,' said Tom. 'If my mother will only harness the horse, I will get into his ear and tell him which way to go.'

'Well,' said the father, 'we will try for once.'

So the mother harnessed the horse to the cart, and put Tom into his ear; and as he sat there, the little lad told the beast how to go, crying out: 'Go on!' and 'Stop!' as he wanted: and thus the horse went on just as well as if the woodman had driven it himself into the wood. It happened that as the horse was going a little too fast, and Tom was calling out 'Gently! Gently!' that two strangers came by.

'What an odd thing that is!' said one. 'There is a cart going along, and I hear a carter talking to the horse, but yet I can see no one.'

'That is queer, indeed,' said the other. 'Let us follow the cart, and see where it goes.' So they went on into the wood, till at last they came to the place where the woodman was. Then Tom Thumb, seeing his father, cried out: 'See, father, here I am with the cart, all right and safe! Now help me down!' So his father took hold of the horse with one hand, and with the other took his son out of the horse's ear, and put him down upon a straw.

When the two strangers saw this they said: 'That little fellow will make us rich, if we can get him, and carry him about from town to town as a show; we must buy him!' So they went up to the woodman, and asked him what he would take for the little lad.

'I won't sell him at all,' said the father. 'My own flesh and blood is dearer to me than all the silver and gold in the world.' But Tom, hearing of the bargain they wanted to make, crept up his father's coat to his shoulder and whispered in his ear: 'Take the money, father, and let them have me; I'll soon come back to you.'

So the woodman at last said he would sell Tom to the strangers for a large piece of gold, and they paid the price.

They journeyed on with little Tom Thumb, till it began to be dusky, and then the little man said: 'Let me get down, I'm tired.' So the man put him down on a mound of earth, in a ploughed field by the side of the road. But Tom ran about amongst the furrows, and at last slipped into an old mouse-hole. 'Good night, my masters!' said he, 'I'm off!'

Then they ran at once to the place, and poked the ends of their sticks into the mouse-hole, but it was no use, Tom only crawled farther and farther in, and at last it became quite dark, so that they were forced to go their way without him, angry and penniless.

By good luck, Tom found a large empty snail shell. 'This is lucky. I can sleep here very well because it is a safe place to spend the night,' he said as he crept inside.

Just as he was falling asleep, he heard two men passing by, chatting together; and one said to the other, 'How can we rob that rich parson's house of his silver and gold?'

'I'll tell you!' cried Tom.

'What was that noise?' said the thief, frightened; 'I'm sure I just heard someone speak.'

They stood still listening, and Tom said, 'Take me with you, and I'll soon show you how to get the parson's money.'

'But where are you?' they asked. 'Look about on the ground,' answered Tom, 'and listen where the sound comes from.'

At last the thieves found him out, and lifted him up in their hands. 'You little creature!' they said, 'what can you do for us?'

'Why, I can get between the iron window-bars of the parson's house, and throw you out whatever you want.' 'That's a good thought,' said the thieves, 'come along, we shall see what you can do.'

When they came to the parson's house, Tom slipped through the window-bars into the room, and then called out as loud as he could bawl, 'How much do you want? Do you want it all?'

At this the thieves were frightened, and said, 'Softly, softly! Speak low, that you may not awaken anybody.' But Tom seemed as if he did not understand them, and bawled out again, 'WHAT'S THAT YOU SAY? YOU WANT TO TAKE ALL THE MONEY? I'LL GIVE YOU EVERYTHING, HOLD OUT YOUR HANDS!'

The cook heard this quite plain, so she sprang out of bed, and ran to open the door. The thieves ran off as if a wolf was at their tails. The maid went away for a light and by the time she came back, Tom had slipped off into the barn; and when she had looked about and searched every hole and corner and found nobody, she went to bed, thinking she must have been dreaming.

The little man crawled about in the hay loft, and at last found a snug place to finish his night's rest; so he laid himself down, meaning to sleep till daylight, and then find his way home to his father and mother. But alas! Poor Tom's troubles had only begun!

The cook got up early, before daybreak, to feed the cows; and going straight to the hay loft, carried away a large bundle of hay, with the little man in the middle of it, fast asleep. He still, however, slept on, and did not wake up until he found himself in the mouth of the cow. He was lucky not to have been crushed between the cow's teeth. After she chewed awhile, she swallowed and down went Tom into the cow's stomach.

'Goodness me,' he said, 'somebody forgot to put any windows in this house. It would be nice to have some fresh air!'

The worst of it was, that more and more hay was always coming down, and the space left for him became smaller and smaller. At last he cried out as loud as he could, 'That's enough! No more hay! I'm quite full thanks!'

The maid happened to be just then milking the cow; and hearing someone speak, but seeing nobody, and yet being quite sure it was the same voice that she had heard in the night, she was so frightened that she fell off her stool, and overset the milk pail. As soon as she could pick herself up out of the dirt, she ran off as fast as she could to her master the parson, and said, 'Sir, sir, the cow is talking!'

But the parson said: 'What, don't be silly!' However, he went with her into the barn, to try and see what was the matter.

Scarcely had they set foot on the threshold, when Tom called out: 'Thank you very much but please don't bring me any more hay!' Then the parson himself was frightened; and thinking the cow was surely bewitched, told his man to kill her on the spot. So the poor cow was killed, and cut up and the stomach, in which Tom lay, was thrown out with the rubbish.

Tom soon set himself to work to get out, which was not a very easy task; but at last, just as he had made room to get his head out, a hungry wolf sprang out, and snapped up the whole stomach in his teeth, with Tom still half in it, and ran away.

Tom, however, was still not disheartened. Thinking the wolf would not dislike talking to him as he was going along, he called out: 'My good friend, why do you want to eat this nasty cow stomach? I can tell you where to find some delicious treats!'

'Where's that?' said the wolf.

'In a house near the forest,' said Tom, describing his own father's house. 'You can crawl through the drain into the kitchen and there you will find cakes, ham, beef, cold chicken and everything that your heart can wish.'

So the wolf, his mouth watering, went to the house and crawled through the drain into the kitchen and ate and drank there to his heart's content. As soon as he had had enough he wanted to get away; but he had eaten so much that he could not go out by the same way he came in.

Tom shouted out to his parents, 'Help! Help! There's a big bad wolf in here! Help!'

The woodsman and his wife, being awakened by the noise, peeped through a crack in the door; but when they saw a wolf was there, the woodsman ran for a big stick. Then he whacked the wolf and sent him howling into the woods. 'Nice work, Father,' said Tom.

Then the woodsman and his wife hugged and kissed their dear little son, and gave him plenty to eat and drink, for he was very hungry. And then they fetched new clothes for him, for his old ones had been quite ruined on his adventures. So Tom Thumb stayed at home with his father and mother, in peace; for though he had been so great a traveller, and had done and seen so many fine things, and was fond enough of telling the whole story, he always agreed that, after all, there's no place like HOME!

Have you heard the saying 'There's no place like home' elsewhere? See more on page 121.

PARENTS: You may want to talk with your child about how stories from different lands can be alike in many ways. After reading 'Issun Boshi' and 'Tom Thumb,' you might begin by asking your child if she noticed some ways the two stories are alike. Perhaps she has heard of the story of Thumbelina by the great Danish storyteller Hans Christian Andersen? For fairy tales and folk tales from different lands, check your local library for such titles as:

Pretty Salma by Niki Daly (Frances Lincoln) 2006: a 'Red Riding Hood' story set in an African township, with Anansi the spider

Snow White in New York by Fiona French (Oxford) 1989

Mariana and the Merchild by Caroline Pitcher and Jackie Morris (Frances Lincoln) 2000: a folk tale from Chile about a woman who finds a mer-baby in a crabshell, whom she comes to love as her own.

The Fire Children, a West African Folk Tale retold by Eric Maddern (Frances Lincoln) 2006: a creation myth in which the first man and woman bake themselves children made of clay, some of whom are pale and some of whom are dark.

Jamila's Clever Cat by Fiona French (Frances Lincoln) 2006: a Bengali 'Puss in Boots' in which a poor weaver contrives to marry a princess with the help of his clever cat Sardul.

Mufaro's Beautiful Daughters by John Steptoe (Puffin) 1997: a 'Cinderella' story from Africa.

It Could Always Be Worse

Read more about the Jewish religion on page 139.

Once there was a poor Jewish man who had come to the end of his tether. So he went to his rabbi, a holy teacher, for advice.

'Holy Rabbi!' he cried. 'Things are in a bad way with me, and are getting worse all the time! We are poor, so poor that my wife, my six children, my in-laws and I have to live in a one-room hut. We get in each other's way all the time. Our nerves are frayed and, because we have plenty of troubles, we quarrel. Believe me – my home is awful, and things could not possibly be worse!'

The rabbi pondered the matter gravely. 'My son,' he said, 'promise to do as I tell you and your condition will improve.'

'I promise, Rabbi,' answered the troubled man. 'I'll do anything you say.'

'Tell me – what animals do you own?'

'I have a cow, a goat and some chickens.'

'Very well! Go home now and take all these animals into your house to live with you.' The poor man was amazed, but since he had promised the rabbi, he went home and brought all the animals into his house.

The following day the poor man returned to the rabbi and cried: 'Rabbi, what misfortune have you brought upon me! I did as you told me and brought the animals into the house. And now what have I got? Things are worse than ever. The house is turned into a barn! Save me, Rabbi – help me!'

'My son,' replied the rabbi calmly, 'go home and take the chickens out of your house. God will help you!'

So the poor man went home and took the chickens out of his house. But it was not long before he again came running to the rabbi.

'Holy Rabbi!' he wailed. 'Help me, save me! The goat is smashing everything in the house – she's turning my life into a nightmare.'

'Go home,' said the rabbi gently, 'and take the goat out of the house. God will help you!'

The poor man returned to his house and removed the goat. But it wasn't long before he again came running to the rabbi, crying loudly: 'What a misfortune you've brought upon my head, Rabbi! The cow has turned my house into a stable! How can you expect a human being to live side by side with an animal?'

'You're right – a hundred times right!' agreed the rabbi. 'Go straight home and take the cow out of your house!'

And the poor, unfortunate man hurried home and took the cow out of his house.

Not a day had passed before he came running again to the rabbi. 'Rabbi!' cried the poor man, his face beaming. 'You've made life sweet again for me. With all the animals out, the house is so quiet, so roomy and so clean! What a pleasure!'

> **PARENTS:** After reading this story, you might want to ask your child, 'What do you think the title means?'

Jack and the Beanstalk

There was once upon a time a poor widow who had an only son named Jack, and a cow named Milky-White. And all they had to live on was the milk the cow gave every morning, which they carried to the market and sold. But one morning Milky-White gave no milk, and they didn't know what to do.

'What shall we do, what shall we do?' said the widow, wringing her hands.

'Cheer up, mother, I'll go and get work somewhere,' said Jack.

'We've tried that before, and nobody would take you,' said his mother. 'We must sell Milky-White.'

'All right, mother,' says Jack. 'It's market day today, and I'll soon sell Milky-White, and then we'll be better off, you'll see.'

So he took the cow and set off. He had not gone far when he met a funny-looking old man, who said to him: 'Good morning, Jack.'

'Good morning to you,' said Jack, and wondered how he knew his name.

'Well, Jack, where are you off to?' asked the man.

'I'm going to market to sell our cow, Milky-White.'

'Oh, yes you look like just the sort of chap to sell a cow,' said the man. 'I wonder if you know how many beans make five.'

Jack thought this was indeed a rather odd question but he answered: 'Two in each hand and one in your mouth.'

'Right you are, and here they are, the very beans themselves,' said the man, pulling out of his pocket a number of strange-looking beans. 'I don't mind doing a swap with you – your cow for these beans.'

'Well now,' said Jack, 'that would be a good deal – for you!'

'Ah! But you don't know what these beans are,' said the man. 'If you plant them overnight, by morning they grow right up to the sky.'

'Really?' said Jack, who was a lot more interested in the peculiar looking beans when he heard that.

'Yes, it's true! And if it doesn't turn out to be true you can have your cow back.'

'Alright then,' said Jack, as he handed over Milky-White, put the beans in his pocket and started off home.

'Back already, Jack?' said his mother. 'How much did you get for her?'

'You'll never guess, mother,' said Jack.

'Oh well done, you clever boy! Did you get five pounds? Ten? Fifteen? Surely - it couldn't be twenty?'

'I said you wouldn't guess!' said Jack. Reaching into his pocket, he said 'Look, Mother, what do you say to these beans? They're magical! Plant them overnight and – '

'What!' shrieked Jack's mother, 'have you been such a fool, such an idiot, as to give away my lovely Milky-White, the best milker in the county for a set of disgusting beans? Off to bed with you and no supper! As for your precious beans here they go out of the window!'

So Jack went upstairs to his little room in the attic, where he eventually fell asleep to the sound of his rumbling stomach.

When he woke up, the room looked very odd. The sun was shining into part of it, and yet all the rest was quite dark and shady. So Jack jumped up and dressed himself and went to the window. And what do you think he saw? Why, the beans his mother had thrown out of the window into the garden had sprung up into a big beanstalk which went up and up and up through the clouds. So the man had spoken truth after all!

The beanstalk grew up quite close past Jack's window, so all he had to do was to open it and give a jump onto the beanstalk which ran up just like a big ladder. So Jack climbed, and he climbed, and he climbed, and he climbed, and he climbed, and he climbed, and he climbed till at last he reached the sky. And when he got there he found a long, straight road. So he walked along, and he walked along, and he walked along some more till he came to a great big tall house, with a great big tall woman on the doorstep.

'Good morning, miss,' said Jack, ever so politely. 'Could you be so kind as to give me some breakfast?'

'It's breakfast you want, is it?' says the great big tall woman. 'It's breakfast you'll become if you don't move off from here! My husband is a giant and there's nothing he likes better than boys buttered on toast. You'd better be moving on before he comes.'

'Oh! Please do give me something to eat. I've had nothing to eat since yesterday morning, really and truly,' says Jack. 'I may as well be eaten if I'm going to die of hunger.'

Well, the giant's wife was not so bad after all. So she took Jack into the kitchen, and gave him a hunk of bread and cheese and a jug of milk. But Jack hadn't half finished these when thump! thump! thump! the whole house began to tremble with the noise of someone coming.

'Goodness gracious me! It's my husband!' said the giant's wife. 'What on earth shall I do? Come along quickly and jump in here.' And she bundled Jack into the oven just as the giant came in.

He was a big one, to be sure. At his belt he had three cows strung up by the heels, and he unhooked them and threw them down on the table and said: 'Here, wife, cook me these for breakfast. Ah! What's this I smell?

> *Fee-fi-fo-fum,*
> *I smell the blood of an Englishman,*
> *Be he alive, or be he dead,*
> *I'll grind his bones to make my bread!*

'Nonsense, dear,' said his wife. 'You're dreaming. Or perhaps you smell the scraps of that little boy you liked so much for yesterday's dinner. Here, you go and have a wash and tidy up, and by the time you come back your breakfast will be ready for you.'

So off the ogre went, and Jack was just going to jump out of the oven and run away when the woman told him: 'Wait until he's asleep. He always has a nap after breakfast.'

Well, the giant had his breakfast, and then went to a big chest and took out a couple of bags of gold. Down he sat and counted the gold until at last his head began to nod and he began to snore till the whole house shook.

Then Jack crept out on tiptoe from the oven and, as he was passing the giant, he took one of the bags of gold under his arm, and off he ran until he came to the beanstalk. Then he threw down the bag of gold, which, of course, fell into his mother's garden, and then he climbed down and climbed down until at last he got home and told his mother all that had happened and showed her the gold. 'Well, mother, wasn't I right about the beans? They really are magical, you see.'

So they lived on the bag of gold for some time, but at last they came to the end of it, and Jack made up his mind to try his luck once more at the top of the beanstalk. So one fine morning he rose up early and clambered onto the beanstalk. Then he climbed, and he climbed, and he climbed, and he climbed, and he climbed and he climbed till at last he came out onto the road again and up to the great big tall house he had been to before. There, sure enough, was the great big tall woman standing on the doorstep.

'Good morning, miss,' said Jack, as bold as brass, 'could you be so good as to give me something to eat?'

'Go away, my boy,' said the big tall woman, 'or else my husband will eat you up for breakfast. Aren't you the youngster who came here once before? Do you know, that very day one of my husband's bags of gold went missing.'

'That's very strange, miss,' said Jack, 'I might be able to tell you something about that, but I'm so hungry I can't speak until I've had something to eat.'

Well, the great big tall woman was so curious that she took him in and gave him something to eat. But he had scarcely begun munching it as slowly as he could when thump! thump! thump! they heard the giant's footstep, and his wife hid Jack away in the oven again.

All happened as it had before. In came the giant who said: 'Fee-fi-fo-fum' and had his breakfast of three boiled cows.

Then he said: 'Wife, wife! Bring me the hen that lays the golden eggs.' So she brought it to him, and the giant said 'Lay,' and it laid an egg of solid gold. And then the giant began to nod his head, and to snore until the house shook.

Then Jack crept out of the oven on tiptoe and caught hold of the golden hen, and was off before you could say 'Jack Robinson'. But this time the hen gave a cackle which woke the giant, and just as Jack got out of the house he heard him calling: 'Wife, wife! What have you done with my golden hen?'

And the wife said: 'Why, my dear?'

But that was all Jack heard, for he rushed off to the beanstalk and climbed down like a house on fire. And when he got home he showed his mother the wonderful hen, and said 'Lay' to it; and it laid a golden egg. Every time he said 'Lay!' another golden egg appeared.

Well, Jack was still not content, so one fine morning he rose up early and got to the beanstalk, and he climbed, and he climbed, and he climbed, and he climbed till he got to the top.

But this time he knew better than to go straight to the giant's front door. When he got near to the house, he waited behind a bush till he saw the giant's wife come out with a pail

We met another bird who could lay golden eggs in one of Aesop's fables. Gretel also used an oven to help her get the better of a cruel person, but she used it in a very different way!

to get some water, and then he crept into the house and quietly shut himself in the oven. He hadn't been there long when he heard thump! thump! thump! as before, and in came the giant and his wife.

So the giant sat down to breakfast and afterwards called out: 'Wife, wife! Bring me my golden harp.'

So she brought it and put it on the table before him. Then he said, 'Sing!' and the golden harp sang most beautifully. And it went on singing till the ogre fell asleep and began to snore like thunder.

Then Jack snuck in, caught hold of the golden harp and dashed with it towards the door. But the harp called out quite loudly, 'Master! Master!' and the giant woke up just in time to see Jack running off with his harp.

Jack ran as fast as he could, and the ogre came rushing after, and when he got to the beanstalk the giant was not far behind when Jack climbed down the beanstalk as fast as he possibly could. As soon as he reached the bottom he called out, 'Mother! Mother! Bring me an axe, bring me an axe!' And his mother came rushing out with the axe in her hand, but when she came to the beanstalk she stood stock still with fright, for there she saw the giant with his legs just through the clouds.

But Jack jumped down, took hold of the axe and gave a chop at the beanstalk. The giant felt the beanstalk shake and quiver, so he stopped to see what was the matter. Then Jack gave another chop with the axe, and the beanstalk was cut in two and began to topple over. Then the ogre fell down dead at the foot of the beanstalk.

From then on, Jack and his mother had all the money and music they wanted, for the hen gave them golden eggs and the harp sang for them all day long – and so they lived happily ever after.

The Knee-High Man

(An African American folktale, retold by Julius Lester)

Once upon a time there was a knee-high man. He was no taller than a person's knees. Because he was so short, he was very unhappy. He wanted to be big like everybody else.

One day he decided to ask the biggest animal he could find how he could get big. So he went to see Mr. Horse. 'Mr. Horse, how can I get big like you?' Mr. Horse said: 'Well, eat a whole lot of corn. Then run around a lot. After a while you'll be as big as me.'

The knee-high man did just that. He ate so much corn that his stomach hurt. Then he ran and ran and ran until his legs hurt. But he didn't get any bigger. So he decided that Mr. Horse had told him something wrong. He decided to go ask Mr. Bull.

'Mr. Bull, how can I get big like you?'

Mr. Bull said: 'Eat a whole lot of grass. Then bellow and bellow as loud as you can. The first thing you know, you'll be as big as me.'

So the knee-high man ate a whole field of grass. That made his stomach hurt. He bellowed and bellowed and bellowed all day and all night. That made his throat hurt. But he didn't get any bigger. So he decided that Mr. Bull was all wrong too.

Now he didn't know anyone else to ask. One night he heard Mr. Hoot Owl hooting, and he remembered that Mr. Owl knew everything. 'Mr. Owl, how can I get big like Mr. Horse and Mr. Bull?'

'What do you want to be big for?' Mr. Hoot Owl asked.

'I want to be big so that when I get into a fight, I can whip everybody,' the knee-high man said.

Mr. Hoot Owl hooted. 'Anybody ever try to pick a fight with you?' The knee-high man thought a minute. 'Well, now that you mention it, nobody ever did try to start a fight with me.'

Mr. Owl said: 'Well, you don't have any reason to fight. Therefore, you don't have any reason to be bigger than you are.'

'But, Mr. Owl,' the knee-high man said, 'I want to be big so I can see far into the distance.'

Mr. Hoot Owl hooted. 'If you climb a tall tree, you can see into the distance from the top.'

The knee-high man was quiet for a minute. 'Well, I hadn't thought of that.'

Mr. Hoot Owl hooted again. 'And that's what's wrong, Mr. Knee-High Man. You hadn't done any thinking at all. I'm smaller than you, and you don't see me worrying about being big. Mr. Knee-High Man, you wanted something that you didn't need.'

Medio Pollito
(A Hispanic folktale)

There was once a large black Spanish hen who had fine little chicks. All of them were ordinary chicks, except for one, who looked as if he had been cut right in half. All his brothers and sisters had two wings and two legs and two eyes, but he had only one of each. And he had only half a head and half a beak. So they called him Medio Pollito [MEH-dee-o poh-YEE-toh], which means 'Half-Chick' in Spanish.

The brother and sister chicks did just what they were told to do, but Medio Pollito did not like to obey his mother. When mother hen called for him to come back to the chicken house, he pretended that he could not hear, because he had only one ear. And the older he became, the more he disobeyed his mother. One day he said: 'I am tired of life in the barnyard. I am going to the city to see the king.' His mother said: 'You aren't old enough yet. When you get older, we will go to the city together.'

But Medio Pollito would not listen to anyone. 'I am going to visit the king, and I shall have a big house in the city and become rich. Maybe I will invite you to visit me sometime.' With that, he hopped down the road toward the city.

His mother called out: 'Be sure to be nice to everyone you meet.' But Medio did not listen, and off he went.

He first hopped to a little stream of water, choked with weeds. 'Oh, Medio,' it cried, 'please help me clear away these weeds so I can flow.'

'Do you think I have time to take from my travels?' said Medio. 'I am off to the city to see the king.' And away he hopped. Later he came to some burning grass, and the fire said to him: 'Medio, please put some sticks on me so I won't go out.'

'Do you think I have time to take from my travels?' said Medio. 'I am off to the city to see the king.' And away he hopped.

As he got closer to the city, he came to a tree where the wind was caught in the branches and leaves, and the wind said to Medio, 'Oh, please climb up here and get me out of these branches so I can fly away.'

'Do you think I have time to take from my travels?' said Medio. 'I am off to the city to see the king.' And away he hopped.

As he entered the city, he saw the royal palace, and hopped right into the courtyard. Who should see Medio but the king's cook, who said: 'I think I shall make the king a nice chicken soup for dinner.' And he reached out, and caught Medio, and put him into a pot of water near the stove.

Medio felt very wet. 'Oh, water,' he cried, 'don't wet me like this.'

But the water replied: 'You would not help me when I was a little stream, so why should I help you?'

Then the fire on the stove began to heat the water. Medio felt very hot. 'Oh, fire,' he cried, 'don't burn me like this.'

But the fire replied: 'You would not help me when I was going out in the grass, so why should I help you?'

The pain was so bad that Medio thought he would die. Just then, the cook raised the lid of the pot to see if the soup was ready. But he saw the ugly little chick, and said: 'I can't send such an ugly chick to the king.' And he threw Medio out of the window.

There the wind caught him and took him so fast he could hardly breathe. 'Oh, wind,' he cried, 'don't carry me like this. Let me rest or I shall die.'

But the wind replied: 'You would not help me when I was caught in the tree, so why should I help you?' And with that he lifted up Medio Pollito, up in the air to the top of the church tower, and left him stuck on the steeple.

There he is to this very day. If you look at the top of many a church steeple, you will see a weather vane in the form of half a chicken. It is Medio Pollito, the chick who would not help others. Now he must help everyone by showing them which way the wind is blowing.

> Does this story make you think of the Golden Rule? In the Year 1 book we learned the saying 'Do unto others as you would have them do unto you.'

The Pied Piper of Hamelin

Rats! Everywhere in the little town of Hamelin, there were rats, rats and more rats. There were so many that no amount of traps could catch them, and no amount of poison could kill them. They fought the dogs and chased the cats. They made nests in the people's hats. They ate the food right off the tables. They ran up and down the streets in broad daylight, flicking their tails and twitching their whiskers. And they made such a squeaking and shrieking that you could not hear yourself speak, or get a wink of good sleep.

In the middle of Hamelin at the Town Hall, a crowd had gathered. The people were shaking their fists and shouting: 'Mr. Mayor! Mr. Mayor! You must get rid of these rats, or we will get rid of you!'

'What do you expect me to do?' asked the mayor. He sat his big round body down in a big wooden chair. 'I've racked my brain again and again, but all in vain.' Then, giving his head a rap, he cried: 'Oh for a trap, a trap, a trap!'

Just then at the door came a gentle tap. 'It's a rat!' cried the mayor.

'Rats don't knock,' said a townsman.

'Oh, yes, of course,' said the mayor. Then, trying to sound brave, he called out: 'Come in!' And in came the strangest-looking person you've ever seen.

He was tall and thin, with sharp black eyes, each like a pin. His frilly green coat and cape matched his green cap with a red feather on top. And those tights! Striped half of yellow and half of red, his tights flashed brightly. In his hand, he carried a silver pipe.

'Who are you?' asked the mayor.

And the strange-looking figure answered: 'People call me the Pied Piper. On my pipe I play music that charms all things under the sun – all creatures that creep, or swim, or fly or run. Whenever I play, they follow me, wherever I go. I can charm the birds of the air. I can charm the fishes of the sea. I can charm the wild beasts that live in the forests.'

'And rats?' said the mayor. 'What about rats? Can you charm them?'

'That I can,' said the Pied Piper. 'I can charm every last rat from your town. Give me a thousand gold pieces and I will set to it.'

'A thousand?' said the mayor. 'Why, you may have fifty thousand if you can do it!' And the townspeople cried: 'Yes, yes, we will gladly give him fifty thousand. Just get rid of the rats!'

'As you wish,' said the stranger. Then, with a strange smile, he stepped out into the street and put the pipe to his lips. And he had hardly played three notes when, from every direction, rats came running, tumbling, tripping, hurrying, scurrying.

Great rats, small rats, lean rats, brawny rats,
Brown rats, black rats, grey rats, tawny rats,
Grave old plodders, gay young friskers,
Fathers, mothers, uncles, cousins,
Cocking tails, and prickling whiskers,
Families by tens and dozens,
Brothers, sisters, husbands, wives –
Followed the Piper for their lives.
From street to street he piped advancing,
And step by step they followed dancing.

The Pied Piper walked slowly down the street, playing his merry tune. And when he came to the river, the rats jumped in and were carried under and away by the rushing water.

The townspeople hurrayed and hurrahed, and rang the bells till they rocked the steeples. But they fell quiet as the Pied Piper returned. He walked up to the mayor and said: 'The rats are gone. It is time to pay the Piper. I will take my thousand gold pieces and go.'

But the mayor hemmed and hawed and harrumphed, and said that really, he didn't see why the Piper should be paid so much for what was such an easy job. After all, what had he done but walk down the street and play on a pipe? And really, wouldn't the Piper think it fair to be paid, say, about ten gold pieces, yes, ten, didn't that seem about right for so easy a job?

And as the mayor spoke, the townspeople nodded and began to whisper among themselves that, indeed, this funny-looking man hardly deserved a thousand gold pieces just for playing a silly pipe – why, the very idea!

'You promised to pay a thousand,' said the Piper. 'You even offered me fifty thousand. Come now, I have no time to waste. I must be on my way. It's a thousand we've agreed on, and a thousand you must pay.'

The mayor put ten gold pieces on the table and said with a huff: 'Take it or leave it. Now, fellow, be off with you.'

Once more the Pied Piper stepped into the street. Once more he began to play. And after only a few notes, there was a rustling, and a bustling, and a sound of small feet pattering, and little tongues chattering. Out came the children, all the children of Hamelin town, tripping and skipping and running merrily after the music with shouting and laughter.

The townspeople could not speak. They could not move. They stood as though they had been changed into blocks of wood. They could not shout or utter a cry as they watched the children skipping by.

As the children danced merrily behind him, the Pied Piper played his tune. And the tune seemed to make a promise, a promise of a joyous land where the sun was shining and birds were singing, and children played in fields in which flowers bloomed brighter than rainbows. And on they danced, as the Piper led them far from town, until they came to a mountainside.

And there, in the rock, a door opened wide. The Piper walked in, and the children followed. And when all were in to the very last, the door in the mountainside shut fast. The townspeople searched high and low, up and down. But they never again saw the Pied Piper or the children of Hamelin town.

Pinocchio

PARENTS: Many children may already be familiar with one version of the story of Pinocchio as told in the Walt Disney film. The Disney film, a compelling animated classic, makes many changes from the original story, published in 1883 by an Italian author who used the pen name of C. Collodi. One big difference is that, from the start, Collodi's Pinocchio is a naughty, mischievous puppet. If your child knows the film, then it may be interesting to talk with him about how it differs from this story. Collodi's story fills a small book; here we retell a few episodes to give you a flavour of how enjoyable this book is.

Pinocchio Runs Away

There was once a poor woodcarver named Geppetto [jeh-PET-toe]. One day, Geppetto picked out an unusual block of wood and said, 'I will carve a fine puppet out of this, one that can dance and jump when I pull the strings.' And he thought that perhaps he could travel with the puppet and put on shows and earn a living.

'What shall I name my puppet?' thought Geppetto. 'I know – Pinocchio. That sounds like a lucky name!' And so he started carving. First he worked on the head. He carved the eyes and, to his surprise, the eyes opened and stared at him! Then he carved the nose. Geppetto jumped back: the nose was growing longer and longer. 'Stop, nose, stop!' Geppetto cried. Finally it stopped growing, but oh, it was long! Geppetto next worked on the mouth. As soon as he finished the mouth, the puppet began to laugh, and it kept on laughing. 'Stop laughing, you!' said Geppetto. The puppet stopped laughing – but it stuck out its tongue!

'Pinocchio!' said Geppetto. 'You're not even finished and already you're a bad boy.' Geppetto kept carving, and he finished the legs and feet. But as soon as he did, the puppet raised a foot and kicked him in the nose!

'Come, you mischief-maker,' said Geppetto. 'Let us see if you can use those legs.' He put Pinocchio on the ground and held him up. At first Pinocchio's legs were so stiff that he could not walk. Geppetto showed him how to put one foot in front of another, and Pinocchio began to walk by himself. Then he began to run around the room. When he saw the door was open, he jumped out and ran away!

Pinocchio ran through the village until he came to the fields and meadows. He leaped over brambles and bushes, and across brooks and ponds. He heard the chirp-chirp-chirping sound of a cricket. Suddenly the cricket began to talk. 'Pinocchio, listen to me,' said the cricket. 'Bad boys who run away and disobey their parents will never be happy.'

'You silly cricket,' said Pinocchio. 'If I go back home, I know what will happen: I'll have to go to *school*, and whether I want to or not, I'll have to *study*. But it's much more fun to chase butterflies, and climb trees, and do just as I please.'

'Then you are a silly wooden-head!' said the cricket. 'If that's the way you spend your time, you'll grow up to be a big donkey, and everyone will make fun of you.'

Pinocchio was angry. He picked up something heavy and threw it – and there was no more talking or chirping from the cricket. As Pinocchio walked away, he felt a new feeling, a strange emptiness inside him. Along with the emptiness came a loud growling sound. 'Why, I'm hungry,' the puppet said. 'I'm hungry as a wolf.'

He ran back to the village. It was dark. The shops were closed, and all the doors and windows were shut tight. 'Oh, I'm so terribly hungry,' he cried. He walked up to a house and rang the bell, again and again. 'That's sure to wake someone up,' he thought. And he was right. A window opened upstairs and a sleepy man stuck out his head. In an angry voice he said: 'What do you want at this time of night?'

'I'm a poor hungry boy,' said Pinocchio. 'Please feed me.'

'Wait a minute, I'll be straight back,' said the man.

The puppet looked up at the window and imagined the wonderful treats that the man might be bringing. Then – *splash!* – Pinocchio was hit in the face by a shower of ice-cold water!

'Maybe that cricket was right after all,' Pinocchio grumbled. He found his way back to Geppetto's cottage. The old man was very glad to see him. 'You must promise not to run away again,' he said. 'You must go to school, like a good boy.'

'Yes, Father, I'll be good,' said Pinocchio.

Pinocchio at the Puppet Show

The next morning Geppetto, who was very poor, sold his only coat in order to buy Pinocchio an ABC book. With his new book in hand, Pinocchio started for school.

'I will be a good boy,' he said. But he had not gone very far when he saw a sign for a puppet show. 'I can go to school any old day,' he thought, 'but I must see that show today.' So he sold his book for the price of a ticket and went to see the show.

The theatre was full of people, laughing loudly at the puppets on the stage. Then a most unexpected thing happened: the puppets on stage cried out: 'Look, it's Pinocchio, our fellow puppet! Pinocchio, come up here!' Pinocchio began leaping over people's heads to get to the stage. Well, you never saw anything like it, or heard such a great clattering, as the puppets knocked their wooden arms and legs together in their rush to hug Pinocchio.

The people in the audience were angry that the play had stopped. 'The play! We want the play!' they shouted.

Suddenly the puppet master came out. He was a fierce-looking man, with a long black beard, sharp yellow teeth, and eyes like glowing red coals. 'What's this? You don't belong here!' he roared as he grabbed Pinocchio. 'So,' he said, 'you're made of wood. Then I will use you for firewood.'

'No, please don't,' pleaded Pinocchio. 'Please spare me. My poor old father will miss me so much. Just this morning he sent me off to school, and he bought me an ABC book with the money he got from selling his only coat. It was an old coat, too, full of patches.'

The puppet master looked fierce, but he wasn't all bad. With a loud sniff he said to Pinocchio: 'I feel sorry for your poor father. Go back to him, and give him these five gold pieces to buy a new coat.'

The Fox and the Cat

Pinocchio thanked the puppet master a thousand times and started on his way home. But he had not gone far when he met a fox who seemed to be lame and a cat who seemed to be blind.

'Good morning, Pinocchio,' said the fox.

'How do you know my name?' asked the puppet.

'I know your father,' said the sly fox. 'I saw him yesterday morning, standing in the doorway of his house, wearing only a tattered shirt. He was cold and shivering.'

'But he will be warm soon!' said Pinocchio. Then, holding out the five gold coins, he said: 'See, I'm rich! I'm going to buy my father a fine new coat.'

When he saw the gold pieces, the fox, who was supposed to be lame, jumped up; and the cat, who was supposed to be blind, stared with wide-open eyes that looked like two green lamps. But all this happened so quickly that Pinocchio didn't notice.

'My, my,' said the fox, 'so much money. And what exactly do you plan to do with it?'

'I'll buy Father a coat and myself a new ABC book,' said Pinocchio.

'An ABC book?' asked the fox in a doubtful voice.

'Yes,' said Pinocchio. 'I'm going to school to study.'

'Study!' exclaimed the fox. 'Do you know what happens when you study? I tried to study once, and now look at me – I am lame!'

'I also tried to study once,' said the cat, 'and now look at me – I am blind.'

'You don't need to study or work,' said the fox. 'Just listen to me, my boy. How would you like to see those five gold coins turn into ten? Or twenty? Or a hundred? Or even a thousand?'

'Really?' said the puppet. 'How?'

'Why, it's very easy,' laughed the fox. 'Do you know the place called the Field of Wonders? You just go there and dig a little hole in the ground. Then you cover the hole with a little earth, water it, and go away. During the night your gold pieces will sprout and grow. And in the morning you'll find a tree loaded with gold pieces!'

'Oh, how wonderful!' cried Pinocchio. 'How can I ever thank you? Oh, I know. When I have picked all the gold pieces, I will give you a hundred of them.'

But the fox cried out, as though he were surprised and embarrassed. 'A present! For us! No, really, we simply could not accept. Our greatest pleasure is to bring happiness and wealth to others.'

'Oh, yes,' said the cat, 'helping other people is all the reward we ask.'

'Come on, then!' exclaimed Pinocchio. 'Let's go to the Field of Wonders!'

'Certainly,' said the fox. 'But shall we stop for dinner on the way? I believe that one of your gold coins should be enough to feed us all.'

The Return of the Cricket, and the Field of Wonders

At dinner the fox and cat stuffed themselves as though they were eating a meal to last a lifetime. Pinocchio was not very hungry, so he stepped outside to think about all the money he would soon have. He heard a small voice calling his name.

'Who is calling me?' asked Pinocchio.

'I am the spirit of the talking cricket,' said the voice.

'What do you want?' asked the puppet.

'I want to give you a few words of advice,' said the voice. 'Return home and give the four gold pieces you have left to your father. Do not listen to those who promise to make you rich overnight. Either they are fools or they will make a fool out of you. Listen to me, Pinocchio, and go home.'

'No,' said the puppet. 'I'm going to do what I want.'

'It is very late,' said the voice.

'I'm going to do what I want.'

'The night is dark.'

'I'm going to do what I want.'

'There are dangers ahead.'

'I'm going to do what I want.'

'Remember that children who insist on doing what they want will be sorry for it, sooner or later.'

'I've heard all that before,' said the stubborn puppet. Just then the fox and cat came out and joined him again. Together they walked on to the Field of Wonders. As they walked,

Pinocchio kept thinking to himself: 'I wonder how much gold the tree will grow? What if it's a thousand pieces? Or maybe two thousand? Or even five thousand? Oh, I will have a grand palace, and a thousand toys, and a kitchen filled with candy and cakes!'

They came at last to a large field. No one was in sight. 'Here we are, my young friend,' said the fox. 'Now dig a hole and put your gold pieces in it.'

Pinocchio dug a hole, placed the four remaining gold pieces in it, and carefully covered them with earth. Then he went to a nearby well and filled his shoe with water, which he brought back and sprinkled on the ground where he had planted the coins.

'Is there anything else?' he asked the fox.

'Nothing else at all,' said the fox. 'Now, you simply have to leave this place for about twenty minutes. And when you return, you will find a tree covered with money.'

'Thank you, thank you, a thousand times thank you,' said Pinocchio as he jumped up and down for joy.

The fox and the cat went one way, and Pinocchio went another. He counted the minutes, one by one. When he thought it was time, he ran back to the Field of Wonders. He came to the field and looked for a tree but saw nothing. He turned around and looked in all directions – still nothing. Then he heard someone laughing. Looking up, he saw a big parrot siting in a tree.

In an angry voice Pinocchio asked: 'Why are you laughing?'

'Oh,' said the parrot, 'only because I just tickled myself under the wing. And because I always laugh at silly people who believe everything they are told.'

'Do you mean me?' snapped Pinocchio.

'Yes, indeed, I mean you,' said the parrot. 'You are foolish enough to think that money can grow like beans or peas. Don't you know that to earn money honestly, you have to work with your hands and with your head?'

'I – I don't understand what you mean,' said Pinocchio in a trembling voice.

'Oh, I think you do,' said the parrot. 'Why don't you check where you planted the money?'

Pinocchio did not want to believe the parrot. Still, he bent down and began to dig the earth out of the hole where he had planted the money. He dug and he dug and he dug until he had made a hole as big as himself. But the money was not there. Every piece of it was gone. And Pinocchio knew, as well as you know, who took it.

Sadly, Pinocchio walked back to the village. On his way he passed a small cottage, and there, standing in the door, was a beautiful blue-haired fairy. 'Pinocchio,' she called out. 'What happened to your gold coins?'

'I, uh, you see, well, I lost them. Yes, that's it, I lost them,' stammered Pinocchio.

No sooner had he said this than his nose grew longer, longer and longer!

'Pinocchio,' said the fairy, 'I hope you've learned your lesson.' Then she called in a flock of woodpeckers, who pecked on his nose until it was back to its old size. But from then on, you could always tell whenever Pinocchio was lying, for his nose would grow and grow.

Pinocchio has many more adventures. He meets a naughty boy named Lampwick. They sneak away from school to go to the Land of Toys. But when Pinocchio leaves the Land of Toys, he finds that he has grown the ears and tail of a donkey! The blue-haired fairy helps Pinocchio, and he decides that he wants to become a real boy. Before he does, he goes through some very hard trials – he is even swallowed by a giant shark! In the end, Pinocchio is reunited with Geppetto, and his wish comes true: he is no longer a puppet but a real boy.

The Princess and the Pea
(from the story by Hans Christian Andersen)

Once upon a time there was a prince who wanted to marry a princess; but she would have to be a real princess. He travelled all over the world to find one, but nowhere could he get what he wanted. There were princesses enough, but it was difficult to find out whether they were real ones. There was always something about them that was not as it should be. So he came home again, disappointed and sad, for he would have liked very much to have a real princess.

One evening a terrible storm came on; there was thunder and lightning, and the rain poured down in torrents. Suddenly a knocking was heard at the gate, and the old queen went to open it.

It was a princess standing out there in front of the gate. But, good gracious! What a sight the rain and the wind had made her look. The water ran down from her hair and clothes; it ran down into the toes of her shoes and out again at the heels. And yet she said that she was a real princess.

'Well, we'll soon find that out,' thought the old queen. But she said nothing, went into the bedroom, took all the bedding off the bedstead, and laid a pea on the bottom; then she took twenty mattresses and laid them on the pea, and then twenty eiderdown quilts on top of the mattresses.

On this the princess had to lie all night. In the morning she was asked how she had slept.

'Oh, very badly!' said she. 'I have scarcely closed my eyes all night. Heaven only knows what was in the bed, but I was lying on something hard, so that I am black and blue all over my body. It's horrible!'

Now they knew that she was a real princess because she had felt the pea right through the twenty mattresses and the twenty eiderdown quilts.

Nobody but a real princess could be as sensitive as that.

So the prince took her for his wife, for now he knew that he had a real princess; and the pea was put in the museum, where it may still be seen, if no one has stolen it.

So the prince married her and was so happy that he had at last found a real princess.

And that, children, is a true story!

Puss-in-Boots

There was once upon a time an old miller, and when he died he left to his three sons his mill, his donkey and his cat. The eldest took the mill, the second the donkey and the youngest was left with nothing but the cat.

The poor young fellow was quite annoyed with his small share. 'My brothers,' he said, 'can make a lot of money by combining their gifts but what can I do with a cat? I suppose I could eat him and sell his skin, but then what?'

The cat heard all of this but pretended he was not paying attention. And when the young man had quite finished, he said to him in a grave and serious voice: 'Don't worry, my good master. If you give me a bag, and have a pair of boots made for me, so that I may scamper through the mud and the brambles, then you shall see that you are not as unlucky as you might think.'

The young man thought to himself: 'What have I got to lose?' After all, he had seen the cat play a lot of clever tricks in order to catch mice. So he fetched the cat a bag and a pair of boots.

With a slinky movement, Puss pulled on the boots and threw the bag about his neck. He put some grain into the bag, pulled the drawstrings and went to a place where he knew there were a great many rabbits. He put the bag on the ground and left it open. Then he stretched himself out as if he were dead, lying very still. There he waited for some young unsuspecting rabbits to come and look into the bag.

Puss had scarcely lain down before he had what he wanted. A rash and foolish young rabbit jumped into his bag; the master cat pulled the drawstrings tight and killed the rabbit with one vigorous shake of the bag.

Proud of his prey, Puss went with it to the palace, and asked to speak with his majesty, the King. He was shown upstairs into the King's apartment and, making a low bow, said to him: 'Sire, I have brought you a plump rabbit from my noble Lord, the Marquis of Carabas,' (for that was the title which the cat was pleased to give his master).

'Tell your master,' said the King, 'that I thank him, and that I am very pleased with his gift.'

The next day, Puss went and hid himself in a field of wheat. He again left his bag open, and when a pair of partridges ran into it, he drew the drawstring tight and caught them both. He presented these to the King, as he had done before with the rabbit. The King received the partridges with great pleasure and gave him some money. Puss continued, from time to time, to present whatever he had caught to his majesty from the 'Marquis of Carabas'. The King began to think of this Marquis as a famous hunter and a generous man, though he was, as we know, only the poor miller's youngest son!

One day, when Puss heard that the King would be taking a coach along the riverside with his daughter, the most beautiful princess in the world, he said to his master: 'If you will follow my advice you will be a rich man! All you must do is to go and have a swim in the river and leave the rest to me.'

The Marquis of Carabas did what Puss advised him to, without knowing why. While he was bathing the King passed by, and the cat began to cry out: 'Help! Help! My Lord Marquis of Carabas is drowning. Save him! Save him!'

At this noise the King put his head out of the coach window and, finding it was the cat who had so often brought him so many gifts, he commanded his guards to run immediately to the assistance of his lordship the Marquis of Carabas. While they were drawing the poor Marquis out of the river, Puss ran up to the coach and told the King that some thieves had come by and stolen his clothes and thrown him in the deepest part of the river, even though he had cried out several times, as loud as he could. In truth, the cunning cat had hidden the clothes under a large stone.

The King immediately commanded one of the guards to run and fetch one of his best suits for the Lord Marquis of Carabas.

The King received the Marquis courteously. And, because the King's fine clothes helped highlight how handsome the young fellow was, the King's daughter took quite a liking to him. The Marquis of Carabas had only to cast two or three glances at her and she had fallen head over heels in love with him. The King asked him to enter the coach and join them on their drive.

Puss, quite overjoyed to see how his plan was succeeding, ran on ahead. Meeting some countrymen who were mowing a meadow, he said to them: 'My good fellows, you must tell the King that the meadow you are mowing belongs to my Lord Marquis of Carabas, or else you shall be chopped up like vegetables for a pot of soup!'

The King did not fail to ask the mowers whose fine meadow it was that they were mowing.

'It belongs to my Lord Marquis of Carabas,' they answered, for the cat's threats had frightened them.

The King was quite impressed and said to the Marquis: 'You own a great deal of very fine land!' Now the princess began to think even more of the handsome fellow.

The capable cat, still running on ahead, came to a stately castle, the lord of which was an ogre, the richest that had ever been known. All the lands which the King had just passed really belonged to the ogre.

At the castle, Puss asked to speak with this cruel ogre, saying he could not pass so near his castle without having the honour of paying his respects to him.

The ogre received him as civilly as an ogre could do, and invited him to sit down. 'I have heard,' said the cat, 'that you are able to change yourself into any kind of creature that you want. You can transform yourself into a lion or even an elephant.'

'That is true,' answered the ogre very briskly. 'Do you not believe me? Well, to convince you, I shall now become a lion!' And suddenly Puss saw before him a huge lion. The cat was so terrified at the sight of a lion so near him that he leaped onto the roof. However, the ogre resumed his natural form, and the cat came down, saying that he had been very frightened indeed.

'I have further been told,' said the cat, 'that you can also transform yourself into the smallest of animals, for example, a rat or a mouse. But I can scarcely believe that. I must say I think that that would be quite impossible.'

'Impossible!' cried the ogre. 'You shall see!'

He immediately changed himself into a mouse and began to run about the floor. As soon as the cat saw this, he fell upon him and ate him up!

Meanwhile the King, who saw this fine castle of the ogre's as he passed, decided to go inside. Puss, who heard the noise of his majesty's coach running over the drawbridge, ran out with his tail twitching and said to the King: 'Your majesty is welcome to this castle of my Lord Marquis of Carabas.'

'What!' cried the King, 'Does this castle belong to you? There can be nothing finer than this castle and all the stately buildings which surround it. Let us go inside, if you don't mind.'

The Marquis gave his hand to the princess, and they followed the King, all of whom were led in by Puss who danced along in his boots. They passed into a spacious hall, where they found a magnificent feast, which the ogre had prepared for himself, for he was very greedy.

The King was charmed with the good qualities of the Lord Marquis of Carabas, as was his daughter, who had fallen violently in love with him. After seeing the vast estate he possessed and after having drunk five or six glasses, the King said to him: 'It will be your own fault, my Lord Marquis, if you do not become my son-in-law.'

It will not surprise you, I am sure, if I tell you that the Marquis of Carabas married the princess that very day, and they were happy together forever after.

Puss-in-Boots, the clever cat, became a great lord, and never again ran after mice, except for fun!

Rapunzel

(A tale from the Brothers Grimm)

There were once a man and a woman who had long wished in vain for a child. They wished for nothing else in the world but a child, but still their wish had not come true.

They had a little window at the back of their house from which a splendid little garden could be seen, which was full of the most beautiful flowers and herbs. However, the garden was surrounded by a high wall, and no one dared to go into it because it belonged to an enchantress, who had great power and was dreaded by all the world.

One day the woman was standing by this window and looking down into the garden, when she saw a bed which was planted with the most beautiful rapunzel, which is a kind of lettuce, and it looked so fresh and green that she longed for it and had the greatest desire to eat some. She longed for it so much that she began to look pale and miserable.

Her husband was alarmed, and asked: 'What might be the matter, dear wife?'

'Alas,' she replied, 'if I can't eat some of that rapunzel in the garden behind our house, I shall die!'

The man, who loved her, thought: 'I cannot bear to see my wife suffer, so I will do everything in my power to bring her some of that rapunzel.'

At twilight, he clambered down over the wall into the garden of the enchantress, hastily clutched a handful of rapunzel, and took it to his wife. She at once made herself a salad and ate it greedily. It tasted so good to her – so very good, that the next day she longed for it three times as much as before.

So her husband knew he must once more descend into the garden. Therefore, in the gloom of evening, he let himself down again, but when he had clambered down the wall he was terribly afraid, for he saw the enchantress standing before him.

'How dare you,' she said with an angry look, 'descend into my garden and steal my rapunzel like a thief? You shall suffer for it!'

'Please,' answered he, 'be merciful, I did it because I had no choice. My wife saw your rapunzel from the window, and felt such a longing for it that she would have died if she had not had some to eat.'

The enchantress allowed her anger to be softened, and said to him, 'If that is the case, I will allow you to take away with you as much rapunzel as you like, on one condition, you must give me the child which your wife will bring into the world, it shall be well treated, and I will care for it like a mother.'

The man was so scared that he agreed.

Not long passed when his wife gave birth to a beautiful baby girl. The enchantress appeared at once, gave the child the name of Rapunzel, and took it away with her.

Rapunzel grew into the most beautiful child under the sun. When she was twelve years old, the enchantress shut her into a tower in the middle of a forest. The tower did not have either stairs or a door, but near the top was a little window. When the enchantress wanted to go in, she placed herself beneath it and cried:

'Rapunzel, Rapunzel!
Let down your hair.'

Rapunzel had magnificent long hair, as fine as spun gold, and when she heard the voice of the enchantress, she unfastened her braided tresses and then let her hair fall down to the ground far, far below. Then the enchantress would hold on to the hair and use it to climb up to the tower window.

After a year or two, it so happened that the king's son rode through the forest and passed by the tower. Then he heard a song, which was so charming that he stood still and listened. It was Rapunzel, who in her loneliness passed her time sweetly singing. The king's son wanted to climb up to her, and looked for the door of the tower, but none was to be found. He rode home, but the singing had so deeply touched his heart that every day he went out into the forest and listened to it.

Once when he was standing behind a tree, he saw the enchantress arrive and he heard how she cried:

> 'Rapunzel, Rapunzel!
> Let down your hair.'

Then he saw Rapunzel let down the braids of her hair and watched the enchantress climb up to her. 'So that is the ladder. Well then, I too will climb it,' he thought, and the next day when it began to grow dark, he went to the tower and cried:

> 'Rapunzel, Rapunzel!
> Let down your hair.'

Immediately the hair fell down and the king's son climbed up.

At first Rapunzel was terribly frightened when she saw the king's son, for she had never seen a man before. But the king's son began to talk to her quite like a friend, and told her that his heart had been so stirred that it had let him have no rest, and he had been forced to see her. Then Rapunzel lost her fear, and when he asked her if she would take him for her husband, and she saw that he was young and handsome, and she said: 'I will willingly go away with you, but I do not know how to get down. Bring with you a bundle of silk every time that you come, and I will weave a ladder with it, and when that is ready I will descend, and you will take me on your horse.' They agreed that until that time he should come to her every evening, for the old woman only came by day.

The enchantress knew nothing of this, until one day Rapunzel said to her quite without thinking: 'Tell me, why is it that you are so much heavier for me to draw up than the young king's son? He is with me in only a moment!'

'Ah! You wicked child,' cried the enchantress. 'What do I hear you say? I thought I had separated you from all the world, and yet you have deceived me!'

In her anger she clutched Rapunzel's beautiful braided tresses, wrapped them twice round her left hand, seized a pair of scissors with the right, and snip! snap! they were cut off, and the lovely braids lay on the ground. And the enchantress took poor Rapunzel down into the forest and led her far away. She left Rapunzel deep in the forest where she had to live in great grief and misery, all alone.

On the same day that she cast out Rapunzel, however, the enchantress fastened the braids of hair, which she had cut off, to the hook of the window. When the king's son came, he cried:

> *'Rapunzel, Rapunzel!*
> *Let down your hair.'*

The enchantress let the hair down. The king's son climbed up, but instead of finding his dearest Rapunzel, he found the enchantress, who gazed at him with wicked and venomous looks.

'Aha!' she cried mockingly, 'you would fetch your dearest, but the beautiful bird no longer sits singing in her nest; the cat has got it and will scratch out your eyes as well. Rapunzel is lost to you; you will never see her again.'

The king's son was beside himself with pain and, in his despair, he leapt down from the tall tower. He escaped with his life, but the thorns into which he fell pierced his eyes.

He wandered quite blind about the forest, ate nothing but roots and berries, and did nothing but cry over the loss of his dearest beauty. At length he stumbled upon the spot deep in the forest where Rapunzel lived. He heard a voice that seemed so familiar to him that he went towards it. When he approached, Rapunzel recognised him, fell on him and wept. Two of her tears wet his eyes and they grew clear again, and he could see with them as before. He led her to his kingdom where he was joyfully received, and they lived happily ever after.

Rumpelstiltskin
(A tale from the Brothers Grimm)

Once there was a miller who was poor, but who had a beautiful daughter. Now it happened that he had to go and speak to the king, and so, in order to make himself appear important, he said to him: 'I have a daughter who can spin straw into gold.'

The king said to the miller: 'That is a talent worth having! If your daughter is as clever as you say, bring her tomorrow to my palace, and I will put her to the test.'

And when the girl was brought to him he took her into a room which was quite full of straw, gave her a spinning-wheel, and said: 'Now set to work, and if by tomorrow morning you have not spun this straw into gold, you must die.'

Thereupon he locked the room and left her alone. So there sat the poor miller's daughter, who for the life of her had no idea of how straw could be spun into gold, and she grew more and more frightened, until at last she began to weep.

But all at once the door opened, and in came a little man saying: 'Good evening, mistress miller, why are you crying so?'

'Alas,' answered the girl, 'I have to spin straw into gold, and I do not know how to do it.'

'What will you give me,' said the ugly little man, 'if I do it for you?'

'My necklace,' said the girl.

The little man took the necklace, seated himself in front of the spinning-wheel, and whirr, whirr, whirr, the wheel spun round until, by morning, all the straw was spun into gold.

By daybreak the king was already there. When he saw the gold he was astonished and delighted, but his heart became only more greedy. He had the miller's daughter taken into another room full of straw, which was much larger, and commanded her to spin that also in one night if she valued her life. Again, the girl did not know what to do and was crying, when the door opened again, and the little man appeared, saying: 'What will you give me if I spin that straw into gold for you?'

'The ring on my finger,' answered the girl.

The little man took the ring, again began to spin the wheel, and by morning had spun all the straw into glittering gold.

The king rejoiced beyond measure at the sight, but still he had not enough gold, and he had the miller's daughter taken into a still larger room full of straw, and said: 'You must spin this, too, in the course of this night, but if you succeed, you shall be my wife.'

When the girl was alone the ugly little man came again for the third time, and said: 'What will you give me if I spin the straw for you this time also?'

'I have nothing left that I could give,' answered the girl.

'Then promise me, if you should become queen, to give me your first child.'

Who knows whether that will ever happen, thought the miller's daughter and, not knowing how else to help herself in this situation, she promised the manikin what he wanted, and for that he once more spun the straw into gold.

And when the king came in the morning, and found all as he had wished, he took her in marriage, and the pretty miller's daughter became a queen.

A year later, she brought a beautiful child into the world, and she never gave a thought to the little ugly man. But suddenly he appeared in her room, and said: 'Now give me what you promised.'

The queen was horror-struck, and offered the little man all the riches of the kingdom if he would leave her the child. But the little man said: 'No, something alive is dearer to me than all the treasures in the world.'

Then the queen began to weep and cry, so that the little man pitied her.

'I will give you three days,' said he. 'If by that time you can guess my name, then you may keep your child.'

So the queen sat up through the whole night, making a list of all the names that she had ever heard; and she sent a messenger over the country to inquire, far and wide, for any other names that there might be. When the manikin came the next day, she began with Caspar, Melchior, Balthazar, and said all the names she knew, one after another, but to every one the little man said: 'That is not my name.'

On the second day she had inquiries made in the country as to the names of the people there, and she repeated to the manikin the most uncommon and curious names. 'Perhaps your name is Shortribs, or Sheepshanks or Laceleg?' she said, but he always answered: 'That is not my name.'

On the third day the messenger came back again, and said: 'I have not been able to find a single new name, but as I came to a high mountain at the end of the forest, where the fox and the hare bid each other good night, there I saw a little house, and before the house a fire was burning, and round about the fire quite a ridiculous little man was jumping up and down. As he hopped upon one leg he shouted:

'Today I brew, tomorrow I bake,
And then the fair queen's child I'll take.
And no one can deny my claim,
For Rumpelstiltskin is my name.'

You may imagine how glad the queen was when she heard the name. And when soon afterwards the little man came in, and asked: 'Now, mistress queen, what is my name?'

At first she said: 'Is your name Jack?'

'No.'

'Is your name Harry?'

'No.'

'Perhaps your name is *Rumpelstiltskin?*'

'The devil has told you that! The devil has told you that,' cried the little man, and in his anger he plunged his right foot so deep into the earth that his whole leg went in, and then in rage he pulled at his left leg so hard with both hands that he tore himself in two. And the queen never feared him again.

Sleeping Beauty
(A tale from the Brothers Grimm)

There were once upon a time a king and queen who for many years were very sad because they had no children. At last, however, the queen had a daughter. There was a very fine christening. The princess had for her godmothers all the fairies they could find in the whole kingdom (they found seven), and the fairies' custom in those days was that every one of them might give her a gift.

After the ceremonies there was prepared a great feast. Placed before each fairy was a magnificent gold plate with a spoon, knife and fork, all of pure gold set with diamonds and rubies.

After the feast, the fairies began to give their gifts to the princess. The youngest gave her beauty; the next, that she should have the laugh of an angel; the third, that she should have a wonderful grace in everything she did; the fourth, that she should dance perfectly well; the fifth, that she should sing like a nightingale; and the sixth, that she should play all kinds of music to the utmost perfection.

But just as the seventh fairy was about to give the child her gift, a very old, evil fairy who had not been invited, because she was believed to be either dead or enchanted, burst into the great hall where the feast was being held.

She was so angry at not having been invited to the feast that she cried out in a terrible voice: 'When the princess is fifteen years of age, she shall prick herself with a spindle and die of the wound!' This terrible gift made the whole company tremble, and everybody began to cry.

At this very instant, the seventh fairy stepped forward and said: 'I cannot undo the evil spell the wicked fairy has cast, but I can change it so that instead of dying, she shall only fall into a deep sleep, which shall last a hundred years, at the end of which a prince shall come and awake her with a kiss.'

The king was determined to avoid the misfortune foretold by the old fairy, and so he ordered that every spindle in the kingdom be burned.

About fifteen or sixteen years after, when the king and queen happened to be visiting their cousins in another country, the young princess was wondering about the palace exploring when she came into a little room on the top of the tower, where a good old woman was sitting alone, spinning with her spindle.

'What are you doing there, good lady?' said the princess, for of course she had never seen a spindle before.

'I am spinning, my pretty child,' said the old woman.

'And what is this?' said the princess, reaching out towards the spindle. Alas, she pricked her finger, just as the fairy had said she would, and she fell into an enchanted sleep.

The good old woman, not knowing very well what to do, cried out for help. People came in from every quarter in great numbers; they cried out and threw water upon the princess's face, but nothing would wake her. So she was laid upon a bed embroidered with gold and silver in the finest apartment of the palace.

The king was so distraught that he did not know what to do with himself. He was afraid that the little princess would awake in a hundred years, all alone in the old palace, so he summoned the good fairy to him and requested her help. And so the good fairy touched with her wand everyone and everything in the palace, and after being touched by her they all fell deeply asleep, not to awaken before their mistress. Even the fire that flickered went out and not a leaf fell from the trees.

Then there grew up all around about the castle a great hedge of thorns, that neither man nor beast could pass through. Nothing could be seen but the very top of the towers of the palace, and only then from a long way off.

A hundred years passed, while the story of the beautiful princess sleeping behind a wall of thorns spread throughout the land.

One day, the son of a king had been hunting when he noticed the towers poking out from the great thicket, and he questioned his servants: 'What is that strange tower in the distance? I have never noticed it before.' An old man spoke up and told the prince that he had heard from his grandfather that there was in this castle a princess, the most beautiful that was ever seen, and that she would sleep there a hundred years until awakened by a king's son.

The young prince, driven by love and honour, decided to go and rescue the beautiful princess from her slumber. He had scarcely entered the wood, when all the great trees, the bushes and brambles parted to let him pass through. He walked up to the castle and was surprised to see that none of his people could follow him, because the trees had closed again as soon as he had passed through them. However, he bravely continued on his way alone.

He crossed a court paved with marble, went up the stairs and came into the guard chamber, where guards were standing in their ranks, with their muskets upon their shoulders, and snoring as loudly as could be. After that, he went through several rooms full of gentlemen and ladies, all asleep, some standing, others sitting. At last he came into a gilded chamber where he saw, upon a bed, the finest sight that was ever beheld: a princess who appeared to be about fifteen or sixteen years of age, and was the most beautiful he had ever laid eyes on. He approached the little princess and gently kissed her. How great was his surprise when she opened her eyes and yawned loudly!

All in the castle then awoke, and there was great feasting and rejoicing. Then the wedding of the prince and princess was celebrated and they lived happily ever after for the rest of their days.

King of the Nogs

(Story by Oliver Postgate, illustrations by Peter Firmin)

In the lands of the north, where the black rocks stand guard against the cold sea, in the dark night that is very long, the Men of Northlands sit by their great log fires and they tell a tale.

They tell of a prince and how he built a long ship and sailed beyond the black ice at the edge of the world to bring home his bride from the land of the Midnight Sun.

Noggin the Nog was the name of the prince. He was the son of Knut, King of the Nogs, the aged ruler of that land of dark forest and snow which men call the land of Nog.

Now, every morning King Knut would rise from his bed, put on his boots, and climb to the hill above the royal castle. At the top of this hill was a rock known as Knut's seat. The aged king would sit on the seat and as the sun rose behind the mountains he would begin to worry.

He would look down on the little town clustered around the castle walls and he would worry about his people and whether their roofs leaked and whether they had warm socks this cold weather. He would look down on his castle and he would worry about his son, Prince Noggin, and what would happen to his people if Noggin did not marry soon; for it is the law in the Northland that the king shall be married. The old king knew that if he died Noggin would have to marry within six weeks of his death or he would not become king, and then the crown would go to his wicked uncle, Nogbad the Bad.

Then, one day, the king rose from his seat as if to go down to his castle. The people watching him saw him shake and stagger and fall to the ground. The king was dead. Great was the sadness and loud the wailing. All were sad, save one. In his black castle Nogbad the Bad heard the distant sounds of sorrow and smiled a greedy smile.

In the Royal Castle, Noggin's mother, Queen Grunhilda rose from her bed and called for the prince.

'Noggin,' she said, 'the time has come for you to choose a bride. I shall summon all the maidens of gentle birth to the castle within seven days, and on the seventh day you shall choose your bride.'

Soon the sound of trumpets was heard throughout the land as, from the battlements of the castles, from the balconies of the tallest houses the royal heralds proclaimed their message.

What excitement there was among the maidens! What twittering and giggling! With hopeful hearts they put on their walking shoes and skipped away to the Royal Castle.

On the seventh day the maidens assembled, dozens of them, in lines across the hall. Slowly Noggin the Nog walked along the lines looking with great care and friendliness. There were tall girls, short girls, girls from the valleys and girls from the castles on the mountain top.

Noggin came to the end of the line and he had not chosen. He had not found one maiden that pleased him enough to make her his queen.

Standing calmly next to the very last maiden of all, Noggin saw a large green bird, a strange bird, the like of which he had never seen before.

'You are not a maiden, you are a bird,' he said.

'Your highness is observant,' said the bird. 'My name is Graculus. I have flown from the land of the Midnight Sun and from my master, Nan of the Nooks, I bring you greetings and a gift.' The bird took from under his wing a knife. He placed it in Noggin's hand.

'Thank you very much,' said Noggin. He looked at the knife. It was made from a single faultless walrus tooth. On it was carved the likeness of a girl's face. Noggin looked at the face and he thought it beautiful, more beautiful than any of the maidens he had seen that day, or any other day for that matter.

'Who is the maiden?' he asked.

'It is the likeness of my master's daughter,' said the bird. 'It is the face of Nooka, Princess of the Nooks.'

Noggin, Prince of the Nogs, turned to his people and, holding up the knife, he cried out: 'This is the maiden I shall marry.'

What alarm and surprise there was in the castle! What grumbling and grumping!

With heavy hearts the maidens put on their walking shoes and trudged back to their homes.

Noggin climbed the steps in the castle yard and addressed the Royal Guard and the people of the town.

'Who will come with me?' he asked.

'We will!' cried the warriors with one voice.

'Who will build me a ship?' he asked.

'We will!' called the carpenters.

'And we will paint it!' called the painters.

'And we will make you sails!' called the sailmakers.

And so it was. The Nogs built a long ship of oak from the valleys. The mast was a single perfect pine tree. The high prow was carved and painted and gilded to a ferocious dragon's head. The sail was a square of stout canvas embroidered with the crest of Noggin and the face of Nooka. To protect the sides of the ship were shields of hammered bronze.

'Do not grieve for me, Mother' said Noggin the Nog as he took leave of Queen Grunhilda. 'The ship is strong, the men are brave. Graculus will guide us through the perils of the deep.'

So the ship was launched. Noggin and his band of warriors raised the great square sail. The wind took the sail and the ship moved away down the fjord towards the sea.

The people watched from the quay and waved goodbye. Everybody was sad to see them go and afraid for their safety on the long and perilous journey. Everybody save one.

In his black castle on the hill, Nogbad the Bad looked down on the little ship and he smiled. He knew that the journey to the land of the Midnight Sun was so long and dangerous that there was little chance of Noggin coming back and, as he thought of the royal treasure, the taxes and jewels and the crown which would soon be his, he chuckled to himself.

'Huh. Huh. Huh!'

They sailed away from the land of Nog. The next day, a storm came up and the boat was tossed about horribly. The storm blew past but then there was no wind at all. The oarsmen began to row. Then they spotted land! They rowed to the island and started to dig into the ground. But it was not an island at all! It was Arup, King of the Walruses, who said 'I say, do you mind? That hurt!'

Noggin and Arup greeted each other as only kings do, and Noggin offered his guest ship's biscuits because Arup was a bit peckish. Then Arup happily offered to give them a tow towards the land of the Midnight Sun. They travelled all day and all night.

Then, as dawn came, they saw before them the land of the Midnight Sun. It was a flat land. No mountains and forests like their own homeland, just flat ice and snow.

Nan of the Nooks was waiting for them on the shore. He was a little man in a fur hood sitting on a throne made of blocks of ice. He was surrounded by other little men in fur hoods all jumping about with excitement.

Nan of the Nooks came down from his throne of ice and shook Noggin by the hand. 'Perishing cold isn't it?' he said. 'Come up to my place and have a cup of something hot.'

Nan of the Nooks led Noggin to one of the round ice houses and went indoors. There was no door, only a sort of arched tunnel to crawl through. Inside, the house was bright and warm with a skin on the floor for a carpet. Nan and Noggin sat on stools and Nan's daughter brought them black tea in silver mugs.

She was Nooka, the girl whose likeness was carved on the bone knife. Noggin looked at her and she was more beautiful than he had expected.

Noggin turned to her father. He said, 'Nan of the Nooks, I have come far, through hail and wind, through snowstorm and sea mist, past the black ice at the edge of the world to ask your daughter to marry me.'

'Yes, I know,' said Nan of the Nooks.

'Well, er …' Noggin faltered, 'now I'm here, I feel a bit shy. Would you ask her for me?'

Nan of the Nooks laughed. 'All right then.' He called his daughter. 'Nooka,' he said. 'Noggin has come through hail and wind through snowstorm and sea mist, past the black ice at the edge of the world to ask you to marry him. Will you marry him and be Queen of the Nogs?'

'Yes Father, I will.'

So Noggin and Nooka were married. There was great feasting and merriment in the land of the Midnight Sun. Fireworks lit up the sky and the Nogs and the Nooks sang drinking songs and ate roasted caribou meat.

The next morning Graculus came to Noggin and Nooka and told them he was going to fly back to the land of Nog and tell the news that Noggin was married and on his way home. Otherwise Nogbad the Bad was sure to try and seize the throne.

Far away, in the land of Nog, Nogbad the Bad stood in his black castle and looked out across the sea.

High in the air he saw a bird, a green bird, flying very slowly like a bird that is very tired. He watched the bird flutter down and with the last of its strength land on top of the flagpole, fold its wings, tuck away its head and go to sleep.

Nogbad held the flag-rope and told his guards to haul down the flag. The guards pulled down the flag and, as they did so, Nogbad was pulled up the other side of the pole. He reached the top and grabbed the bird by the throat.

'Aaark!' cried Graculus.

'Lower away, guards,' said Nogbad.

They lowered him. He held out the bird to the guards. He said, 'Take this and put it in the dungeon.'

The guards took Graculus and put him in a dungeon. He sat there with a bowl of water and a bowl of birdseed and he wept. The days passed. Then one day the door was thrown open and there stood Nogbad in purple robes carrying a golden crown.

'Look at me, Bird,' he said. 'It is six weeks since Noggin went away. He has not returned and so, today, I go down to the council of elders in the town and they have to proclaim me King!'

Graculus watched from the barred window of the dungeon. He saw Nogbad set out in a golden carriage.

A robin perched on the window sill. 'Robin,' said Graculus. 'Do you want Nogbad to be king?'

The robin shook his head.

'Take this feather,' said Graculus. 'Put it in the hand of Queen Grunhilda and tell her I am here.'

Down in the town, Nogbad the Bad drove in state past the crowds of silent people. Nobody cheered or smiled but Nogbad did not care. He thought of the royal treasure and the taxes and he smiled to himself.

In the royal castle, Queen Grunhilda stood alone by her window and looked out across the cold sea.

'Alas, my poor Noggin!' she sighed and stretched out her hand towards the horizon.

A robin landed on her hand. It was carrying a green feather.

'This is one of Graculus's feathers,' said the old queen. 'Where is he?'

The robin pointed with its wing towards Nogbad's castle. The queen wasted no time. She called the guards.

'Take horses and go to the castle of Nogbad the Bad. Graculus is imprisoned there. This bird will show you the place. I am going down to the council of elders to deal with Nogbad.'

At the council of elders, Nogbad was explaining what a good king he was going to be and how many extra taxes everybody would pay.

Queen Grunhilda entered the hall, 'Nogbad!' she cried in ringing tones. 'What is the penalty for obstructing the king's messenger?'

'The penalty is banishment, Grunhilda.'

'Nogbad,' she commanded, 'go and pack your bags!'

The elders laughed, but Nogbad twirled his moustache and scowled.

'Madam,' he began. 'I could have you thrown into the dungeons, but as you were once Queen of the Nogs I will be merciful. I will let you go back to your castle, but you must stay there and mind your own business, for I am the king.'

'Oh no you are not,' came a voice from the doorway. There was Graculus perched on the shoulder of the captain of the Queen's Guard.

'Slink away Nogbad, your time is up!' and Nogbad slunk away.

'Smoke!' cried the boy who sold winkles.

'Smoke!' cried the harbour master.

The signal fire on the headland was burning to show that a sail had been sighted.

They saw a ship. It was tiny and far away, but Grunhilda, looking through the harbour master's telescope, could make out the crest of Nog and the face of Nooka embroidered on the sail.

Soon the ship sailed up the fjord to the harbour where, amid great rejoicing, Noggin and Nooka stepped ashore to be greeted by their people.

Graculus told Noggin of Nogbad's wickedness and he sent soldiers to seek him out. They did not find him. Nogbad had put on his climbing boots and set off over the pass to stay with his granny in Finland.

So Noggin and Nooka came home to their kingdom.

They were crowned that day in the royal castle, Noggin and Nooka, King and Queen of the Nogs, and their reign was long and happy.

Drama

Do you like to pretend? Maybe sometimes you and your friends pretend to be knights and princesses, or space explorers, or doctors and nurses. Maybe you like to play with dolls, and dress them up and speak for them.

When you do this, you are play-acting. Another word for play-acting is drama. Many television shows and movies are drama. Have you ever seen or been in a play, with actors and actresses in costume on a stage? That's drama, too.

You and some friends can perform your own drama. You can be the actors and actresses. You can put on costumes. You can decorate the stage with scenery, to show where your play is taking place. You will need to remember some words to speak: those words are called your lines. All the lines for the actors and actresses to say are written in the script. The script also gives some special directions, such as telling you when to come on the stage and when to go off.

Speak your lines in a big, clear voice so that the people watching the play – the audience – can hear you. When you're acting onstage, people are watching you, but you have to pretend they're not there!

Here is a script for a play called *The Boy Who Cried Wolf*. It's a drama based on one of Aesop's fables (which you can read in this book on page 32). What kind of costumes will you use? What kind of scenery will you make?

The Boy Who Cried Wolf: A Play

Cast of Characters

Announcer
John the Shepherd Boy
Farmer Brown
Second Farmer
Third Farmer
The Wolf
Sheep

(Note: Boys or girls can play any of these parts. If a girl plays the shepherd, you can change the name if you want.)

The curtain opens. The Announcer comes onstage and talks directly to the audience.

ANNOUNCER: Hello. Our drama is called *The Boy Who Cried Wolf*. This play comes from a fable by Aesop. A fable is a story that teaches a lesson. We hope you enjoy the play. Thank you.

[*The Announcer leaves the stage. Farmer Brown and John the Shepherd Boy enter from opposite sides of the stage and meet in the middle.*]

FARMER BROWN: Good morning, John. What are you doing out so early?

JOHN: Good morning, Farmer Brown. I'm going to the pasture to watch the sheep for my father. I've been watching them all summer.

FARMER BROWN: That's a big job for a young boy. I'm sure your father is very grateful to you.

JOHN: Oh, yes, he is. But I wish that I had someone to talk to or play with. There's no one around but the sheep.

FARMER BROWN: Do you see that valley way over there! [*Points to one side of the stage*] I will be working there with my friends for a few weeks. We will be working very hard, so we cannot play. But if any trouble comes up, you can come and get us.

JOHN: Thank you, Farmer Brown. Goodbye.

FARMER BROWN: Goodbye, John. Take good care of your sheep. [*They exit on opposite sides of the stage. Now the Sheep come onstage.*]

SHEEP: We are a flock of fleecy sheep,

Baa! Baa! Baa!

We like to eat and play and sleep,

Baa! Baa! Baa!

The shepherd boy keeps watch all day,

Baa! Baa! Baa!

He keeps the big bad wolf away!

Baa! Baa! Baa!

[*John enters. He moves the Sheep toward a back corner of the stage. Meanwhile, Farmer Brown and the two other farmers enter and stay at the opposite end of the stage, where they 'work' by pretending to dig, hoe, pick crops, etc.*]

JOHN: Oh, I'm so tired of watching sheep! I wish I had someone to talk to. Nothing exciting ever happens here, not even a wolf. [*He looks across* *to where the three farmers are working*] I wish Farmer Brown and his friends would come here. I know! I'll cry 'Wolf!' and make them think a wolf is eating the sheep. Then they'll come running. [*He runs toward the farmers and cries loudly*] Wolf! Wolf! [*The farmers drop their work and come running.*]

FARMER BROWN: Where is he? Where's the wolf?

SECOND FARMER: Where did he go? I don't see him.

THIRD FARMER: Has he gone already? Are we too late?

[*The farmers suddenly notice that John is laughing but trying to hide it.*]

FARMER BROWN: Why are you laughing, John? What's so funny about a wolf?

SECOND FARMER: Are you playing a joke on us, boy?

THIRD FARMER: If you are, I don't think it's very funny.

JOHN: [*Embarrassed*] There wasn't any wolf. I was tired of staying here alone, so I cried 'Wolf!' just for fun to have you come.

FARMER BROWN: John, you had better not play any more jokes like that.

SECOND FARMER: That's right. You'll be sorry if a real wolf comes.

THIRD FARMER: Come on, friends. We have work to do!

[*The farmers leave the stage. John lets out a big sigh, hangs his head, and exits on the opposite side of the stage. The Announcer enters.*]

ANNOUNCER: Do you think that John learned his lesson? I am sorry to say he did not. A few days later, he played the same trick again. The farmers ran to help him, and when they found out there was no wolf, they were very angry. Now a few more days have passed. And once again John the Shepherd Boy is watching the sheep.

[*The Announcer exits. Enter the Sheep, followed by John, sighing loudly and looking very tired and bored. Also enter the farmers, who go to work in their field.*]

SHEEP: We are a flock of fleecy sheep,

Baa! Baa! Baa!

We like to eat and play and sleep...

JOHN: [*Interrupting the Sheep*] Oh, blah, blah, blah! I don't think I can stand this anymore. Every day it's the same old thing. [*As John talks, the*

Wolf creeps onto the stage, looking very dangerous. The Sheep start baaing nervously but quietly, so that John can be heard] I never get to see anyone, or talk to anyone, or play any games. I want to have fun. I want some excitement. I want a... [*The Wolf has pulled one sheep from the flock. As he does, that sheep lets out a loud 'BAA!' just as John is speaking. John turns and sees the Wolf – and finishes his sentence*] wolf! [*The Wolf pulls the sheep off the stage. All the sheep are baaing in fear. John runs toward the farmers, crying loudly*] Wolf! Wolf! Help, come quick!

FARMER BROWN: A wolf? Really and truly, John?

JOHN: Really and truly! Hurry, come quick!

[*Farmer Brown starts to walk toward John, but the Second Farmer stops him.*]

SECOND FARMER: Wait a minute. Don't let the boy make a fool of us again.

THIRD FARMER: That's right. He's already played the same trick twice.

FARMER BROWN: But what if it's a real wolf?

SECOND FARMER: Then that's the boy's fault. How can we trust him when he plays so many tricks on us?

FARMER BROWN: I suppose you're right. Let's get back to work. [*The farmers go back to their work. John runs back to the sheep. He walks around the flock, looking as though he has lost something and can't find it.*]

JOHN: Oh, I have lost a poor little lamb. Why wouldn't they come to help me? What did I do to deserve this? Why didn't they believe me? Why? Why?!

SHEEP: [*All turning to stare directly at John*]: BAAAAAAA!

JOHN: All right, I know, I know. I didn't tell the truth before, so they didn't believe me this time. I'll never do that again, I promise – really and truly! [*John leads the Sheep, baaing, off the stage. Curtain closes.*]

One of the best parts of being in a play is hearing people applaud when it's over. That's when it's time for you to come out and take a bow. Usually only one actor / actress at a time comes out on the stage. For this play, you would come out in this order: The Wolf, Sheep (all together), Third Farmer, Second Farmer, Farmer Brown and, lastly, John. When all of you are onstage, you can take one last bow together. And enjoy all the clapping – it's for you!

Familiar Sayings

See the Year 1 book for more on these two sayings.

PARENTS: Every culture has phrases and proverbs that make no sense when carried over literally into another culture. To say, for example, 'the early bird gets the worm' does not mean you are actually talking about real birds and real worms. Nor – thank goodness – does it literally 'rain cats and dogs'! The sayings and phrases in this section may be familiar to many children, but the inclusion of these sayings and phrases in the *Core Knowledge Sequence* has been singled out and much appreciated by many parents and teachers who work with children from home cultures in which they may be unfamiliar with these sayings and phrases.

An apple a day keeps the doctor away

People use this saying to mean that if you adopt a healthy way of life you won't have so many problems with your health, so you won't need to see the doctor so often.

When she unpacked her lunch, Tulsi groaned: 'An apple again!'

'But that's good,' said her friend Sangeeta. 'An apple a day keeps the doctor away.'

You can't judge a book by its cover

Although someone or something may look one way on the outside, they may not be as they seem to be.

When the princess kissed the frog in the story of the Frog Prince, she found out that you can't judge a book by its cover.

Read the story of the Frog Prince on page 48?

Hit the nail on the head

When you use a hammer, you have to hit the nail right on its head to make it go in straight. So, when someone says that you 'hit the nail on the head,' they mean that you have said or done something just right.

Joanna was frustrated with her costume for the play. 'There's just something wrong with it, and I can't figure it out,' she said.

'Why don't you take off the crown and use this feather instead?' suggested Natalie.

'That's it!' cried Joanna. 'Thanks, Natalie. You hit the nail right on the head!'

If at first you don't succeed, try, try again

People use this saying to mean: don't give up; keep trying.

Robert the Bruce became King of Scotland after driving out the English. He fought the English army seven times and lost, so he felt like giving up. Hiding in a cave, he watched a spider spinning its web, trying again and again to spin the thread from one part of the cave's roof to another. Eventually the spider did it. 'If at first you don't succeed,' said Robert to himself, 'try, try, try again.'

Land of Nod

To be in the 'Land of Nod' means to be asleep.

'I can't sleep' Tina said to her big sister Jodie. Both girls had been in bed for half an hour. The room was dark and cool, and they could hear the raindrops falling on the windowpane.

'Close your eyes, Tina,' said Jodie, 'and I'll sing you a lullaby.'

She began to hum a tune to her little sister, and it was not long before Tina drifted off into the Land of Nod.

Let the cat out of the bag

If you 'let the cat out of the bag', you tell something that was meant to be a secret.

'Jack let the cat out of the bag: he told Hannah about her surprise party.'

The more the merrier

People use this saying to welcome newcomers to a group. They say this because it means: the more people who take part, the more fun it can be.

The house was full of children playing. Still, when the doorbell rang, Mr. De Niro opened the door and waved in more children, saying: 'Come in, come in, the more the merrier.'

Never leave till tomorrow what you can do today

People use this saying to mean: don't put off things you have to do.

'Let's clean up in the morning,' said Tom.

'No,' said Petra, 'let's clean up now. You know what Grandma always says: "Never leave till tomorrow what you can do today."'

Many hands make light work

People use this saying to mean: when a lot of people work together on a task, they can finish their work more easily and quickly.

'It will take me ages to cook everything for the big dinner party all by myself,' Eleanor said.

'Don't worry,' replied Anne, 'Everyone coming will each make a different dish so it will be easier for all of us. Many hands make light work.'

> It was a lot of work for brave little Peter from 'The Boy at the Dyke' to plug the hole in the dyke by himself. When the townspeople came to help, their many hands made light work of fixing the dyke.

There's no place like home

People use this saying to mean that travel may be pleasant, but home is the best place of all.

'What a great trip!' said Yoshiko. 'We saw the Eiffel Tower and the Mona Lisa in the Louvre!'

'Yes,' said her mother, 'we did have a wonderful time, but I'm glad to be back. There's no place like home.'

See the Aesop fables in this book (pages 32–37) for more sayings:

- 'A wolf in sheep's clothing'
- 'Don't count your chickens before they're hatched'
- 'Sour grapes'

Suggested Resources

Books for Teaching Reading

Liz Baldwin, *Sounds Fun* (Learning Development Aids) 2011

Big Cat Phonics series, and CD-Rom (Harper Collins) 2006

Mona McNee, Step by Step Reading: *A 50 Step Guide to Teach Reading with Synthetic Phonics* (Galore Park) 2007

Irina Tyk, *The Butterfly Book* (Civitas) 2007

Mo Willems, The Elephant and Piggie series (Walker Books)

Books for Beginning Readers

Ronda and David Armitage, Lighthouse Keeper series (Scholastic)

Blue Banana series (Egmont)

Tony Bradman, Dilly the Dinosaur series (Egmont)

Nick Butterworth, *The Whisperer* (Harper Collins) 2005

Dot Cleeve, *The Feather* (Tamarind) 2003

June Counsel, *But Martin!* (Random House) 2005

Roald Dahl, *Fantastic Mr. Fox* (Puffin) 2012

Julia Donaldson, *Charlie Cook's Favourite Book* (Macmillan) 2006

Alan Durant, *Burger Boy* (Andersen) 2006

Vivian French, Walker Blue Starter series (Walker Books)

Sally Grindley, The Ark Adventures series (Orchard)

Rose Impey, Animal Crackers series (Orchard)

Rose Impey, Titchy Witch series (Orchard)

Julia Jarman, *Class Two at the Zoo* (Hodder) 2008

Julia Jarman, *Class Three all at Sea* (Hodder) 2009

Arnold Lobel, Frog and Toad series (HarperCollins)

Peggy Parish, Amelia Bedelia series (Harper Collins, Greenwillow Books)

E. B. White, *Charlotte's Web* (Puffin) 2003

Online Resources

BBC KS1 Bitesize Literacy online activities: http://www.bbc.co.uk/bitesize/ks1/literacy

BBC Schools online activities:
http://www.bbc.co.uk/schools/websites/4_11/site/literacy.shtml

Galore Park online phonics activities: http://www.galorepark.co.uk/downloads-1.html

Mobile Apps (Free)

ABC Phonics Long Vowel Words (Abitalk) app for iPad or iPhone

ABC Phonics Rhyming Words Lite (Abitalk) app for iPad or iPhone

ABC Pocket Phonics Lite (Apps in My Pocket Ltd) app for iPad or iPhone

Prof's Phonics 1 (Ruth Fielding-Barnsley) app for iPad or iPhone

History and Geography

Introduction

For many years British primary schools have taught history through topics, such as Florence Nightingale, Henry VIII and his six wives and the Great Fire of London. These topics are all interesting, and have an obvious appeal to children, but their popularity often results in children going over this material several times in the course of their school career, whilst not covering other very important areas. By treating history as a series of topic projects, there is a danger that children never learn the sequence of events in British history which makes it clear to them how one thing has led to another, and how each generation builds on the experiences of those who have gone before them.

Learning history is not simply a matter of being able to recall names and dates, though the value of getting a firm mental grip on a few names and dates – such as 1066 and 1688 – should not be discounted. Year 2 pupils have not, of course, developed a sophisticated sense of chronology that allows them to appreciate the vast expanses of years between, say, the Ice Age, ancient Egypt and the Norman conquest, all of which, to the Year 2 child, happened long, longer or *really* long ago. Nevertheless, the development of a chronological sense is aided by having at least a few dates fixed in the mind and associated with specific events, so that later, as children grow, they can begin to place these dates and events into a more fully developed sense of what happened when.

The thematic approach to history – looking at the development of toys or houses through the ages – is also appealing to children, and can be a useful means of conveying information about things with which the child is already familiar. However, with no chronological framework at all, it becomes difficult for the child to grasp even the development of these familiar concepts.

As anyone knows who has witnessed children's fascination with dinosaurs, knights in armour or kings and queens, young children are interested not just in themselves and their immediate surroundings but also in other people, places and times. In Year 2, we can take advantage of children's natural curiosity and begin to broaden their horizons. An early introduction to history and geography can foster an understanding of the broad world beyond each child's locality, and make the child aware of varied people and ways of life. Such historical study can also begin to develop a child's sense of our nation's past and its significance.

In the following pages, we begin to share with children the long and fascinating story of both the country they live in and the wider world beyond it. Each corresponding chapter in the Core Knowledge UK series of books is divided into sections including world history and geography and British history and geography. The extent to which children can appreciate the complexities of a given period will obviously increase with age. However, our aim is that children should have an overall grasp of the major outlines of the history and geography of both the world and of Britain by the time they finish their primary education.

While it's good to help children grasp a few important facts, for young children the best history teaching emphasises the story in history. By appealing to children's naturally active imaginations, we can ask them to 'visit' people and places in the past (for example, we take children on a trip down the Nile River with King Tut in ancient Egypt). We encourage parents and teachers to go beyond these pages to help children to learn about history through art projects, drama, music, television programmes and discussions.

World History and Geography

History: Everyone's Story

History. Listen closely to the word: history. Do you hear another word in it? Do you hear the word story? History is a story. It's the story of all the people who have lived before us. It helps us remember who we are and what we've done.

When you study history, you learn stories of great men and women who have done extraordinary things. You will learn about people who survived in a hot desert by growing food beside the longest river in the world and who built amazing pyramids very, very long ago. You will meet a brave queen who fought against a huge empire to keep her people free. You will learn about kings and warriors who were so strong that they could sail through icy seas in wooden boats.

History is not just the story of emperors, kings and queens. It's also the story of ordinary people, of farmers, builders, artists, sailors, soldiers, teachers and children. Their stories are worth knowing. They are our stories. History is about how we have changed and how we have stayed the same. And so history is everyone's story.

The Birth of Civilisation

In the Year 1 book, we looked at the way people lived in the Stone Age, the Bronze Age and the Iron Age in Britain. For thousands of years, people lived by hunting animals and gathering plants. But in some other parts of the world, people were already living in a way that was much more like the way we live today. We talk about these people and their ancient civilisations – a civilisation is a big word for a group of people who live in a highly developed society. Let's think of some of the things that make civilised people different from those Ice Age hunters of long ago: things like living in one place, farming, building cities and having a written language. This means that people in a civilisation have a set order to their society so everyone knows the rules and laws.

The first civilisations began in Africa and Asia. Can you find those continents on a globe or world map? Now let's learn about two of the earliest civilisations. Let's go first to ancient Egypt.

Why are Ancient Civilisations Called 'Ancient'?

When you hear the Egyptians or other people in this book described as ancient, it doesn't mean that they grew to be very old. It means that the people were part of a civilisation that existed a long, long, long time ago. Ancient Egypt is the civilisation in Egypt thousands of years ago.

Egypt: Gift of the Nile

Egypt is in Africa. It's in a giant desert. Do you know what the weather is usually like in a desert? It's dry. It doesn't rain much at all.

Even though they lived in a desert, the ancient Egyptians were among the first people to learn to farm. Now wait a minute; how could that be? To grow crops, you need enough water. But what about Egypt, with all that burning sun and so little rain?

Read more about the desert and the animals living there in the science chapter on pages 290–291.

In fact, the Egyptian soil wasn't as dry as you might think. Egypt had very little rain, but she had a great treasure – a fantastic flooding river called the Nile.

The Nile is the lo-o-o-o-ngest river in the world. Do you see it on the map? It begins high in the rain-soaked mountains of central Africa and flows down the mountainsides. It twists and splashes into calm lakes and beautiful waterfalls. The Nile travels north for thousands of miles, and when it finally reaches the desert, this river does more than flow. It floods!

Once a year the Nile overflows its banks. The river's yearly flood turns one of the driest parts of the world into fertile ground ('fertile' means that plants can grow there very easily). After the Nile floods, for about ten miles along either side of the river the soil turns a rich black colour. It's full of minerals

This is how the River Nile looks today

and other good things that help crops grow.

Five thousand years ago, the Nile's gift of rich black soil meant so much to the early Egyptians that they named their country 'Black Land'. We call such moist, rich soil 'silt'. If you mix silt, sunshine and seeds together, plants will grow. Along the banks of the Nile, warm breezes blew wild barley seeds into the soil, and food crops sprang from the ground.

The Egyptians didn't just wait for nature to blow the seeds into the soil. They began planting seeds on purpose along the banks of the Nile. They grew big crops of grains like barley and wheat, whose seeds can be ground up into flour. You still eat these grains in foods like cereal and bread.

When the Egyptians began to grow crops they could eat, then they didn't have to hunt as much. They began to stay in one place in order to be near their fields and take care of their crops. They began to build villages and cities. They began to build a civilisation.

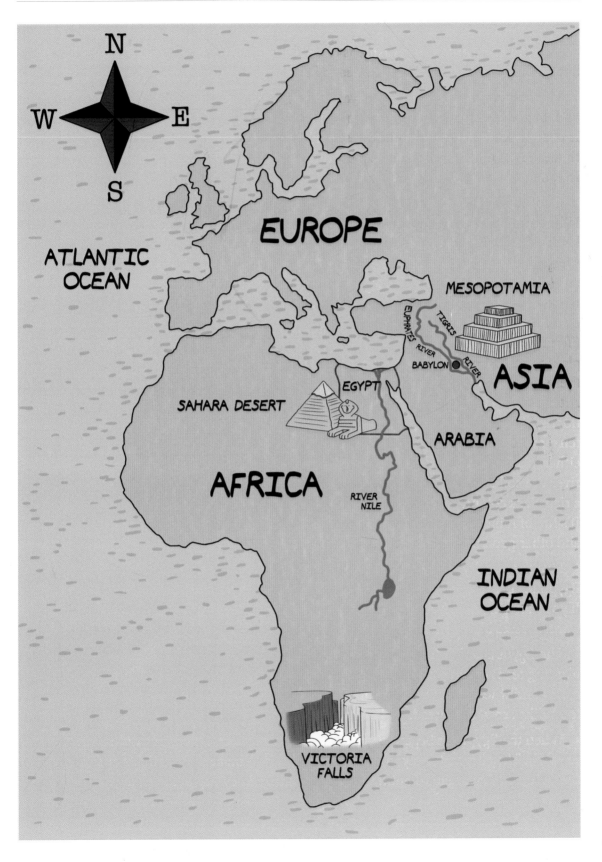

Fantastic Pharaohs and Marvellous Monuments

What a civilisation! In the next two thousand years, the Egyptians built enormous buildings and monuments that are still among the biggest ever made. They built huge stone temples and pyramids (you'll learn more about pyramids soon). Why did they do it?

Well, one reason was that the pharaohs [FAIR-rows] ordered them to do it. Who were the pharaohs? They were the rulers of ancient Egypt. The pharaohs had wonderful names that are fun to say – Rameses [RAM-ee-sees], Akhenaten [ah-ken-AH-ten], Amenhotep [ah-men-HOE-tep], Tutankhamun [toot-AN-CAR-moon] and Hatshepsut [hat-SHEP-soot]. They were like kings and queens, but in some ways they were even more powerful. The people of ancient Egypt thought the pharaoh was divine which means they thought he (or she!) wasn't just a powerful person but also a god. This belief in the pharaoh as a living god-king made his or her commands very powerful indeed!

A huge statue of Rameses II

The pharaohs wanted to inspire and amaze people with their greatness. Each pharaoh wanted to show his people that he was even more powerful and important than the god-king who had come before him.

Imagine for a moment that you're the pharaoh. You are very proud and boastful. To show everyone how powerful and important you are, what would you do? Would you have someone write a story about the great things you've done? Would you make a huge statue of yourself for everyone to see? Those ideas occurred to the pharaohs, too.

Lots of sculptures of Queen Nefertiti have been made to show her beauty and her power as the wife of the pharaoh Akhenaten. See a famous portrait bust of Queen Nefertiti on page 180.

Were all the pharaohs of Egypt men? Most were, but once there was a woman pharaoh named Hatshepsut. She didn't want to be called 'queen'. She wanted to be known as 'pharaoh' because she did the work of a pharaoh! She led armies into battle, and she ordered the building of great monuments.

The pharaohs ordered thousands of slaves to build great monuments to themselves and to the gods they worshipped.

They ordered workers to carve large images of their faces in stone. Now, imagine for a moment that you're one of the workers: you sweat and strain in the sun as you drag massive, heavy stones across the hot sand. Maybe you don't think as highly of the pharaoh as he does of himself!

One very important pharaoh, Rameses II, thought he was so great that he even erased from the monuments the names of many pharaohs who had come before him. He made sure only his stories were written on the walls of the buildings!

Do you think that this statue of the pharaoh Hatshepsut makes her look more like a male pharaoh rather than a female one?

Hieroglyphics: Picture Writing

Do you remember the reason we know only a little about the early humans in the Ice Age? It's because those early humans did not have a way to write anything about themselves. But we know a lot more about the ancient Egyptians. Why do you think we know more?

Did you say that the Egyptians knew how to write? Yes, the Egyptians did have a form of writing. Instead of writing with letters, as you're learning to do, they used picture writing. This picture writing is called hieroglyphics [hi-row-GLIFF-icks]. Some modern scientists who are called archaeologists [ar-key-OLL-oh-jists] study the things that were left behind by people who lived long ago. Archaeologists studied the Egyptian hieroglyphics and have figured out what many of them mean by using the Rosetta Stone. The Rosetta Stone used three different forms of writing to record the same message three times. Because archaeologists knew the other two languages, they were able to decode the hieroglyphics so we can learn a lot about the Egyptians from what they wrote.

When Rameses II ordered his workers to tell his stories, they carved hieroglyphics in stone. Each picture – whether of a falcon, a snake or a shepherd's staff – had a meaning. One of the reasons we know so much about Rameses II is that he had a lot written about himself!

Egyptian Hieroglyphs

The Rosetta Stone in the British Museum in London

A Journey Down the Nile

Are you ready for an adventure? Imagine you can travel back thousands of years to ancient Egypt. We're going for a sail down the Nile!

There's a boat floating on the river. And look, there's a young man wearing a fancy headdress. He's nodding to you. You're lucky to have him as your host. Although he's young – only a teenager – he is very important. In fact, he's the pharaoh!

His name is Tutankhamun. Let's call him 'King Tut' for short. Come on, hurry up, pharaohs aren't used to waiting for anyone. In a very dignified voice, King Tut says: 'Welcome aboard. I am so pleased that you can join us for the crocodile hunt.'

The Great Sphinx and an Egyptian Pyramid

'Crocodile hunt?!' you splutter. 'But I don't even know how to fish!'

'Do not worry about a thing,' King Tut responds. 'My servants will spear the creatures for you.' You look around and see that there are many people on the boat who are ready to wait on the young pharaoh's every need. They bow very low before him. You wonder what their lives are like. Are they afraid of this young pharaoh? Do they get tired of having to wait on him and do whatever he asks?

A servant brings King Tut a fruit drink and offers you one, too. You sip your drink and enjoy the sights as the boat floats along the Nile. 'Look over there,' says King Tut. 'Do you see that enormous statue – that huge figure with the body of a lion and the head of a human? That is the great Sphinx. The Sphinx is like a pharaoh: the pharaoh rules as a man, and he is as powerful as a lion.'

'And look there,' says Tut, 'near the Sphinx. Do you see the pyramids?' How could you miss them? They're huge! The biggest pyramid covers a space on the ground as big as thirteen football fields, (of course, they didn't play football way back in Tut's time)!

You look at the young pharaoh and ask: 'Why did you build the pyramids, King Tut? What are they for?'

Tut laughs and says: 'Oh, I did not build them! Those pyramids have been around for a thousand years. They are the sacred tombs of the god-kings before me. They are the burial places of ancestor pharaohs from long ago.'

'But King Tut,' you ask, 'why do you go to all that trouble to bury someone?'

'For us,' the young pharaoh explains, 'it is not a simple matter of just putting a pharaoh in the ground after he dies. No, what is important to us is the way the pharaoh lives after he dies.'

Tut can tell that you're puzzled, so he goes on. 'You know,' he says, 'that Egyptian pharaohs are god-kings. After our bodies die, we believe that our spirits keep on living if we make the necessary preparations. First, our bodies must be well preserved, because the body provides a home for the spirit after death. So our priests prepare the bodies of dead pharaohs in a special way. They do many things, such as wash and clean the body with fragrant spices, and rub it with special oils. One of the last things they do is wrap the body in rolls of white cloth, to make a mummy.'

Tut goes on: 'The mummy is very important. It's a home for the pharaoh's ever-living spirit. If the mummy is damaged, the spirit cannot live. So the mummy must be kept safe. That is why the pyramids were built. The pyramids are very safe places to protect the pharaoh's mummy.'

Horus

Animal Gods

The ancient Egyptians believed in many gods. They often pictured their gods as having human bodies with the heads of animals, such as lions, rams (male sheep with horns) or crocodiles!

The god of the sun, called Amon (sometimes Amon Ra), had a ram's head. Here you can see a picture of the god of the sky, Horus, who had the head of a bird called a falcon.

To see a picture of King Tutankhamun's magnificent gold sarcophagus – his mummy case – turn to page 134

'Still,' you ask, 'why do the pyramids have to be so big?'

'Oh, there is much more in the pyramid than just a mummy,' Tut answers. 'The pyramids are filled with different chambers and passageways. The room where the mummy lies contains everything the pharaoh needs in the afterlife.'

'What does he need?' you ask.

'Why,' says Tut, 'his spirit needs almost everything he needed in his earthly life – food, furniture, jewellery, games and much more.'

Tut leans over and motions for you to come very close. Then he whispers to you: 'If you can keep a secret, I'll tell you where I am to be buried.'

The ancient Egyptians made mummies for their pharaohs and their favourite animals – here are some at the British Museum

'You can trust me,' you whisper back. 'Where?'

'There,' he says as he points to the distant hills.

'Is that where you'll have your pyramid built?' you ask.

'No, no,' says Tut with a frown. Then he explains that pharaohs don't use pyramids any more, because too many robbers, who have no respect for the dead, have broken into the monuments of the great pharaohs and stolen all the treasures. So, when Tut dies, he will be buried in a tomb hidden underground in this place, called the Valley of the Kings.

Thinking about tombs has made Tut very serious. In a friendly but firm voice he tells you: 'It is time for you to go now.' You're just about to speak up and point out that you haven't caught a crocodile yet, but then you remember: it's not a good idea to talk back to a pharaoh!

The Treasures of King Tut

King Tutankhamun was a real pharaoh who lived thousands of years ago. He did a very good job hiding his tomb. It wasn't so very long ago – in 1922 – that a hardworking archaeologist, after searching for five years, finally found Tut's tomb in the Valley of the Kings. As he entered the tomb, his eyes opened wide in amazement: it was in almost perfect condition! The tomb was full of decorated chairs, shining jewellery, fancy clothes

A jewel treasure buried with King Tut

King Tut's golden mask

and thousands of other objects that had been buried with the pharaoh.

Here you can see some of the treasures buried with Tut, including a beautiful gold mask that shows what he looked like.

Mesopotamia – Another Gift

In Egypt the Nile flooded every year. East of Egypt, on the continent of Asia, two other rivers flooded yearly. These neighbouring rivers are called the Euphrates [yoo-FRAY-teez] and the Tigris [TIE-gris]. Like the Nile, when these rivers flooded, they gave the gift of rich soil. That meant that the people who lived beside or between the rivers could farm, grow plenty of food and build their homes.

An Ayyab letter written in cuneiform, on display at The Louvre in Paris

This warm and pleasant region has a long name, Mesopotamia [MESS-oh-puh-TAY-me-uh].

Mesopotamia means 'the place between two rivers'. (Look at the map on page 127). What happened between the Tigris and Euphrates rivers? A lot!

Mesopotamia is known as 'the cradle of civilisation' because history was born here. Remember, history is a story: so, when we say history was born in Mesopotamia, we mean that it's the place where people first began to write down the story of human lives. Even before the ancient Egyptians started writing with hieroglyphics, the early people of Mesopotamia had begun to write. We call their kind of writing cuneiform [KYOO-nee-form]. It's a strange-sounding word, and it means 'wedge-shaped', which is exactly what cuneiform was: a thin, triangular, wedge-shaped kind of writing.

A Great Mesopotamian Story

A statue of Gilgamesh

Not so long ago, archaeologists were digging in this cradle of civilisation. They found twelve clay tablets covered with cuneiform. The tablets were over five thousand years old! They told an exciting story – the oldest story in the world. We do not know what the people of Mesopotamia called it, but we call it the Epic of Gilgamesh [GILL-guh-mesh].

An epic is a long story filled with the adventures of heroes. *The Epic of Gilgamesh* tells the story of a mighty king named Gilgamesh, who rules harshly over his people. He forces them to build high walls and tall monuments and never lets them rest. But another hero, named Enkidu, fights Gilgamesh. Although they begin as enemies, Enkidu and Gilgamesh eventually become friends. Enkidu teaches Gilgamesh what it means to rule wisely.

Because the Epic of Gilgamesh was written down, we can learn a lot from it about how the people in long-ago Mesopotamia saw the world. It tells us what they admired in a hero, what gods they worshipped and how they thought the gods wanted them to behave.

What's a Ziggurat?

Like the ancient Egyptians, the Mesopotamian people worshipped many gods. They prayed to a sky god, a sun god, a water god, a storm god and many more. From what you know about ancient peoples and the importance of growing crops, why do you think weather gods were so important to them?

This is a reconstructed Ziggurat

To honour their gods, the people of Mesopotamia built temples called ziggurats [ZIG-uh-rats]. Ziggurats were enormous monuments with sides that looked like stair steps. They were not quite as tall as the pyramids, but if you saw one today, you'd feel very tiny standing next to it! You can still see the remains of a very large ziggurat in a city called Ur.

The Mesopotamian people believed in a powerful goddess they called Ishtar. To honour Ishtar, they built a wall around their largest and most important city, Babylon. The wall had a beautiful blue gate called the Gate of Ishtar. This blue-tiled gate was decorated with golden bulls and lions, which were Ishtar's favourite animals. In this way the people of Babylon warned their enemies: 'Do not mess with us, for we are protected by Ishtar!'

The restored Gate of Ishtar in the Pergamon Museum in Berlin, Germany

A Leader and the Laws

Think about it: Why do people need laws? What would happen without them?

In early Mesopotamia the people did not have pharaohs as rulers. They had kings. One very important king was named Hammurabi [ha-muh-RAH-bee]. He ruled over Babylon. He also ruled the land around the city, because he had sent his armies out to conquer it. He was known for miles around as a strong and fair king.

Hammurabi decided that, to make Babylon strong, the kingdom needed to have good laws. Do you know what laws are? Laws are the rules we obey. Today, for example, we have a law that says that all cars have to stop when you walk across a zebra crossing. Do you know of any other laws?

Of course, Hammurabi lived a very, very long time before there were cars. In fact, he lived in a time when people were first beginning to understand why it's important to have laws. Hammurabi collected laws from as many kingdoms as he could, and then he put

together the Code of Hammurabi. This was a very long list of laws, and some of them seem strange or cruel to us today. For example, one law said that if a doctor operated on a patient and the patient died, then the doctor's hand should be chopped off! This is definitely not the way we would do things today. But not all of Hammurabi's laws were so harsh. In fact, many of his laws protected those who could not protect themselves. For example, one law said that if a man was poor, a doctor should charge him less than a rich man for the same operation.

The Code of Hammurabi is carved into this stone

Justice: An Important Idea

Hammurabi was one of the first people to recognise how important laws are. Although we would not agree with some of the harsh laws he made, we share today Hammurabi's concern with an idea called justice. Justice is a big and important idea. When we think about justice, we think about what is fair for everyone. And we ask, what can we do to make life in our communities more just – better and fairer – for everyone?

Religions:
What Different People Believe

PARENTS: In the World History and Geography section, we introduce children not only to ancient civilisations but also to topics in the history of world religions. As the many people who contributed to the development of the *Core Knowledge Sequence* agreed (see pages xxi–xxii), religion is a shaping force in the history of civilisation and thus should be part of what our children know about. The pages on religion have benefited from the critiques of religious scholars and representatives of various faiths, whom we wish to thank for their advice and suggestions. In introducing children to the history of world religions, we focus on major symbols, figures and stories. Our goal is to be descriptive, not prescriptive, and to maintain a sense of respect and balance.

Have you noticed that when we talk about early civilisations, we keep mentioning 'the gods'? When we talk about the gods, or God, that people believe in, we are talking about their religion.

For thousands of years, different religions have helped many different people try to answer some big questions. These are not just questions that people asked long ago in ancient times. People still ask these questions today, questions like: How did the world begin? Where did people and animals come from? Why is the world the way it is? How should people behave?

Today there are many religions in the world. Let's find out more about three religions that have been important to many people for thousands of years. These three religions are called Judaism, Christianity and Islam.[1] Today these religions have millions of followers. But thousands of years ago, each of these religions was just getting started. We're going to look back to these long-ago times and learn about how Judaism, Christianity and Islam began.

But first, think about this: do you remember that people in ancient Mesopotamia and ancient Egypt believed in many gods? They believed in gods of nature, such as a sun god and an earth god. They believed in many other gods, such as a god of the dead and a god to protect the city. Well, there's a big difference in the religions you're going to learn about now. Judaism, Christianity and Islam do not believe in many gods. Instead, all of these religions believe in just one God, and they spell the name with a capital 'G', because that's how you begin a name – with a capital letter. Thousands of years ago, this belief in just one God was a new idea. And this new idea came first from the religion called Judaism.

---

[1] Later books in the Core Knowledge UK series discuss other religions. *What Your Year 3 Child Needs to Know* introduces children to Hinduism and Buddhism.

Judaism

The followers of Judaism today are called Jews. The Jewish people believe in one God. To worship God, they go to a place called a synagogue. The holy book of the Jewish people is called the Bible, or sometimes the Hebrew Bible. It is written in Hebrew, a language that is still spoken by many Jews today. The first part of the Hebrew Bible is called the Torah: it tells the history of the Jewish people and their God. Many Jewish people believe that the Torah was written by a man named Moses.

The Star of David, an important symbol of the Jewish religion

The Story of Moses

Moses was a great leader of the Jewish people. Way back in the time of Moses, the Jewish people were known by another name: they were called Hebrews. Sometimes the Bible also calls them Israelites or the Children of Israel. Here is some of the story of Moses, as told in the Hebrew Bible.

The story of Moses begins in ancient Egypt more than three thousand years ago. It was an awful time for the Hebrews because they were forced by the Egyptians to work as slaves. The Hebrews had to work long and hard days in the hot sun, carrying the heavy rocks used to build big monuments. Now, the pharaoh of Egypt noticed something that bothered him. He saw that among the Hebrews more and more children were being born every day. He began to worry that one day there might be so many Hebrews that they would rise up and fight against their Egyptian masters. And so Pharaoh gave a cruel command. He ordered that all boy children born to the Hebrew people should be drowned in the River Nile!

Just at this time a Hebrew woman gave birth to baby boy. She knew of Pharaoh's awful command. She decided she must do something to save her boy, but what? What could she do?

For a few months she did her best to hide him, but she could not keep him hidden forever. And so this is what she did. She wove a basket out of a long grass called bulrushes. She put tar on the bottom of the basket so that it would float. Then she carried her baby down to the River Nile and put him in the basket. She left the basket, with the baby in it, floating among the long grass by the riverbank. Hidden in the distance, the baby's older sister, named Miriam, watched the basket and waited to see what would happen.

Soon a group of women came walking along the riverbank. It was Pharaoh's daughter, along with the maidens who served her, coming to bathe in the river. Pharaoh's daughter saw the basket in the bulrushes, and she sent a maid to fetch it. When she looked inside,

'The Finding of Moses by Pharaoh's Daughter' *by Sir Lawrence Alma-Tadema*

she saw a crying baby boy! 'He must be one of the Hebrew children,' she said. She felt sorry for the little child, all alone. She named him Moses, which, it is said, means 'drawn out of the water'.

Just then the baby's older sister, Miriam, came out of her hiding place. She approached Pharaoh's daughter and asked: 'Shall I go and find a Hebrew woman to help you take care of the child?'

'Yes, do,' said Pharaoh's daughter. Now, who do you think Miriam went to get? Moses's own mother! So, with two mothers to take care of him, Moses was raised as a prince in the palace of his people's enemies!

When Moses grew up, he saw something that upset him. He saw an Egyptian beating a Hebrew slave. Moses fought the Egyptian and he killed him. And now Moses was in very big trouble. He had to leave Pharaoh's palace. He left behind his comfortable life and went far away to live as a shepherd.

The Hebrew Bible tells us that one day, as Moses was keeping watch over the sheep, he saw an amazing sight: it was a bush covered with flames, yet the bush itself was not burned by the flames. Then a voice spoke from the burning bush and said to Moses: 'I am the God of your fathers. I have seen the suffering of my people who are in Egypt. I will send you to Pharaoh that you may bring forth my people out of Egypt to a good and broad land, a land flowing with milk and honey.'

Moses was afraid. He said: 'O Lord, who am I to do this? Pharaoh will not listen to me. I am not a man of words. I do not speak well.' Then God became angry and asked Moses who had given him the power to speak in the first place? God told Moses: 'I will teach you what to say.'

So Moses, together with his brother, named Aaron, went to Pharaoh and said: 'God has commanded you: "Let my people go."' But Pharaoh said: 'I do not know your God, and I will not let your people go.' And Pharaoh made the Hebrews work even harder.

Then, says the Hebrew Bible, God punished the Egyptians. He sent a plague of frogs: the River Nile was filled with frogs and the people found frogs in their beds and in their food bowls. Still, Pharaoh refused to let the Hebrews go. So God sent more punishments. The land was covered with gnats, flies and locusts. The crops died, and the cattle died. The people of Egypt found their skin covered with terrible sores. Thunder crashed in the sky as a terrible hail battered the earth.

Finally, Pharaoh had had enough. He let the Hebrews leave Egypt. They gathered their few belongings and set off to the land that God had promised to Moses and his people, the Promised Land 'flowing with milk and honey'.

The journey of the Hebrews out of Egypt is called the Exodus. It was a long, hard journey. Soon after they started, the Hebrews came to the shore of a sea, where they stopped to rest. They didn't know, however, that Pharaoh had changed his mind about letting the Hebrews leave. He wanted them back to work as slaves. So he sent his soldiers after them. When the Hebrews saw Pharaoh's mighty troops approaching, they were terrified. The soldiers, riding fast in their horse-drawn chariots, were coming at them from one side. On the other side was the sea. What could they do? They turned to Moses and cried out: 'Have you brought us out of Egypt only to die here?'

But Moses raised his staff and a great wind began to blow. It blew so hard and so strong that the waters of the sea parted in two. The Hebrews were amazed to see a dry path between two walls of water! Moses led his people across this path through the sea. Not far behind came the soldiers of Pharaoh. But as the soldiers came across, the walls of water came crashing down, and all of Pharaoh's men were drowned.

The Hebrews were safe. Moses led them to their promised homeland, which is now called Israel. The escape of the Hebrews from Egypt is still celebrated by Jewish people today as an important holiday in the Jewish religion. It is called Passover.

Moses parting the sea to let the Hebrews escape

Another popular holiday in the Jewish religion is called Hanukkah [HAH-nuh-kuh; sometimes spelt Chanukah]. It is usually celebrated in December, and is sometimes called the Festival of Lights. On each night for eight nights, a candle is lit in a special holder called a menorah.

Christianity

The religion called Christianity began about two thousand years ago. It grew out of the religion you've just learned about, Judaism. It happened like this.

As you know, Moses led the Hebrews to their promised homeland, called Israel. But there were still many hard times ahead. More than once, the Jewish people were conquered and ruled over, as they had been by the Egyptians.

The Bible is a holy book for both Christians and Jewish people. But the Hebrew Bible of the Jewish people does not include a part of the Christian Bible – the part that tells the story of Jesus.

The Jewish people, as well as many other people, were conquered by the powerful Romans. The Romans had strong armies with thousands and thousands of soldiers. It was hard for the Jewish people to be ruled by the Romans. Many people in Israel hoped for a saviour – a person who would come and save them. The Jewish people called this saviour they hoped for the Messiah. Many Jewish people thought that when the Messiah came, he would lead the Jews against their Roman conquerors and make them free.

Into this world was born Jesus of Nazareth. Many people believe that Jesus was the Messiah the Jewish people were waiting for. These people are called Christians because Jesus was also called the Christ (which means something like 'the chosen one').

Jesus was not the son of a king or a powerful warrior. His parents, named Mary and Joseph, were humble people. The story of Mary, Joseph and the birth of Jesus is told in the holy book of Christians, called the Bible.

The First Christmas

Christians celebrate the birthday of Jesus on the day called Christmas. Here, from the Bible, is the story of the first Christmas. In the city of Nazareth, there lived a young woman named Mary. She did not know that something amazing was going to happen to her.

The Bible tells us that one day Mary was visited by an angel sent by God, an angel named Gabriel. 'Hail, O favoured one!' Gabriel said to Mary ('Hail' means 'Hello'). Mary was amazed and scared. 'Do not be afraid,' said the angel. But what Gabriel told her made her more afraid and very excited. The angel said that Mary would have a son, and that this son would be the Messiah, the promised one, the saviour of Israel.

Then Mary asked the angel: 'How can I have a son? I do not even have a husband.' The angel told her that the baby would be sent from God, and that her child would be called the Son of God.

Months later, Mary prepared to go on a trip with her new husband, Joseph. It was a hard time to travel, for indeed, Mary was now expecting a child. But they had to make the trip. The ruler of the Romans, called the emperor, had sent out an order. The Roman emperor wanted to tax all the people he ruled (that means he wanted to get money from them). He ordered them to return to the town of their ancestors to pay their taxes.

So Mary and Joseph went to the town of Joseph's ancestors, the little town of Bethlehem. It was a hard journey. When they arrived, Mary could feel that it was time for her baby to be born, that very night.

But they could find nowhere to stay: there was no room at the inn. The innkeeper told them they could stay in the stable where the animals were kept. In there they would at least find some straw to rest on.

And there in the stable, with the cattle and other animals moving softly about, Mary gave birth to her baby son. And since there was no crib or bed, she placed him in a manger, which held the feed for the animals to eat.

Nearby there were shepherds in the field, keeping watch over their flock by night. An angel appeared to them and said: 'Fear not: for, behold, I bring you good tidings of great joy. For unto you is born this day a Saviour, which is Christ the Lord.'

Cribs are a popular way of reminding people about the birth of the baby Jesus in a stable, surrounded by animals.

The shepherds were amazed. For so many years their people had waited for a saviour, a mighty leader. Could it be that their saviour was born here, among such plain and humble people?

The shepherds hurried to Bethlehem to see the child. They found Mary, and Joseph and the baby, who was lying in a manger. The shepherds told Mary what the angel had said.

143

Then they went to tell everyone the good news. But Mary remained quiet and thought deeply about all that had happened.

And that is what the Bible tells us of the first Christmas. Christians today remember and celebrate the first Christmas each year on the twenty-fifth of December by putting on special plays, giving gifts and singing songs about Bethlehem, the angels, the shepherds and the baby Jesus. Sometimes they make a 'crib' like the one on page 143.

Jesus the Teacher: The Parable of the Good Samaritan

When Jesus grew to be a man, he started teaching. People flocked to listen and Jesus soon had many followers. When Jesus taught people, he often told parables. A parable is a story that teaches a lesson.

Aesop's fables are also stories that teach lessons

A painting of the parable of the Good Samaritan by Van Gogh, whose self-portrait is on page 195.

Jesus taught that you should love your neighbour as you love yourself. Once a lawyer asked Jesus: 'Just exactly who is my neighbour?' To answer this question, Jesus told the parable of the Good Samaritan. (A Samaritan is a person from the region called Samaria.)

Once, said Jesus, a man was travelling along a road. Suddenly he was attacked by thieves. They robbed the man and beat him. He lay half-dead by the side of the road. Soon a priest came along. He saw the man lying in pain but did not stop to help him. Then another man came down the road; he, too, walked right on by without helping. Then along came a Samaritan. When the Samaritan saw the half-dead man, he went to him and took care of his wounds. He took the man to a nearby inn. He told the innkeeper that he would pay whatever it cost to take care of the man.

When Jesus had told this story, he turned and asked the lawyer: 'Which now of these three was neighbour unto him that fell among the thieves?' And that, from the Bible, is the story of the Good Samaritan. What do you think? Who was most like a neighbour to the man who was robbed and beaten? Why? Today, people sometimes call anyone who goes out of his or her way to help someone in need a 'good Samaritan'.

Easter

Many people listened to Jesus and believed him. But many others got angry with Jesus. They expected a saviour who would lead them in a great fight against the Romans. Instead, Jesus said that people should forgive their enemies.

Although many people began to follow Jesus, other people became his enemies. His words made them angry and scared. And so they hurt Jesus, and eventually they killed him. He was put to death on a cross, so the cross has become the main symbol of Christianity. Christians believe that on the third day after Jesus died, he rose from the dead; Christians celebrate his rising from the dead at Easter. Easter and Christmas are the two most important holidays and celebrations for Christians.

Islam

A long time after Jesus lived – in fact, more than five hundred years later – a man named Muhammad was born in the land then called Arabia (look at the map on page 127).

The religion of Islam began in the time of Muhammad. Followers of Islam are called Muslims.

Muhammad was a merchant, a person who buys and sells things for a living. He was a respected man in his hometown of Mecca (sometimes spelled Makkah). Many people called him al-Amin, which means 'the Trustworthy'.

Because he was a merchant, Muhammad travelled a lot to buy and sell his goods. In his travels he met many different people. Some of them were followers of the two religions you've already learned about: Judaism and Christianity. From these Jews and Christians, Muhammad learned about the idea of one God. And from the Christians he learned about the teachings of Jesus.

Muhammad thought about what he learned during his life and travels. When he returned home, he looked around at what he saw in his own land and he became troubled. He saw that many of the people still worshipped many gods. He felt that too many people in the city of Mecca had become proud and greedy. He did not like the rich rulers of the city. He believed they fought too much and were too concerned with money.

Beautiful Arabic writing in the tiles of the Wazir Khan mosque

Here is the story that Muslims tell about how their religion began. Muhammad liked to go off to sit alone in a quiet cave, where he could think about things that were worrying him. One day, when he was forty years old, he went to the cave and there he had a vision (a vision is like a dream, except you're awake). Muhammad saw an angel, the angel Gabriel. Is that name familiar to you? Gabriel is the same angel that, the Bible says, came to Mary to tell her that she would give birth to the baby Jesus.

Muslims believe that God spoke to Muhammad through the angel Gabriel. The angel told Muhammad to tell everyone in Arabia that there was only one God, whose name is Allah. 'Allah' is the Arabic word for the English word 'God'. So, you see, Muslims worship the same God that Jewish people and Christians worship.

Muhammad set out to tell people that they should worship only the one God, Allah. Some people listened to Muhammad's teachings and believed him. But most people were not very happy to hear what he said. He told them that their ideas about religion were wrong and that they should change what they believed and how they behaved. Some people got so angry with Muhammad that they even killed some of his followers and forced him to leave Mecca, the city that was his home.

The Regent's Park Mosque in London

But Muhammad was determined to spread his message. He continued to teach about Allah, and more people began to follow him. The people liked Muhammad's lessons about being kind to each other and about helping the poor. They prayed many times every day. They tried hard to live better lives.

The rulers of Mecca were still angry with Muhammad, and they were worried as many more people began to follow him. More than once the rulers of Mecca sent soldiers to attack the Muslims. But the Muslims fought back and, in the end, they beat the soldiers of Mecca. Muhammad returned to his home city and his many followers came with him.

Soon all of Arabia accepted Muhammad as the messenger of God. Since the time of Muhammad, the religion of Islam has spread from Arabia to many parts of the world. Muslims everywhere study the Qur'an (sometimes spelt Koran), which is the holy book of Islam. They worship Allah in buildings called mosques [MOSK-s].

Today Judaism, Christianity and Islam are three of the world's biggest religions. Jews, Christians and Muslims have much in common. All the followers of these religions believe in the same God, though they call this one God by different names. The holy books of the three religions tell some of the same stories. In the Qur'an there are many stories that are also told in the Torah and the Bible, such as the story of Noah and the flood and the story of Moses. In later books in this series, you'll learn more about the place of these religions in the story of world history, and you'll learn about other religions too.

British and European Geography

Do you remember from Year 1 how we talked about maps? They are pictures of an area of land from above. If you imagine flying high above the world like a bird, what would you be able to see? You might see streets and houses or shops and people; you might even see fields and rivers and big hills. If you were to go higher, you would even be able to see the shape of the continents and the oceans and seas in between them. A map is a drawing of a part of the world so that people can know where they are and what is around them.

Draw a map of your school that shows where all the buildings and paths are. Imagine yourself walking around the school. Where would you be on the map? Which building you have your lessons in? What do you walk past every day? What is next door to the school? Can you see these places on the map?

When you look at a map of the world, can you find the British Isles? Once you have found them, you can see

that these islands are separated from the bigger piece of land by water, but together we are all part of the continent of Europe. Can you see the area we call Europe? This is one of the seven continents of the world. Europe is a big place, with lots of different countries and people, and it would take a long time to travel from one end of the continent to the other. But it is not as big as some of the other continents of the world. Can you name the other continents? (Asia, Africa, North America, South America, Australia, Antarctica.)

Some of us live in cities, close to lots of other people, and some of us live in smaller communities like villages in the countryside. Can you name the community you live in? Villages, towns and cities across the British Isles are often grouped together in counties. There are lots of counties, over one hundred across the British Isles. Can you name the one you live in?

The Countries of the British Isles

The British Isles are made up of different countries. We call the biggest island Britain. In Britain there are three countries: England, Scotland and Wales. The smaller island is called Ireland. There are two countries in Ireland. In the south there is the Republic of Ireland, and in the north is Northern Ireland. Can you find where all these countries are on a map of the British Isles? Which one do you live in?

England, Scotland and Wales have their own flags. Together England, Scotland, Wales and Northern Ireland are the United Kingdom of Great Britain and Northern Ireland. They share one flag called the Union Flag or Union Jack. The Republic of Ireland also has its own flag. Can you see these flags on page 153?

> In Year 1 we read about the Union Flag and how it was put together.

England is the biggest country in the British Isles and lots of people live there. The English flag is a red cross on a white background, and it is known as St. George's cross. St. George is the patron saint of England.

> Do you remember the story of St. George and the Dragon that we read in Year 1?

A rose is the flower of England. The capital city of England is London, which is also the capital of the United Kingdom. It is the biggest city in the whole of the British Isles, and it is one of the biggest cities in the world. The river that runs through the middle of the city is called the River Thames. The south of England is mostly quite flat, which means it is good for growing food, but it is hillier in the north of England and the tallest mountain in England is in the county of Cumbria. It is called Scafell Pike.

The Oxford and Cambridge boat race

England is full of different types of people and different sorts of places, but there are some things that people think of when they think of England. What do you think of? Could it be fish and chips, a very popular meal in England, or maybe the sport of cricket, which was an English invention?

Or perhaps the annual boat race between teams from the universities of Oxford and Cambridge?

Have you heard the story of Robin Hood? It is an English story that has been popular for a very long time.

Geoffrey Chaucer wrote traditional English stories like *The Canterbury Tales,* but the most famous English writer is William Shakespeare. He was born a long time ago in a small English town called Stratford-upon-Avon, but today he is known all around the world.

We will read about Robin Hood in Year 3.

We will read about William Shakespeare's play *A Midsummer Night's Dream* in Year 6.

The Tower of London

England also has lots of big, old castles, such as Windsor Castle and the Tower of London, where you can see Beefeaters. It is not only England that has famous old castles. Edinburgh Castle is in Edinburgh, the capital city of Scotland, and it is one of the most famous castles in the world. Scotland is the country to the north of England. Scotland's patron saint is St. Andrew, and the St. Andrew's Cross, which is a white cross on a blue background, is the Scottish flag. The flower of Scotland is the thistle. The south of Scotland is where the big cities of Edinburgh and Glasgow are, but the north of the country is called the Highlands. Here it is very hilly. There are massive mountains called Munros, vast valleys called glens and large lakes called lochs [loCK-s]. The tallest mountain in Britain is in Scotland. It is called Ben Nevis and is in a mountain range called the Grampians. One of the deepest lakes in Britain is Loch Ness. It is so deep that there is a story about a monster living at the bottom called the Loch Ness Monster!

Most people in Scotland speak English today, but an older language called Gaelic still exists. It is part of Scottish culture, but what else do you think of when someone says Scotland? It might be the kilt, which is traditional Scottish clothing made from tartan. Tartan is a pattern woven from different colours. The different patterns represent Highland

Scottish dancers

communities called clans, but today the tartan kilt is worn by people all across Scotland. You might also think of bagpipes, a musical instrument often used to play traditional Scottish folk songs. The national poet of Scotland was Robert Burns. He wrote many famous and popular folk songs, but one of the best known is 'Auld Lang Syne', which is still sung today all over the world on New Year's Eve.

But it is the Welsh who are most famous for their singing. Wales is the country to the west of England. The capital of Wales is Cardiff in the south of the country and, even though the patron saint of Wales is St. David, the Welsh flag is not St. David's cross, but a red dragon instead. The flower of Wales is a daffodil. The highest mountain in Wales is Mount Snowdon in the north of Wales. It is in a mountain range called Snowdonia, but the south of Wales also has a mountain range called the Brecon Beacons. This means Wales is a very hilly country. The river Severn, which rises in Wales, is the longest river in Britain.

The Welsh have their own language, which is very different from English, and even from Scottish Gaelic. Many people in Wales can speak both English

Mount Snowdon in Wales

and Welsh. But the most famous Welsh poet was Dylan Thomas who always wrote in English. He wrote a famous play called *Under Milk Wood*. The Welsh celebrate their tradition of poetry and folk music in festivals every year called Eisteddfods. As well as music, the Welsh are famous for playing rugby.

England, Scotland and Wales are all part of Britain, but do you remember the other big island in the British Isles? It is called Ireland – which sounds like island!

The Welsh national rugby team are seen here playing against France

It is west of Britain and is made up of two countries: the Republic of Ireland and Northern Ireland. Ireland has two big cities: Dublin, which is the capital of the Republic of Ireland, and Belfast, which is the capital of Northern Ireland.

The patron saint of Ireland is St. Patrick, and Irish people across the world celebrate St. Patrick's Day on the 17 March. The flower of Ireland is a shamrock, but a gold harp is also a symbol of Ireland. Since the colour of Ireland is green, it is sometimes called the Emerald Isle. The longest river in Ireland is the River Shannon, and it is also the longest river in the whole of the British Isles. It runs from the middle of the country all the way to the city of Limerick in the south of the country where it meets the Atlantic Ocean. Lough Neagh is the biggest lake in the British Isles, found in Northern Ireland.

These dancers have learned to keep their arms by their sides while they dance

Even though most people in Ireland speak English, just like Wales and Scotland, Ireland has its own language too. It is called Gaelic and is similar to Scottish Gaelic. Ireland has its own sports too. People in Ireland like to play Gaelic football and hurling, as well as sports like football and rugby. Irish people have a love of words, and many great writers have come from Ireland. Every year, thousands of people visit Blarney Castle to kiss the Blarney Stone. They think it will give them 'the gift of the gab'! The Irish love to dance. They have a tradition of step dances, such as the reel, jig and hornpipe. In the best-known style, dancers keep their arms by their sides while moving their feet very quickly.

How many of the people and places can you name in this map of the British Isles? The clues are all in the text!

The North is Cold

If somewhere is usually very cold and snowy, we say it has a cold climate. The climate is the kind of weather a place normally has. The further north you go, the colder the climate gets, and there are some places where it is so cold it is snowy all year round! Look at the map of the British Isles on page 153. Using the compass points that you have learned, you can see that Scotland is north of England, England is east of Wales, and Ireland is west of Britain. In the science chapter you will learn about the North and South Poles. It's very cold in these places because there is not a lot of warmth from the sun. Scotland is further north than England, and closer to the North Pole. This means that generally Scotland gets more snow and is colder than the south of England. Also, the west of Ireland and the west of Britain get more rain than places in the east. This is because big clouds full of rain come from the Atlantic Ocean and drop most of their rain on the west before the wind blows them towards the east. Where do you live in the British Isles? Is it very cold and wet, or do you have warm, sunny weather?

Even though there are differences in the types of weather between the different countries in the British Isles, generally the climate is not too hot and not too cold. In countries in the south of Europe like southern Spain and Italy, it can be very, very hot in the summer. And if you were to go to some of the countries in the very north of Europe, it could be really, really cold.

The Scottish village of Braemar in the snow

Scandinavia

The British Isles are quite far north, but there are other countries in Europe that are even further north. Norway, Sweden, Finland, Denmark and Iceland are often known together as Scandinavia. Can you find these countries on a map? Some of them are quite a long way north of the British Isles. Now, as you know that it gets colder the closer you get to the North Pole, you can probably guess what the climate is like in these countries. It can be very, very cold in winter. Because of this cold climate, it can be difficult for plants and animals to survive. They have to have ways of dealing with the snow and ice and freezing weather. If you were going out in the snow, you would put your coat on. In the same way, many animals in these northern European countries have thick fur all over to keep them warm.

Trees and other plants also have to deal with not getting a lot of sunlight. Have you noticed how many trees lose their leaves in the autumn? Well the further north you go, the more trees you will find that stay green all year round to make sure they have enough energy to survive the really cold winter. They also have to have very thin leaves (or 'needles') so that they don't get covered in lots of cold and heavy snow. Plants and animals need lots of special tricks like these to survive in these really cold places, but if you go really far north in Scandinavia, not far from the North Pole, it is so cold that no trees can grow at all.

A Reindeer

We will learn more about the habitats of different animals on pages 286–292.

It is not just plants and animals that have to be clever to survive in the north of Scandinavia, but it is hard for the people who live there too. It can be exciting when it sometimes snows in winter, but can you imagine what it would be like to have lots of snow for many months? That is what it is like for some people in the north of Scandinavia. It means that it is important to keep warm and wear lots of clothes. It is also very dark in winter, and even dark all day and all night in the middle of winter very far north in Scandinavia. However, those who live that far north might have the chance to see the beautiful Northern Lights.

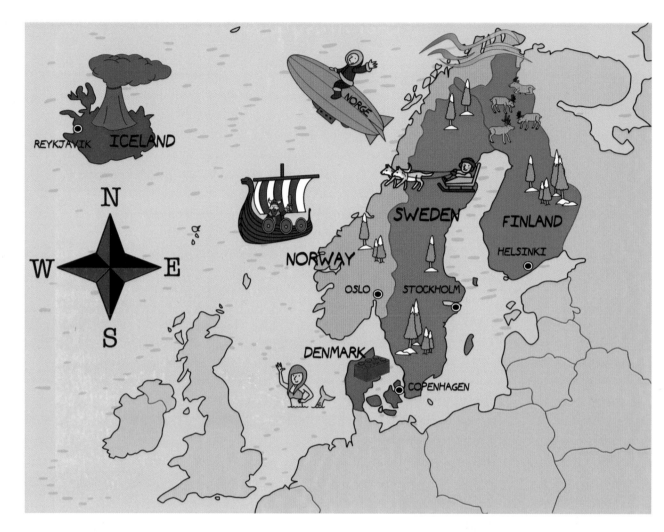

The northern parts of the Scandinavian countries are full of mountains and valleys and lakes. It is hard for people to live there, so most people in these countries live farther south, where is it usually a bit warmer. The capital cities of Norway, Sweden, Finland, Denmark and Iceland are: Oslo, Stockholm, Helsinki, Copenhagen and Reykjavík (in that order). These places are big, important and modern capital cities, and living there is very different from the cold, snowy northern areas.

This famous statue of Hans Christian Andersen's Little Mermaid can be seen on the seafront in Copenhagen.

Great Explorers: Roald Amundsen

Roald Amundsen [AM-oond-sun] was born in 1872 in Norway. He became a famous explorer of the coldest places on the surface of the Earth. He was born into a rich family, which owned many ships, but he had a hard early life. His father died when Roald was only 14 years old. His mother died when he was 21. His mother had made him promise to become a doctor. But when she died, Roald Amundsen decided to follow his heart and become an explorer.

In 1903, Amundsen was the captain of the first ship to sail through the Northwest Passage. This is the icy water north of Canada, on the continent of North America. It connects the Atlantic and Pacific Oceans. Can you find this area on a world map?

Roald Amundsen

During this voyage, Amundsen met many Inuit [IN-you-it] people who lived in the Arctic Circle. They have to survive in the cold climate for their whole lives. Amundsen learnt some of their ways of life. They wore clothes made from thick animal skin, not woolly clothes. They also travelled over the snow using sledges pulled by dogs. Learning these things was very useful for Amundsen in later expeditions.

In 1911, Amundsen led the first successful expedition to the South Pole. He had wanted to be the first to reach the North Pole, but when another explorer, Robert Peary, announced that he had already reached the North Pole, Amundsen decided that he would try to be the first person to get to the South Pole.

The South Pole is on Antarctica, a continent of ice all the way at the bottom of the Earth. Amundsen's team sailed as far as possible before the water was nothing but ice. Then they had to go the rest of the way on foot using sledges pulled by dogs to carry supplies. It took them nearly two months. Amundsen beat his rival, English explorer Robert Scott, by just a few days. The Amundsen-Scott South Pole Station is named after the two explorers in their honour.

Amundsen's expedition succeeded because he planned everything very carefully. He made sure his team could keep as warm as possible, and that they had enough food for the trip. They walked a set distance each day. Amundsen wrote later: 'Victory awaits him who has everything in order'.

In 1926, Amundsen reached the North Pole too. He didn't go by foot this time though! He flew over it in a big airship called the Norge [NOR-guh]. It was built and piloted by an Italian engineer called Umberto Nobile [NOB-bi-lay]. Although some people claimed to have reached the North Pole before, this is the first group of people that we can be sure got to see it.

Roald Amundsen led a life of adventure. He walked and skied over snow and ice, sailed ships and flew aeroplanes. But his life was also very dangerous. He died in 1928 while bravely trying to save his friend Nobile whose aeroplane had crashed. His body was never found but people believe that his own aeroplane also crashed in the Arctic.

> Can you see the Norge on the map on page 156? Amundsen didn't really sit on top!

British History

Romans in Britain

The Romans were a famous ancient civilisation, just like ancient Egypt or Mesopotamia. They came from the city of Rome, which is now the capital of Italy, but was then the centre of a huge empire. Like ancient Egypt or Greece, Roman civilisation was very advanced compared with others at that time. The thing that made the Romans different was that they used their technology and large army to explore and rule places all across the continent of Europe and North Africa. Have a look at a map of Europe. At its height, the

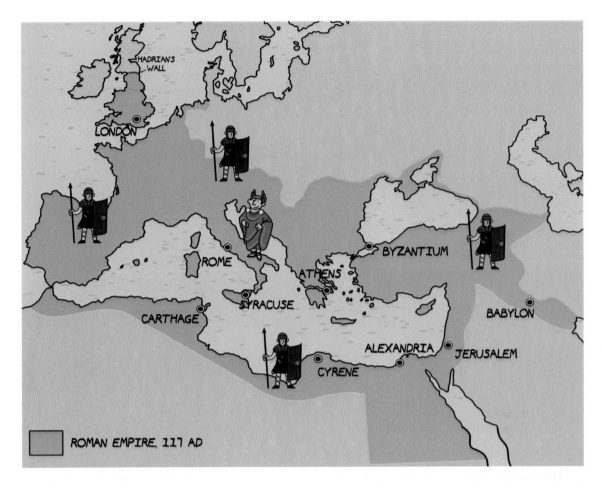

ROMAN EMPIRE, 117 AD

Roman Empire stretched from Britain to the north of Africa and to the Middle East.

At the same time as many Romans lived in large towns and cities, with roads and big buildings under the rule of a huge empire, the people in the British Isles were still living in what was known as the Iron Age. Can you remember what this means?

Before the Roman invasion, the British Isles were much less developed and life was very different from life in Rome. There were no roads in Britain, like there were in Rome, and people still lived in small huts made from wood. These buildings did not last as long as the

We learned about the Iron Age in Year 1

stone ones that the Romans had. This is just one reason why we know more about what happened in Britain after the Romans arrived than before. Romans also had emperors who ruled over the whole empire with their armies, but in Britain there were lots of smaller tribes, each with their own king. This made it easier for the Romans when they decided to invade Britain because they only had to defeat smaller tribes rather than one big country where everyone fought together.

Despite their large, organised army and modern weapons, the Romans did not find it easy to conquer Britain. The famous general Julius Caesar invaded first, in 55 BC, but he thought it would be a big job to conquer Britain. So it was not for almost one hundred years that the Romans tried again, in 43 AD. This time the invasion was led by Emperor Claudius, who sent a large army to Britain. The invading Roman army was a terrifying sight for all the tribes in Britain.

Some tribal kings decided not to fight and accepted Roman rule. This meant that they could remain as the head of their tribe, but they had to accept Roman law and pay taxes to the Romans. Other tribes fought back. The Catuvellauni, a tribe from the south-east of Britain, led the resistance to the Romans. Eventually, the Romans beat the native tribes, defeating the Catuvellauni at the Battle of the Medway.

Julius Caesar

Even after the Romans had taken control of the south of Britain, people fought back. Some were happy to be ruled by the invading Romans, but others were angry. If you had lived in Britain at this time, would you have been friendly with the Romans, or would you have fought them? Some did fight back, and one of the most famous rebellions against the Romans was led by Boudicca, the queen of a tribe

Queen Boudicca's Chariot

called the Iceni. Her husband had been king and he had made peace with the Romans, but after he died the Romans tried to take control of his lands. Queen Boudicca led her people in revolt, burning down Roman towns such as Colchester, St Albans and even London.

They were so successful that the Romans even thought about leaving Britain altogether! But eventually the Romans defeated the rebellion and killed Boudicca. Since then, Queen Boudicca has been remembered as a heroine of British history, and there is even a statue of her opposite the Houses of Parliament in London, the city she invaded and destroyed!

Once the Romans had control of the south of Britain, they tried to invade the rest of the island and conquer the area they called Caledonia in modern day Scotland. Some of the people there were called Picts and they fought against the invasion. They were beaten by the Roman General Agricola at the Battle of Mons Graupius in the north east of Scotland. But this was not the end of the Caledonians and the Romans had to keep sending armies to Scotland to control the Picts. Eventually, the Romans decided that Scotland was too cold and difficult a place to conquer. Instead, they decided to build a wall across Britain and leave the north of the island. The wall was called Hadrian's Wall and it stretched from one coast to the other with lots of Roman forts and soldiers along it. Because it was the edge of the Roman Empire, it had to be well-defended and there were battles along the wall as the Picts tried to invade Roman Britain. The wall was so well built that some of it still exists, and you can still see it today, thousands of years after it was built.

It was not just walls that the Romans were good at building. They built roads and cities as well. Unlike the tribes who lived in Britain before them, the Romans lived in big towns and cities with lots of people. They also had lots of soldiers who needed somewhere to live. The Romans built big cities in Britain, including York (which they called Eboracum) and London (Londinium). There are still Roman buildings that you can see in these cities, but some of the best preserved Roman buildings are the Roman villa at Fishbourne and the Roman baths in the city of Bath.

Hadrian's Wall

The Romans built roads to connect their cities, villas and baths. Before the Romans came, people in Britain travelled on dirt tracks or by boat. The Romans knew how to build long, straight roads that were made from stones so they were easier to travel on. This was important for the Romans to keep control of Britain because it meant they could march soldiers to different parts of the country very quickly.

Do you remember another important wall from the Year 1 book? Yes, the Great Wall of China!

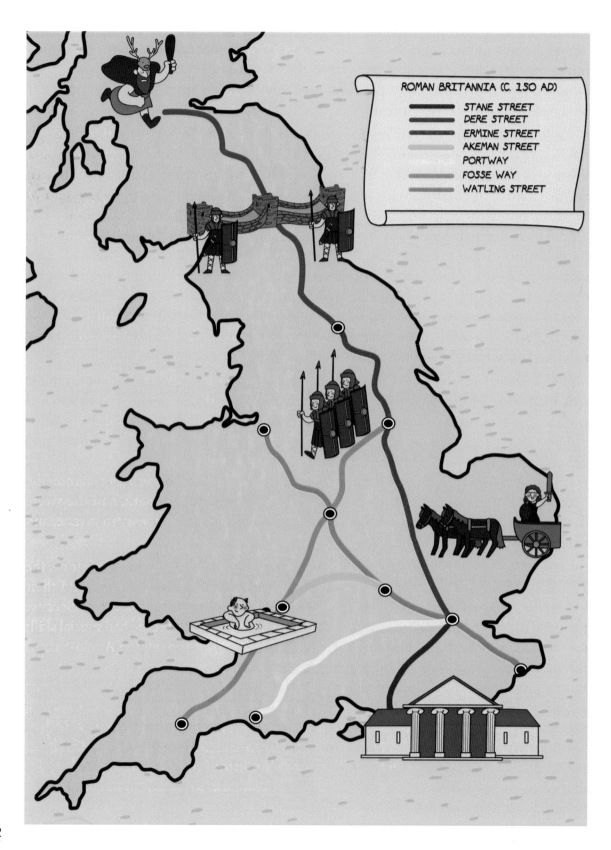

ROMAN BRITANNIA (C. 150 AD)

STANE STREET
DERE STREET
ERMINE STREET
AKEMAN STREET
PORTWAY
FOSSE WAY
WATLING STREET

The Romans brought other new things too. They built canals and aqueducts to bring water to towns and cities and a sewage system to remove the smelly waste from these growing cities. These are all things that we now take for granted, but they were brought over by the Romans.

Of all the things that the Romans brought to Britain, possibly the most important were reading and writing. Before the Romans, people in Britain

Roman baths in Bath

did not write things down, but the Romans kept written records. This means we have a better idea of what actually happened all those years ago. Also, just like in ancient Egypt and Mesopotamia, it meant there could be written laws and that tribal leaders could rule over much larger areas and many more people.

The Romans stayed in Britain for hundreds of years. Eventually, the Roman Empire collapsed and the Roman armies left Britain. But they left their influence on the way we speak, read and write; they also left behind the roads and buildings they had built.

Post-Roman Britain

After the Romans left, new people arrived in Britain. They came from across the North Sea, the place we now know as northern Germany and Denmark, and they were called the Anglo-Saxons. With the Roman armies gone, they found it easy to invade, and the Anglo-Saxons won an important victory over the native Britons.

Unlike the Romans, who liked to live in big towns and in buildings made of stone, the Anglo-Saxons mostly lived in smaller communities and they used wood to build their houses. This means that there are not a lot of Anglo-Saxon buildings left today. Because they lived in the countryside, most Anglo-Saxons were farmers. But some had special skills and could make metal jewellery and decorated swords. Even though the Anglo-Saxons mostly fought with axes, swords were very special because they were so difficult to make. Objects like these have been found buried in the ground. When one Anglo-Saxon king of East Anglia died, he was buried in a ship with many of his treasures. It is known as the Sutton Hoo ship burial. Does this sound similar to how the ancient Egyptian pharaohs were buried?

Discover more treasure from the Sutton Hoo ship burial on page 182.

Archaeology

How do we know what happened all these years ago and how people lived in those days? Often people did not write down what happened, so we have to find out other ways of knowing about it. Archaeology, [arr-kee-OLL-oh-gee] finding the things that used to belong to these people, is the main way we know about them.

Excavation at Sutton Hoo

When people saw odd-looking mounds in a place called Sutton Hoo (that was once part of the kingdom of East Anglia), they were curious to learn what was inside. They decided to explore these mounds in 1938 and the archaeologist Basil Brown made a great discovery! Inside the mounds, he found lots and lots of Anglo-Saxon treasure including military helmets, armour and swords. You can still see these amazing things from centuries ago that people used to fight with in the British Museum in London, or you can visit the Sutton Hoo National Trust site in East Anglia.

Burial mound, Sutton Hoo

Helmet from Sutton Hoo

King Arthur and the Knights of the Round Table

The Anglo-Saxons liked to tell stories, and a few of these legends are still known today. They told stories about great warriors such as Beowulf, a prince who defeated a monster. The native Britons also told stories. One of the most famous was about King Arthur, a king of the Britons who had fought bravely against the invading Anglo-Saxons.

The Romans had ruled all of England, but there were lots of different Anglo-Saxon and Celtic tribes. They were not 'English' or 'Scottish', but they belonged to lots of smaller groups of people, each ruled by their own king or queen. These different groups of people were part of what we call 'kingdoms'. They sometimes fought against each other for land and money, and sometimes they were peaceful and got on with one another. Sometimes a king of one of the kingdoms might proclaim himself king of Britain. At different times, some kingdoms were more powerful than the others.

There were seven main kingdoms in England and two in Scotland. In the north of England there was a kingdom called Northumbria. South of that in the middle of England was the kingdom of Mercia. The kingdoms of Northumbria and Mercia both had great power at different times. In the south of England was also the kingdom of Wessex. These were the three biggest kingdoms. In the east of England there were the kingdoms of East Anglia, Essex, Sussex and Kent. Do you recognise these names? Some of them are still used for counties in England. Scotland's kingdom of Pictland was in the north and the east, and in the west was a kingdom that also included part of the north of Ireland. It was known as Dál Riata. Have a look at the map to see where these different kingdoms used to be. Where in Britain do you live? Can you work out what kingdom you would have lived in if you had been alive then, hundreds and hundreds of years ago?

Do you remember the story we read about King Arthur pulling his sword from a stone in Year 1? We will read more about him in Year 3.

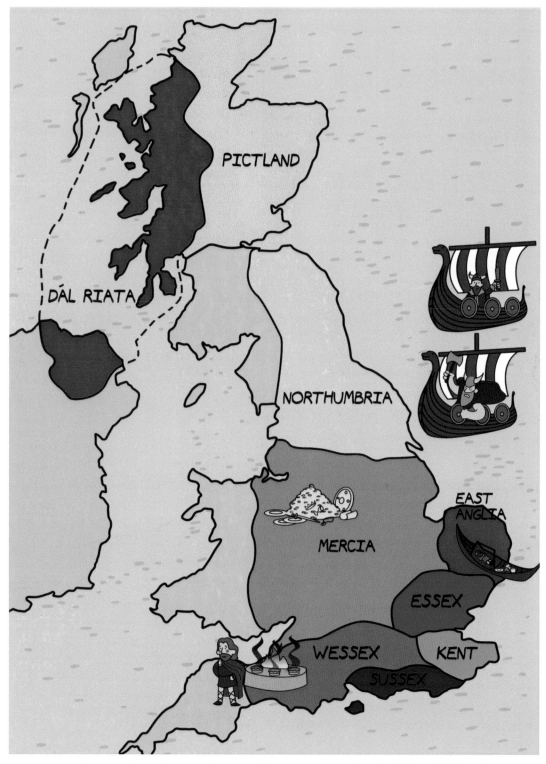

Anglo-Saxon kingdoms. Can you see where the Staffordshire Hoard and the Sutton Hoo ship were found?

Just a few years ago, in 2009, Terry Herbert was in the farmland near his home in the Midlands and discovered the largest collection of Anglo-Saxon items ever found! He discovered many objects from the kingdom of Mercia and, when he reported his great find, archaeologists from the Birmingham Museums & Art Gallery came to dig out the objects. They found many pieces of metal jewellery, armour and swords that are together called the Staffordshire Hoard. What do you think we can learn from the objects that were found? People who study this period of history can tell all sorts of things about the way people lived in those days, such as what they believed in and how they fought in battles.

Top: *Items from the Staffordshire Hoard*
Middle: *Bracelet from the Hoard*
Bottom: *Uncleaned pommels from the Hoard*

Look at the Sutton Hoo shoulder clasp on page 182.

Does it look similar to these uncleaned pommels?

By comparing the newly found objects from the Staffordshire Hoard with other items, archaeologists can learn more about them. Since we know that the shoulder clasps were made by the Anglo-Saxons, do you think other Anglo-Saxons made the pommels? They did!

The Vikings

The Anglo-Saxons were not the only people who wanted to rule Britain.

The Vikings were explorers and warriors from Scandinavia. They were mainly from the countries that we know today as Denmark and Norway, and so the Vikings are sometimes called 'Norsemen'. As well as being strong soldiers, they were also very good sailors and were able to build boats to take them very far from their homeland. These boats were called longships, and the Vikings used them to row and sail to new countries. Why do you think the Vikings travelled so far from home? One of the reasons they travelled was to trade with different peoples. They sometimes settled in the new lands they explored. They went to central Asia and were able to trade with people there and bring back exciting and unusual things such as silk and spices.

Dragon's head from a replica of a Viking ship located in Scotland

The Vikings were also warriors, and were known for being violent. Sometimes they would sail somewhere just to attack the place and take anything they wanted. The people who were threatened by the Vikings sometimes gave the Vikings money not to attack their area. This was known as 'Danegeld'. But it often did not stop the Vikings from attacking.

The Vikings started attacking monasteries along the east coast of Britain, taking gold and other valuable things. The Vikings were strong and fought with swords and axes. There was little the English monks could do when they were attacked. One of the first and most famous Viking attacks was a raid on the monastery at Lindisfarne in the English kingdom of Northumbria in 793 AD. After these raids, the Vikings invaded other parts of the British Isles, especially in the North East. They fought battles against kingdoms across England and Scotland. Some Vikings went to Ireland and settled in the city that today we call Dublin. The Vikings called it Dublinia. It is on a river and very near the sea so it was perfect for the seafaring Vikings!

When the Vikings came to Britain, the different Anglo-Saxon kingdoms stopped fighting against each other because they now had the same enemy. At one time, the only

Viking Religion

The Vikings were not Jewish, Christian or Muslim. They did not think there was just one God, but many gods. Odin was the king of their gods. The Vikings used to tell stories about their gods, and this was one of the ways they passed their culture on to their children. One of the most famous gods was Thor. He controlled thunder and lightning and was fierce in battle, so he was very popular with the fearsome Viking warriors! He carried a very powerful hammer, so powerful the Vikings believed this weapon could destroy mountains, and they often carried a small copy of it with them. Vikings believed that if they died in battle they would go to Valhalla, a Viking heaven, and so they were often buried with their belongings to take with them. Some important Viking chiefs were even given ship burials on longboats that were filled with their possessions and treasure. This is similar to the Anglo-Saxon Sutton Hoo ship burial but, with Viking chiefs' burials, their ships were usually set on fire and pushed out to sea.

Alfred the Great

major kingdom left that was not ruled by the Vikings was Wessex. Led by the famous King Alfred the Great, the other English kingdoms joined with Wessex to fight against the Vikings. King Alfred stopped the Vikings invading the south of England and, for many years, the two sides were at war. Eventually Wessex drove out the Vikings and the other kingdoms joined together with Wessex to become England.

In Scotland, the two kingdoms also joined together to fight the Vikings who had invaded. Scotland's first king was called Kenneth MacAlpin. In Ireland a great warrior called Brian Boru, who was the High King of All Ireland, was determined to drive the Vikings from his land. He defeated them at the Battle of Clontarf, near Dublin, but one of the Viking leaders who was retreating from the battle killed Brian. The Viking army was crushed but the Vikings didn't all leave Ireland. They stayed, married Irish people and gradually became just like the Irish themselves.

After the battles with Alfred the Great, the Vikings settled in the north and east of England in an area that became known as the Danelaw. The Vikings now ruled the old English kingdoms of Northumbria and East Anglia. People in the Danelaw lived by Viking laws and customs as many Vikings had settled there. However, the battles between the Vikings and other English kingdoms did not stop. Eventually the English defeated the Vikings and the Danelaw became ruled by England again. In later years the Vikings came back, and for a while England was ruled by a Scandinavian king called Cnut [ka-NEWT]. He had a big Viking empire that included Norway and Denmark. After King Cnut's death, England got an English king called Edward the Confessor in 1042. But in the north of Scotland, some places were still under Viking rule hundreds of years later!

The Danelaw

Tall Tales

There are lots of famous stories about people who lived in the past and who were really important in history, but sometimes we're not sure if the stories are true. Perhaps they just tell us something about those people and the way they dealt with things in a way that's easy to remember. We call these Tall Tales. Here is a Tall Tale about Alfred the Great and some cakes.

King Alfred of Wessex was a great warrior and a wise king, and he became the leader of the Saxons in their fight against the Vikings. They fought bravely, but the Vikings defeated them in battle after battle. Eventually Alfred's supporters deserted him, and he had to flee to Somerset with his wife and children.

He was so poor that he went to live in the cottage of a cowherd called Denewulf. His clothes were so old and worn that the cowherd's wife thought that he was a friend of her husband, and so she treated him as if he had been a common man and not a great king.

One day Denewulf's wife was very busy. She had been baking cakes, and still had many things to do. Alfred meanwhile was sitting by the fire. Thinking deeply about his kingdom and his people, and of how he could free them from the Vikings, he had forgotten all else.

It seemed to Denewulf's wife that Alfred was a lazy sort of fellow. She did not know the great matters he had to think of, and she wondered how anyone could sit for hours by the fire doing nothing. Now, she said to herself, this lazy fellow can at least look after my cakes, while I go to do something else.

'Here, good man,' she said to him, 'just mind my cakes for me. And don't let them burn. When they are nice and brown on one side, turn them over on to the other side, like this—' and she showed him how to do it.

'All right, good lady, I will look after your cakes for you,' replied Alfred.

But when the good woman had gone, Alfred sank once more deep in thought. As he watched the cakes, he looked into the fire. Soon, in the red glow of the burning ashes, he saw amazing things. The cakes and the cowherd's cottage vanished. Once again he was leading his army, his banner fluttering in the breeze, his crown upon his head. He heard the shout of his soldiers as they charged the Vikings. Alfred's soldiers overcame their enemies, and the Vikings fled to their ships. Fast behind them came the English. They set fire to the Viking ships. He smelt the smoke as it rolled upward, heard the crackle of the flames, the shrieks of the dying, the shouts of victory. England was saved.

Then suddenly he was awakened out of his dream by a blow to his shoulder and an angry voice in his ear. Alas! The cakes, and not the Viking ships, were burning, and the cowherd's wife was very angry. She scolded him well, little thinking that she was scolding her king. Then Denewulf came in. 'Hush thee, woman, hush thee,' he said, ashamed and frightened.

'Hush, shall I?' she cried angrily. 'The lazy loon, the idle good-for-naught, to sit by the fire, and see the cakes burn, and never stir a finger.'

'Hush thee, woman,' said Denewulf again in despair. 'It is the King.'

'The King!' cried the good wife, astonished, and a little frightened too. 'Well, king or no king,' she added grumblingly after a minute, 'he ought to have minded the cakes.'

Alfred was not angry, as Denewulf feared he would be, and afterwards, when he came to his kingdom again, Alfred made the cowherd a bishop, for he had found out while hiding in his cottage that Denewulf was a good and wise man. So the cowherd's wife became a great lady, and perhaps never baked any more cakes. Certainly she never again had a king to watch them for her.

Can you see King Alfred burning the cakes on page 166?

Life with the Vikings

The Vikings settled in some areas, becoming farmers, traders and craftsmen. After it was captured, the city of York, which had before been known as the Roman city of 'Eboracum', became the Viking settlement of 'Jorvik'. People who study Vikings have found the remains of Viking Jorvik under the modern-day city of York. From this we know that it was a big, busy place at the time, and full of people who lived crowded close together. It would have been a very smelly and dirty place because the Vikings did not have toilets. They dug pits outside their houses and went to the toilet there!

Jorvik was also visited by people from across Northern Europe who came to trade at the markets and buy things that the Viking craftsmen had made. They were well known for their blacksmiths, who were skilled at making things like swords and coins from metals. The Vikings' swords had to be very strong and sharp because they did so much fighting.

Even after the Viking chiefs left, the Viking people continued to influence the British Isles. Viking people stayed in Britain and settled down, and many people in Britain (possibly even you!) are related to Vikings from a long, long time ago. Vikings influenced all sorts of things, and many of the words we use today were first used by the Vikings. Did you know that 'Thursday' was named after the Viking god Thor, and used to be called 'Thors-day'?

Christianity in Britain

When we learn about people in the past, it is important to learn the way they thought about their lives and their world, and this often means knowing about their religion. For many people, religion shaped the way they lived and the groups of people they belonged to. For different kings and queens, the religion they chose helped them to decide how they would rule their kingdoms.

Do you remember learning about Christianity in the 'History of World Religions' section? It has been important in British history, because its rules helped people to decide what was right and wrong, and how to treat one another.

The religion of Christianity started a long way from Britain, in the Middle East. But how did it get here? Just like with roads and big stone buildings, it was the Romans who brought Christianity to Britain.

But the Romans were not Christians themselves when they first came to Britain. They believed in lots of different Roman gods, like the ancient Egyptians had done. People in different parts of the Roman Empire were deciding they wanted to be Christian and, to begin with, the Romans were not happy with this. Eventually, though, Emperor Constantine realised that, to keep his empire together, he had better allow people to be Christian. He even converted to Christianity himself. He claimed the reason for this was that on his way to fight a big battle, called the Battle of Milvian Bridge, he saw a Christian sign in the sky that told him his army would win the battle. He did win the battle, and he made Christianity even more popular. Years later, Christianity became the official religion of the Roman Empire.

Because Britain was part of the huge Roman Empire, Christian missionaries came here, and some people in Roman Britain began to convert to Christianity. St. Patrick is the patron Saint of Ireland because he spread Christianity in Ireland. The new religion soon became popular in Ireland, and missionaries travelled across to different parts of Britain. St. Columba left Ireland for Scotland and St. Aidan travelled to the kingdom of Northumbria in the north of England to spread Christianity. St David was born in Wales and spread Christianity in his own country.

The Anglo-Saxons were not part of the Roman Empire and they were not Christians. So when they came to southern Britain, Christianity became less popular. Do you remember the different Anglo-Saxon kingdoms in England at this time? One of these kingdoms was Kent, and their king was called Aethelbert. St. Augustine came from Rome to convert Aethelbert and his kingdom to Christianity. Augustine was so successful that he became the first Archbishop of Canterbury, and there is still an Archbishop of Canterbury today.

St Augustine preaching to King Aethelbert

This was how Christianity came to Britain, but why is that important? Well, Christianity changed the way people did lots of things, like getting married and owning property. Christianity also brought monks and monasteries. Monks were religious men who spent their lives living away from other people in monasteries, where they prayed and studied religion.

Monks also studied important things such as reading and writing, maths, law and even medicine. There were monks and monasteries all across Europe at this time, so lots of new ideas about these subjects arrived in Britain. Over time, some of these monasteries became universities, places where students could learn about these subjects.

The monks even wrote history books because they knew it was important to understand the past. In the kingdom of Northumbria, there was a monk called Bede who is famous for writing the first history book about England. It was called *The Ecclesiastical History of the English People*. It told people about the different kings in England and how people had lived.

The Irish missionaries St. Columba and St. Aidan founded monasteries in Britain. St. Columba founded an important monastery on the island of

Bede was a great teacher and writer

Iona in Scotland. St. Aidan, when he came to Northumbria, founded a monastery on the island of Lindisfarne. The monastery at Lindisfarne is very, very old but it is still there. In these monasteries, monks wrote out and decorated copies of the Bible and some of these books still exist today. Often no one was allowed to read these books because they were so important. The monks used special methods and real gold and silver to make beautiful, shiny designs. One of the most famous books is the Book of Kells, which can be seen today in Dublin in Ireland. It is lucky that so many of these amazing books have managed to survive for so long. The Book of Kells was once stolen and found buried in a bog! At the monastery on Lindisfarne the monk Eadfrith created the famous Lindisfarne Gospels. Luckily, they survived the violent Viking attack on the island that marked the beginning of the Viking invasions!

Can you see the saints in the map on page 153?

You can see a page from the Lindisfarne Gospels on page 183.

Remains of the Lindisfarne Priory today

Normans in Britain

1066 is a famous year in English history. It was in this year that Britain was successfully invaded for the last time. England had only recently been free of Viking rule when Edward the Confessor died. After he died, no one knew who was going to be king, and there were several people who claimed they had a right to rule. Harold Godwinson, a noble from Wessex, initially claimed the throne and was crowned but, as soon as he had become king, he had to defend his position against other people.

Harold Godwinson took his army up to the north of England and fought and defeated the king of Norway, Harald Hardrada, who wanted to be king of England as well. This battle was called the Battle of Stamford Bridge, and took place in Yorkshire. After Harold Godwinson had won, he heard that another nobleman, this time from Normandy in northern France, was attempting to invade and take the crown. His name was William, Duke of Normandy.

William landed on the south coast of England. So Harold had to march his army all the way down from the north of England to the south. Can you imagine how tired they would have been? Harold's men had just fought a battle and now had to walk hundreds of miles to fight another one! They were really, really tired when they arrived to fight William's army at Hastings.

The Battle of Hastings took place on the 14 October 1066 and is one of the most famous events in English history. William's army was about three times bigger than Harold's, but Harold and his men fought hard and they held the Normans back. At last, tiredness and numbers took their toll and William broke though the English defences.

This whole story – from Edward the Confessor's death to Harold Godwinson's battles against William, Duke of Normandy – is told in the Bayeux Tapestry. This is a really long piece of cloth with pictures sewn into it. It was made by William's supporters after the battle to celebrate his victory. Do you think it tells the truth about what happened? People who study history actually think it is quite close to the truth. The tapestry shows Harold being hit in the eye with an arrow, and once the English king had been killed, William had won the battle.

William was now known as William the Conqueror, but his job was not done. He wanted to be king of England, but all he had done was win one battle. He now had to take control of the rest of the country. William and his army went around the south of England over the next few months fighting battles and attacking towns. Eventually most of the important nobles decided that they would be better off accepting William as king because William promised some of them that they could keep their power. Because he wanted people to accept him as king, William was crowned king in Westminster Abbey, where the other English kings had been crowned.

Even though William was now king, it was not easy for him to take control of the country. William tried to convince some nobles to be loyal to him, but he also brought some with him from France because he knew he could trust them. It was not easy to travel around the country, so William relied on trust and loyalty from important people throughout England. Would you have wanted William to be your king? There were many people who didn't like having William as king. In the north of England there were people who opposed William, so he sent an army to attack them, burning towns and cities and destroying fields so the people had nothing to eat. Can you imagine how scary this must have been? He also replaced the important nobles with his own people who would make sure that everyone was loyal to William. He built lots of castles to show people how powerful he was and remind them that he was still the ruler. Many of these castles still exist and you can visit them today.

Part of the Bayeux Tapestry

The making of the Domesday Book

The Domesday Book

William realised that he didn't really know much about the country he now ruled because, at this time, people did not keep many records. He didn't know who owned what and he didn't know how much money he could collect in taxes. To solve this problem he created the Domesday Book. This was a record of all land and property in the country. It even counted individual cows and pigs! Can you imagine what a long and difficult job that must have been, counting everything in England? Now William knew what he was owed in taxes and, just as important, who could provide soldiers to fight for him. This was the first time that the government had collected information in this way. It has been useful for governments to collect information like this ever since. For people who study the Normans, the Domesday Book provides lots and lots of interesting information.

This was how William gained control of England so that when he died he was able to pass the crown on to his son so that Norman control of England could carry on.

Suggested Resources

World History and Geography

Bill and Pete Go Down the Nile, written and illustrated by Tomie dePaola (Puffin Books) 1996
I Wonder Why Pyramids Were Built and Other Questions About Ancient Egypt by Philip Steele (Kingfisher) 1995
Tut's Mummy Lost… And Found by Judy Donnelly (Random House) 1988
The Usborne Internet-linked Children's World Atlas by Gill Doherty (Usborne) 2005
National Geographic Kids World Atlas (National Geographic Society) 2010

British and European History and Geography

Our Island Story by Henrietta Marshall (Civitas/Galore Park) 2006
Britannia: 100 Great Stories From British History by Geraldine McCaughrean and Richard Brassey (Orion Childrens) 2004.
This Sceptred Isle: Julius Caesar to William the Conqueror 55BC-1087 (Audio CD collection, MP3 Download) by Christopher Lee (BBC Audiobooks) 1999
Smashing Saxons (Horrible Histories) by Terry Deary (Scholastic) 2007
Stormin' Normans (Horrible Histories) by Terry Deary (Scholastic) 2007
Vicious Vikings (Horrible Histories) by Terry Deary (Scholastic) Reissue 2007

Visual Arts

Introduction

Doing, making, creating!

For a child in Year 2, making art is just as important as looking and talking about it; the sheer pleasure of doing, making and creating should be encouraged. Throughout the chapter we suggest activities which relate to the works of art discussed; they are intended to deepen children's understanding and memory of the things you will read and talk about. They are also meant to be easy to do at home, making use of readily available or inexpensive materials.

While art is doing, it is also seeing and thinking

By reading this section aloud with your child, you can both learn some of the ways that we talk about art. Looking closely at art, and talking about it, will help your child develop a love of art and a habit of enjoying it in thoughtful, active ways. Sometimes we suggest questions to help direct your conversations, but you should feel free to move beyond these and follow your child's curiosity. By helping your child to become comfortable talking about art, not just making it, you will be supporting their developing language skills and literacy, as well as their creativity.

PARENTS: Create, Learn and Grow! Did you know that for children creativity is not only fun, but can support their learning in many ways? Exploring the arts is great for self-confidence and self-expression as well as for knowledge and understanding. If it is not suitable to do more than drawing at home, or if you are not confident about how to help your child create, then join in with one the practical sessions run in galleries and museums. They are often free, with materials, direction and inspiration provided for you!

People Have Been Making Art for a Very Long Time

Queen Nefertiti

Thousands of years before you or I were born, the people of ancient Egypt were making beautiful and amazing works of art. Much of their art and architecture was so well made that it is still in fantastic condition today. One such piece is the famous portrait bust (which is a sculpted head and shoulders) of Queen Nefertiti. She is wearing an unusual-looking flat-topped, tall hat. This distinctive hat helped people recognise the image as Nefertiti and many copies of this bust are known, telling us Nefertiti wanted people all over Egypt to recognise her. The hat served another purpose too: it allowed the artist to show us Nefertiti's elegant long neck; her hair must have been piled up inside. Also unusual – especially for an ancient work of art – is that we know who made this Nefertiti, because it was found in the remains of the workshop of an artist called Thutmose. By modelling a chalk-based plaster mix over a stone core, he created a realistic face. The chalky material would have been quite flexible while it was still damp (a little bit like plasticine), allowing Thutmose to build details like the thickening in the bridge of Nefertiti's nose and the tendons in her neck.

In Year 1 we learned about 'all around art', or sculpture. Can you remember what a sculpture is? It is a work of art which is not flat but has three dimensions – or can be walked all around – like the bust of Nefertiti on this page.

To bring her to life, next Thutmose painted the plaster surface using natural colours. Nefertiti's skin looks so fresh that it is difficult to believe she is over three thousand years old! Thutmose couldn't decide on the best way to treat her eyes, however. One has been inlaid with crystal and given a pupil of black wax, whereas the other is plain. Why might this be?

Activity 1: Eye spy

Take a good look at Nefertiti's face and eyes from the photograph of her bust on the opposite page. Using a thick pencil or a black pen, draw several pairs of eyes trying to copy the shape of Nefertiti's. Using coloured pencils or pens, first try to draw the eyes as Thutmose made them, one detailed with crystal and one plain. For the other pairs on your page, try out different ways of completing the eyes, using different colours, different sized irises or pupils, giving her eyelashes and so on. How do the different colours and details you have drawn change Nefertiti's expression? Does she look happier, younger or something else? Has this activity helped you think of other reasons why Thutmose left one of Nefertiti's eyes unfinished?

If you have read the World History and Geography section of this book, then you will already know about other wonderful creations of the ancient Egyptians like the pyramids, the Great Sphinx and mummy cases. The most famous mummy case, or sarcophagus as it is properly known, was made for a young Egyptian king named Tutankhamun, who died aged 19 in 1325 B.C. No expense was spared in the making of Tutankhamun's sarcophagus. Instead of being made of wood and painted, it was made from solid gold. Imagine how heavy it must be!

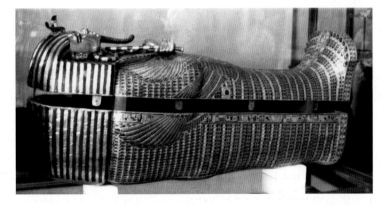

The solid gold sarcophagus of Tutankhamun

Masterpieces in Metal and Manuscripts

It was not only in ancient Egypt that important people were buried with metal artworks and priceless treasures. Raedwald, the Anglo-Saxon king of East Anglia in the east of England, was buried with the finest metal treasures in the seventh century. Unlike Tutankhamun, Raedwald was not laid in a sarcophagus, but in a full-sized boat! The boat tells us he had overseen great victories at sea, and the metal treasures tell us he was powerful and wealthy. The cooking pot, the helmet, sword, purse and spoon which were found with Raedwald sound like practical items when they are listed like this, but when you see them you realise they were made to be looked at and admired, not really to be used. Look at the shoulder clasp, pictured here. Can you see how carefully the gold has been shaped to curve and be symmetrical? The gold, valuable enough on its own, has been enhanced with expensive red garnet

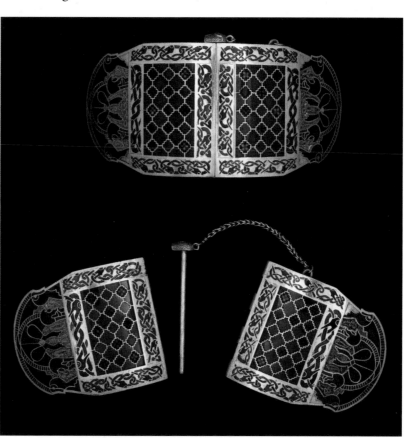

Shoulder clasp from the Sutton Hoo ship burial

stones as well as pieces of rare blue glass. On the tips of the clasp these materials have been used to show wrestling or entwined boars. The boar was a symbol of fearlessness and strength. Combined with the luxury materials used and the time and skill which it must have taken to create, we can be sure that the clasp was made to be seen. If you could pick it up, you would also find out how heavy it is – heavy enough that you wouldn't want to be wearing it on your shoulder for very long.

Metal treasures like the Sutton Hoo shoulder clasp began to change the way that artists who used paint and inks worked. They started to decorate the pages of books, for example, to look like carefully worked metal and jewellery. The *Lindisfarne Gospels,* shown here, is one of the finest examples of this, and is particularly amazing because there are pages and pages of its jewel-like decorations. It is also special because it was the work of just one man; a monk named Eadfrith. Imagine how long it must have taken him to decorate, or illuminate as we call it, a whole book in this way. It is thought to have taken him years; it was literally his life's work.

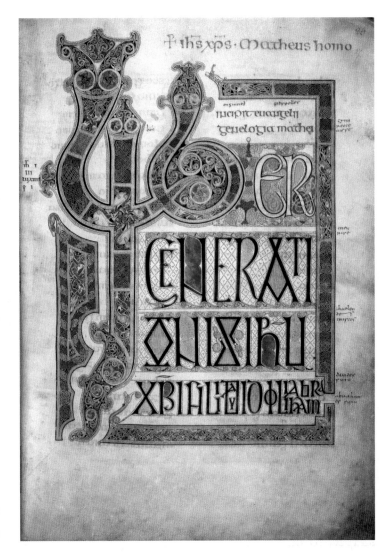

Lindisfarne Gospels, *Gospel of Saint Matthew, initial page*

Activity 2: Illuminating and decorating

Have a go at decorating a page of text – illuminating it – like Eadfrith did. Choose a poem or a song you like from another chapter of this book. Copy the text out on a piece of paper in your finest handwriting. Make the first letter of the first word over-sized and ornate, and then colour this letter and the borders to look like metal work or the *Lindisfarne Gospels.* Time yourself. How long did you spend?

A World of Colour

The Beach at Trouville

Do you have a favourite colour? Let's look at colour in a painting by French artist Claude Monet [MON-ay]. Monet loved colour and was fascinated by how changing light conditions alter the way colours look. What do you think the weather was like the day Monet painted his *Beach at Trouville*? How can you tell the sun was bright but that it wasn't very warm? How can you tell it was windy? The women are wearing heavy dresses and hats but they also hold parasols to keep the sun off their faces. The younger lady (the one on your left) seems to need two hands to hold on to her parasol. In the distance flags are flapping, and the clouds are broken and diagonal in places, chopped by the wind. The colours are mostly pale, as if lightened by strong sunlight. Monet became famous for doing so many of his paintings outside. We know he made this one on the windy beach shown because tiny grains of sand and chips of shell were blown into the wet paint and are still stuck there!

What is the first colour you notice in Monet's painting? Do you see how he was not worried about giving each object a sharp outline? When you draw, I expect you usually start with an outline, but Monet worked in patches of colour instead. Look at the pale-coloured dress of the younger lady. It is made up from thick, rough stripes of buttery-like paint. Monet has chosen to paint the patches of colour and light as

Do you remember from Year 1 how some colours seem 'warm', such as yellow and red, while others – like blue and green – seem 'cool'?

he saw them, rather than to paint the details and texture of the dress and its fabric. Similarly her flowered hat, when you look closely, is simply daubs of contrasting brightly coloured paint and seems almost blurred. It is only when you look at the picture as a whole that these stripes and dabs of coloured paint come together to create an impression of smartly dressed women at a bright and breezy beach. Monet actually used this word 'impression' (which is the same in French and English) as a title for one his paintings. *Impression: Soleil Levant (Impression: Rising Sun)* of 1872, is in Paris at the Musée Marmottan, and used patches, stripes and dashes of colour to show the sun rising over Le Havre harbour. This led to him being known as the first 'Impressionist'.

Monet liked to balance the colours in his paintings, so cool colours, like the blues, greys and whites which dominate this beach, are set off by the warm tones in the sand and the brightly coloured hat. Which colours catch your eye when you look at *Trouville*? Were you drawn to the bright flowers on the hat? Warm colours, like red, seem to jump forward and cool colours, like blue, are less forceful, often appearing further away.

The American painter James McNeill Whistler approached colour in a very different way from Monet. Instead of balancing warm and cool colours, Whistler challenged himself to work with a limited range of colours, and rarely chose bright ones. Can you spot any bright or warm colours in this painting? Only the patches of white stand out. We know that

Whistler's main interest when he painted this was how to balance cool and dark colours, because he did not name it after the sitter, who was actually his mother. Instead he called it *Arrangement in Gray and Black No.1.* Do you think this room is a warm place to be? How do the colours make it appear? Whistler's mother rests her foot on an old-fashioned wooden foot warmer; this tells us that it was not just Whistler's colours that were cold.

Arrangement in Gray and Black No. 1

185

Activity 3: Primary and secondary colours

Using paints of the three primary colours – red, yellow and blue – discover what other colours you can make by mixing them together. Use the illustration on this page to guide you. Remember to wash your brush each time you touch it into a new colour and to use clean water so that you don't muddy your experiments. By the time that Monet and Whistler were painting you could buy paints ready-mixed in many colours. Before the industrial age, artists had to be able to mix up colours for themselves.

red   yellow   blue

blue + Yellow = green

blue + red = purple

red + yellow = orange

red + blue + yellow = black

Get in Shape!

When lines join together they make shapes. You create shapes whenever you draw an outline or cut something out. Here is the shape of a person, cut out of card. The shape of a real person changes as the person moves. Other shapes, like these basic shapes shown below, remain the same, even when their size changes. Can you name them?

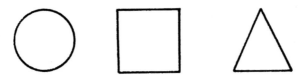

Here are three other shapes: a rectangle, an oval and a diamond.

We call shapes like these ones basic shapes. In art we can use them as building blocks to create the shape of something else. A Spanish artist called Picasso became very interested in doing this, instead of just using line or colour as other painters had.

$e^{i\pi} + 1 = 0$

Find out more about basic shapes in the mathematics chapter of this book

Compare these two paintings by Pablo Picasso. They are both of a girl he knew called Sylvette. He met her one summer holiday and drew and painted her many times. As you can see he really admired her pony tail. In the first picture, Picasso has shown Sylvette in a conventional way, using outlines, to which he has added colours for shading and detail. In the second, however, he has created her from shapes. Can you spot the triangles, circles and a square?

Activity 4: Mini Picassos!

Choose a face, a toy or a house. First draw it concentrating on outlines. Then on a new piece of paper create an image of the same thing but this time using a collage of basic shapes. You could use a packet of pre-cut shapes or stickers (available from most stationers), or you could cut out shapes from coloured paper to arrange and glue down. Can you believe that both your pictures show the same object?

Now that you have looked at one of the ways Picasso used shape, and had a go at doing the same yourself, let's try to focus our eyes just on the shapes in this next painting. Try not to notice all the colours and patterns, but instead look at the way the painter uses basic shapes in his painting. The painting is by a living English artist called David Hockney.

Activity 5: Shape up!

If you have a piece of tracing paper, or very thin plain paper, place it over the image of Hockney's painting here. Trace over the basic shapes you can see: squares, triangles, rectangles, squares and even circles. When you finish, look at your tracing. Which kind of shape do you see the most of? In a painting with no buildings, do you think Hockney would have used another shape more?

We looked at David Hockney's painting *A Bigger Splash* in Year 1

The Road to York Through Sledmere

189

Texture: Oh, What a Feeling!

Close your eyes and imagine you're holding a kitten. How does it feel? Which words come in to your mind? 'Soft' perhaps, or maybe 'furry'? Now imagine a magic wand has been waved and the kitten has turned into a frog, fresh from a pond! How does it feel, do you imagine? Soft and furry are not the right adjectives to describe the frog. Are 'slimy' and 'damp' better? Did you have others in mind? Finding words to talk about how things feel to touch is called describing their texture.

Activity 6: Texture in text

Collect a few things with different textures from your home or outside. A leaf would do, so would a marble, a key, a twig and a cotton wool ball. Feel each object and then try to think of a word to describe its texture.

You have been using words to describe the textures you have imagined and felt. Artists use their materials and the marks they make in place of words. They can choose to paint a dress looking smooth or crumpled, a mountainside appearing rough or icy, by changing the kind of brush they use, the strokes they make and the colours. You might not be able to touch what they have shown but you can imagine how the texture would feel just from looking. We call this 'visual texture'.

Look at this painting called *Young Hare* by the German artist Albrecht Dürer [AL-brekt DEW-rah]. To give us the fluffy feeling of the hare's fur, Dürer used a delicate brush to paint hundreds of separate strokes. Some overlap and some are blended, some curve while others are straight. His brushstrokes imitate the hare's fur so well that it's almost as if it might hop off the page!

Young Hare

Other artists, like the Dutch painter Johannes Vermeer (yo-HAN-es ver-MIR), painted a collection of textures within one picture. How many different surfaces can you imagine the texture of in *The Music Lesson*, below. There is the large rug draped over the table (bristly or silky?), the marble floor tiles (cold and slippery?), the polished wood of the stringed instrument lying on the ground (smooth and warm?). This painting belongs to Her Majesty the Queen, Elizabeth II. It is said to be one of her favourites.

The Music Lesson

Looking Good: Portraits

Have you had your photograph taken at school? Is there a picture of you on a wall or shelf at home? If there is, it is your portrait. 'Portrait' is the word we use to describe a picture of a real person.

Portraits can be taken with a camera, they can be drawn, painted or sculpted. One of the most famous portraits in art is the *Mona Lisa*. It was painted by an Italian master, Leonardo da Vinci [leo-NAR-do da-VIN-chi]. Look at the expression on her face. For hundreds of years, people have been fascinated by it. Is she happy or sad? Is she looking at you, or at something else? Leonardo managed to keep the *Mona Lisa* looking alive (despite being over five hundred years old now) by painting small shadows at the corners of her mouth and eyes. As we look at her we can't quite read her expression because these places are not quite clear. We try out different feelings in our imaginations and see if they fit on the picture. Mona Lisa is not the real name of the person in Leonardo's portrait: it is thought to show a young lady named Lisa Gherardini.

Mona Lisa

Sometimes portraits don't just tell us about how a person looked or felt, they tell us about the times in which they lived. Look at the portrait called *Edward VI as a Child* by Hans Holbein (hol-BINE), the Younger. Edward's father was a king, King Henry VIII of England (who lived more than five hundred years ago). The writing at the bottom of the painting (in the ancient language of Latin) tells Edward to grow up to be like his father. In this portrait, Edward is just over one year old. Did you look like this when you were one? I expect you wore much comfier, and less fancy, clothing than this stiff-looking red and gold outfit, and hat with ostrich feather. Would you be allowed to play wearing

Edward VI as a Child

Rembrandt's self-portrait

such finery? Perhaps Edward was not allowed to run around – it might not have been suitable for a future king! What sort of toys did you play with aged one? I don't expect you had a rattle made of solid gold! These clothes and the rattle show us how important the child in the portrait is, as well as how differently he lived from how we do now.

Self-Portraits: A Good Look at Yourself

Sometimes artists make portraits of themselves. We call these self-portraits. Some artists want to record a feeling, others are using their own faces for practice. The Dutch artist Rembrandt van Rijn (REM-brant fan RINE) made self-portraits for both of these reasons. Sometimes he painted himself when he didn't have paid work or 'commissions' to do. Sometimes he wanted to say something. In the self-portrait shown here Rembrandt was at his most successful. What clues has he included to show us this? He wears expensive fabrics, like velvet and fur. Thick golden chains hang around his neck. He has also hidden his hands. As a painter and printmaker, his hands would have been permanently stained. By hiding them, he shows himself as a wealthy gentleman, not as a working painter.

William Hogarth's self-portrait

Unlike Rembrandt, English artist William Hogarth has shown himself at work painting in his self-portrait. He is holding a wooden palette, which is what painters use to carry and mix their paints, and he holds a selection of brushes. Would he really have sat down to paint in such special looking clothes? Wouldn't you get into trouble for painting without an apron on, especially in fine things? With his lace cuffs, velvet trousers and buckled shoes, is Hogarth keen to make sure we know that although he is proud to be a painter, he is also a gentleman? Do you know why all the brushes Hogarth is holding are the same size? It could be so that he didn't have to keep cleaning one every time he wanted to change colours.

Sometimes artists don't want to show us how they look on the outside. They want to show us how they are feeling on the inside. Sometimes Rembrandt did this. The Dutch painter Vincent van Gogh [Fan-HOCK], learned this from looking at paintings by Rembrandt, but developed what he did. He often left out details of clothing and setting, and used his brushstrokes and colours to communicate instead. How would you say van Gogh was feeling in this self-portrait? Have you noticed the swirling background, and how the movement creeps up van Gogh's jacket too? Have you seen the bright green lines in his face, and the short, sharp brushstrokes used there?

Can you remember the naughty Graham children, whose portrait we looked at in Year 1? They were also painted by William Hogarth.

Van Gogh's self-portrait

We will learn more about Michelangelo's
Sistine Chapel paintings in Year 6

Activity 7: Mirror, Mirror on the Wall!

Try making your own self-portrait, using a mirror to really look at yourself, or paint a portrait of someone in your family who will pose for you. Use some of the techniques you have seen Leonardo, Rembrandt or van Gogh using. Point out to a parent or a friend which things in your artwork you learned from these artists.

Murals: Paintings on Walls

When we think of paintings most of us think first of works of art which can be framed and hung on a wall. But since the earliest times artists have been painting on walls (remember the cave art from Year 1?). This is called mural painting, from the French word *mur*, meaning wall. Murals are usually large. The most famous mural in fine art is probably Michelangelo's work at the Sistine Chapel in the Vatican, Rome. Here Michelangelo didn't just do one wall, he did the whole ceiling too!

Murals are a great way of decorating a large space and creating paintings which can be enjoyed by lots of people at once. (Many paintings in galleries can only be looked at by one or two people at a time). Paula Rego, an artist who is active in England, was asked to paint a mural at London's National Gallery to help decorate a new extension (called The Sainsbury Wing). Her mural is called *Crivelli's Garden*, after the paintings by a 15th century artist from Venice called Carlo Crivelli, many of which hang on the walls of this new building. Rego has used large characters, who can be seen from a distance and tell her main story, supported by smaller ones, who are easier to look at when you are close to the wall, and who add details and mystery.

The Visitation from Crivelli's Garden

In the 'Visitation' scene, shown here, you can see how these large and smaller characters share the same space. What is the large lady in brown whispering the lady in white, do you think? The title 'Visitation' makes us think about a story from the Bible, but this picture does not look religious; details like the clothes make it look more like a traditional tale from an illustrated book. Who might the boy carrying a lamb be? Where is this? What is the seated girl in black doing? Rego's paintings often make us ask questions as we try to figure out who is who and what they are doing. She doesn't always give us clear answers! Rego has realised that one of the best ways to enjoy art is by asking questions and talking over the possible answers. As long as you remember to look for clues in the details you can see, you can't go wrong.

Activity 8: Chalk it up!

Would you like to make your own mural? Your parents or teachers probably won't want you painting on walls, so instead you can use chalks and draw on an outside wall or pavement (but check with your parents first!). Next time it rains the chalk will wash off. Plan before you start. Think what you want your mural to be about: the story of your family, your school, your favourite things to do, your favourite books? Which characters do you need to include, what will your setting be and which details can you include to bring it all to life? Like Paula Rego, will you use differently sized characters? Will your story be clear or mysterious? Will you work alone, or ask a friend to help you?

Suggested Resources

Resources to help you explore the art in this chapter further:

Art activity books

Carole Armstrong, *My Sticker Art Gallery: A Tour of Western Art* (Frances Lincoln) 2006

Emily Bone, *Egyptian Things to Make and Do* (Usborne) 2009

Ana Salvador, *Draw with Pablo Picasso* (Frances Lincoln) 2007

Louise Spilsbury and Richard Spilsbury, *Self Portrait (Start Up Art & Design)* (Evans Brothers) 2007

Looking at and talking about art book

Amanda Renshaw and Gilda Williams Ruggi, *The Art Book for Children: Book One* (Phaidon) 2005

Art story books (which include works in this chapter)

Laurence Anholt, *Picasso and the Girl with a Ponytail: A Story of Pablo Picasso (Anholt's Artists)* (Frances Lincoln) 2003

James Mayhew, *Katie and the Mona Lisa* (Orchard Books) 2009

Colouring/complete the masterpiece books

Doris Kutschbach, *Colouring Book Monet* (Prestel) 2006

Mallory Pearce, *Celtic Animals Colouring Book* (Dover) 1997

Annette Roeder, *Coloring Book Vincent Van Gogh* (Prestel) 2009

Where to find the works of art in this chapter:

Sarcophagus of King Tutankahmun, circa 1323 BC (National Museum of Egyptian Antiquities) Cairo.

Bust of Queen Nefertiti (Limestone, gypsum, crystal and wax), circa 1340 BC, (Egyptian and Papyrus Collection currently in the Neues Museum) Berlin.

Sutton Hoo Site and Excavation Museum, 7th century (National Trust) Woodbridge, Suffolk.

Sutton Hoo Shoulder Clasp, 7th century (now British Museum) London.

Lindisfarne Gospels, late 7th or early 8th century (British Library) London.

Claude Monet, *The Beach at Trouville*, 1870 (The National Gallery) London.

James A. McNeill Whistler, *Arrangement in Gray and Black No. 1* (also called *Portrait of the Artist's Mother*) 1871 (Musée d'Orsay) Paris.

Pablo Picasso, *Portrait of Sylvette*, 1954 (Private collection) England.

Pablo Picasso, *Sylvette, 20 May*, 1954, (Private collection) Paris.

David Hockney, *The Road to York Through Sledmere*, 1997 (Artist's collection).

Albrecht Dürer, *Young Hare*, 1502 (The Albertina) Vienna.

Johannes Vermeer, *The Music Lesson*, 1662-65 (The Royal Collection) London.

Leonardo da Vinci, *The Mona Lisa*, 1503-06 (Louvre) Paris.

Hans Holbein the Younger, *Edward VI as a Child*, 1538 (National Gallery of Art) Washington D.C.

Rembrandt van Rijn, *Self-portrait in a Flat Cap*, 1642 (Royal Collection) London.

William Hogarth, *Self-portrait at an Easel*, 1757 (National Portrait Gallery) London.

Vincent van Gogh, *Self-portrait*, 1889 (Musée d'Orsay) Paris

Paula Rego, *Crivelli's Garden*, 1990 (Sainsbury Wing Restaurant, National Gallery) London.

Music

Introduction

We encourage you to give your child a wide range of musical experiences – singing songs, listening to all kinds of music, dancing around at home, attending local musical performances.

One of the best activities, and one of the easiest, is singing with your child. We suggest some favourite songs in this section (see pages 222–234). If you don't feel confident about your own singing voice, remember that in your own home you're the star! It's fine to play recordings for your child (we suggest some below), but the more you sing with your child, the more comfortable you'll feel and the more you'll both enjoy music together.

The previous book in this series, *What Your Year 1 Child Needs to Know*, introduced activities in which children played with the basic elements of music, such as rhythm, pitch and tempo. We encourage you to continue these activities with your child in Year 2.

In this book, we introduce many kinds of music, including jazz, classical music and opera, as well as different kinds of dance. We suggest ways to become familiar with great composers. We introduce some basic terms and concepts, such as melody, harmony and rhythm, and the notion that music is written down in a language of its own. Further knowledge of musical notation will be developed in later books in this series.

Some families will choose to provide lessons that will lift children to a level of musical competence beyond what we describe in the following pages. Different children will develop musical appreciation and skills at different rates and to different degrees. It's important for everyone to enjoy music and we hope this book will increase that enjoyment through experience and understanding.

Instruments and Their Families

What is a family? Who is in your family? Does everyone in your family look the same?

Musical instruments have families, too. And, just as in your family, some instruments in the same family look alike but are not exactly the same. There are different families of instruments. Let's meet the *percussion* family, the *string* family, the *woodwind* family and the *brass* family.

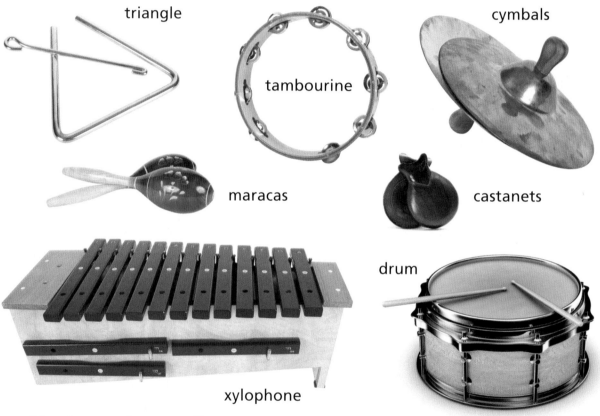

triangle

tambourine

cymbals

maracas

castanets

drum

xylophone

The Percussion Family

Percussion instruments are fun to play: you shake them or hit them with your hand, a stick or a mallet. Can you name a percussion instrument? Did you think of a drum? A xylophone? A tambourine? One percussion instrument is easy to recognise: it's called a triangle. When you hit it, it makes a ding-a-ling-a-ling sound. Another member of the percussion family looks like lids from two big saucepans. These are cymbals and, when you hit them together, they can make a sound like a loud crash!

The String Family

Do you know any instruments with strings? How about a guitar? A banjo? A violin? These instruments don't look the same, but they all have strings. You play stringed instruments either by strumming or plucking them with your fingers, or by playing them with a bow.

guitar

banjo

violin

The Woodwind Family

How do you think you play instruments in the woodwind family? Think about the name – wind. You play these instruments by blowing air. Sometimes the woodwind family is called the wind family. Some wind instruments are made of wood, but some aren't. In the pictures here, the recorder is made of wood, but the flute is made of metal. A flute can sound like a bird singing.

A man playing a Peruvian flute

clarinet   oboe   bassoon

recorder

flute

Many woodwind instruments have a small piece of cane near where you put your mouth. That small piece of cane is called a reed and it helps the instruments to make sounds when you blow into them. Some examples of woodwind instruments with reeds are the clarinet, the saxophone, the oboe and the bassoon. The recorder and the flute do not have reeds. Instead, you blow air past an edge. A recorder has a mouthpiece to blow into and direct the air but a flute's mouthpiece is different. You blow across it, like blowing across a bottle.

The Brass Family

Most instruments in the brass family are made of a hard, shiny metal called brass. If you have ever watched a marching band in a parade, you've seen and heard some brass instruments – and you've probably felt like marching as they went by. You play brass instruments as you play wind instruments: by blowing, but with your lips more inside the mouthpiece. A trumpet, a trombone, a French horn and the big tuba are members of the brass family.

tuba

French horn

trumpet

You can have fun making home-made instruments. This book shows you how: *Make and Use Musical Instruments* by Anna-Marie D'Cruz, Make and Use Series (Wayland) 2007.

A conductor directs an orchestra

The Orchestra

Members of all the families of instruments – percussion, strings, woodwind and brass – come together in an orchestra. It takes many musicians playing many instruments to make up an orchestra.

With so many musicians playing so many different instruments, you might think that an orchestra could sound like a mixed-up mess. But the musicians all play together and the orchestra makes beautiful music! Partly that's because they have a conductor. The conductor does not play an instrument. The conductor is a man or woman who stands in front of the orchestra and helps the musicians stay together and play when they are supposed to. The conductor is like the manager of a sports team: he or she makes sure that all the members of the orchestra play their best and do their job at the right time. To show respect, people sometimes address the conductor as 'Maestro' [MICE-troh], which means 'Master'.

Here are some ways to get to know the instruments in the orchestra:

- A fun way to meet the orchestra is to listen to *Peter and the Wolf* by the Russian composer Sergei Prokofiev [SAIR-gay pruh-KOF-yef]. Many fine recordings of this work are downloadable as well as being available on CD or DVD. *Peter and the Wolf* introduces the orchestra by telling a story in which different instruments play the parts of different characters. A oboe plays a duck; a clarinet plays a cat; stringed instruments play the hero, Peter; and brass instruments play the wolf. Many recordings feature a narrator who tells the story of Peter's adventures along with the music.

- Read *The Hoffnung Symphony Orchestra* by Gerard Hoffnung (The Hoffnung Partnership) 2000. The different intruments of the orchestra are shown in a series of light-hearted cartoons (right).

- Attend a school band concert, or watch an orchestra on television. Notice how the families of instruments sit together on the stage. Watch the conductor and see what kinds of things he or she does during the concert.

Great Composers

Some people are so good at what they do that almost everybody knows who they are. Can you think of a great footballer whom almost everybody knows? Or someone who sings popular songs on the radio? Or someone who has written famous books?

In music, there are some people who write such great music that almost everyone knows who they are. A person who writes music is called a composer. Some great composers wrote their music long before you, your parents or even your grandparents were ever born. But because their music is so wonderful, people still listen to it, play it and enjoy it today.

Let's meet one of these great composers. His name is Wolfgang Amadeus Mozart [MOTES-art]. That's a long name, so most people call him Mozart. He lived a long time ago in a Central European country called Austria. Mozart only lived to be thirty-five years old, but he wrote over six hundred works to sing and to play on instruments.

Mozart started writing music when he was just a little boy. He was an amazing child, a real genius. He had an older sister, Maria Anna, who was a very good musician herself. He called her by a nickname, 'Nannerl'.

Let's hear a story about Mozart when he was a child. Some words in this story may be new to you. Here is what they mean:

clavier [kla-VEER]: an old-fashioned instrument that, like a piano today, has a keyboard

minuet [min-yoo-ET]: a kind of dance

allegro [a-LEG-ro]: an Italian term used to describe music that is fast and lively

Mozart

'Mozart the Wonder Boy'

While Nannerl was having her music lesson with Father Leopold Mozart, three-year-old Wolfgang watched carefully and listened to every word that Father said. Wolfgang enjoyed listening to music and was particularly delighted to hear the harmonies that different instruments produced. When his sister's lesson had finished, Wolfgang asked: 'Can I please have a lesson with you, too, Father?'

'You are only three, Wolfie. When you are older you will have your lessons,' Father Mozart replied.

Wolfgang sat at the clavier's keyboard and began to play a few notes on his own. Hearing the music he produced was ever so much fun.

When Wolfgang was four, Father Mozart started to teach him to play simple songs on the clavier. He soon started to play extremely well. After only half an hour of Father Mozart teaching him to play a minuet, he would learn it perfectly, memorising it and playing it correctly in time. Father Mozart was impressed, and soon Wolfgang played as well as Nannerl.

Wolfgang Mozart's first opera was such a success that the audience clapped loudly

When Wolfgang was only five, he began to compose – to write – his own music pieces. Now Father Mozart became very excited about Wolfgang's progress, and he wanted to share with the world Wolfgang's and Nannerl's talents.

That year, 1762, Father Mozart decided to bring Wolfgang and Nannerl on a concert tour of the grand courts in Munich [MEEYOO-nik] in southern Germany. The trip by stagecoach from Salzburg, where they lived, took many hours and was very bumpy, but Wolfgang and Nannerl still practised their pieces on their imaginary keyboards.

The children were scheduled to perform for the Prince! Wolfgang knew how important this performance was and he felt a little nervous before his concert. Nannerl and Father

Mozart encouraged him, and he performed beautifully. The Prince and his court enjoyed the performance and clapped loudly when it finished. The children and their father stayed in Munich for three weeks. Father Mozart showed off his talented children during many concerts, and all of the people of Munich began to talk of the Mozart children.

When Wolfgang arrived home after his first big trip, he was very excited to see his mother and his little dog named Bimperl because he had missed them so much. He was so happy to be home that he wrote a minuet, one that was particularly *allegro*, to celebrate coming home.

Wolfgang played the clavier very well by now, and Father Mozart decided to give him a present. It was a violin. The boy immediately ran off to try his hand at playing it. Later, when his parents' friends came to the house to play their instruments together, Wolfgang asked: 'Father, can I play my new violin with you?'

'Play your clavier, Wolfie. Wait until you have had lessons to play your violin with us.'

Wolfgang had been so excited about his violin that he now became very disappointed.

'Oh, Leopold,' replied Father Mozart's friend. 'Let Wolfgang play his violin with us. I don't mind. He can stand next to me and he will be fine.'

The musicians began to play, and Wolfgang played along perfectly. He played exactly in harmony with the others. At the end of the piece, everyone clapped wildly and complimented Wolfgang on his astounding violin performance. Father Mozart beamed.

When Wolfgang was six, the Mozart family received an important invitation. Wolfgang and Nannerl were invited to play at the palace in Vienna before the Empress, her family and young Marie-Antoinette. The whole Mozart family travelled to Vienna. There was much excitement – the children practised their pieces, their best clothes were prepared and their shoes were polished until they shone brightly. At the palace, Wolfgang and Nannerl performed beautifully and the concert was extraordinary. Their parents were very proud of them. The trip was so successful that the Mozart family decided to go on a European tour later that year, one that would last three and a half years!

The Mozart family visited many places on their European tour, and they performed concerts everywhere they went. They played for royalty, visited influential courts and met some of the most important people in Europe. Everyone loved watching (and hearing!) the Mozart children perform, and they became well known. They called Wolfgang 'Mozart the Wonder Boy'.

Wolfgang grew up to become a great composer. Even now, so many years after Wolfgang lived, people all over the world still enjoy performing and listening to Wolfgang Mozart's brilliant music.

Get to Know Great Composers and their Music

- Try to hear recordings of Mozart's music. A good place to start is the BBC Radio 3 series (90 – 92 FM), *Composer of the Week*, which combines stories and music. Their Mozart programmes are available as podcasts at http://www.bbc.co.uk/podcasts/series/cotw/all. The series covers many different composers. Presenter Donald Macleod guides you through an aspect of a composer's life, with illustrations from their music.

- The best place to hear any music is live, in the same room as the people performing it. All the UK's major orchestras have junior programmes. There are orchestras in Bournemouth, Belfast, Birmingham, Manchester, Liverpool, Edinburgh, Gateshead, Cardiff and Glasgow as well as London. The City of Birmingham Symphony Orchestra stages family concerts on Sunday afternoons, often with their own children's chorus taking part. The Ulster Orchestra sometimes invites its audience to come dressed as film characters.

- Many musicians work in churches. At the end of a service, the organist often chooses a *voluntary* to play as closing music. He sits in a 'loft', high above the rest of the church. The music can be written by a famous composer, like Bach or Elgar. Be warned. Organs in large churches can be very loud, but you do not have to sit still for as long as in a concert. Some special churches, like cathedrals, also employ choirs to sing most days, with children singing the high notes and men singing the lower ones. If you are near a cathedral in the early evening, you can hear a lot of music as part of the evensong service.

- Music by Mozart and other composers, such as Bach, Beethoven and Tchaikovsky, is often called classical music. One special kind of classical music is called a *symphony*. A symphony is written to be played by an orchestra. Symphonies are usually long pieces of music, sometimes half-an-hour or more. Mozart wrote forty-one symphonies. A composer named Ludwig van Beethoven wrote nine great symphonies. The beginning of Beethoven's Fifth Symphony is one of the most famous moments in all of classical music. Try to hear it sometime, but be prepared – when the music starts, it may make you jump.

- If you prefer listening to recordings, try the Naxos label. They sell a compilation, *My First Classical Music Album* (Naxos 8758203) and an illustrated book to go with it. If you have favourite composers, they have albums for Mozart, Beethoven and Tchaikovsky too. Remember that there is a lot of beautiful music beside the most famous bits. If you like a track, look up the whole work that it is taken from and try listening to it all. You may like the less famous bits even more.

Music Can Tell a Story

Ask your local library for these picture books based on songs that tell stories:

Sing Me a Story: Song and Dance Tales from the Caribbean by Grace Hallworth (Frances Lincoln) 2007

Ten in the Bed by Penny Dale (Walker) 2011

Number Rhymes Tens and Teens by Opal Dunn (Frances Lincoln) 2009

Little Rabbit Foo Foo by Michael Rosen (Walker) 1989

What are some of your favourite stories? Sometimes music and stories go together. Some songs tell stories. If you've ever sung 'Run Rabbit Run' you've sung a story. Let's try it:

On the farm, every Friday,

On the farm, it's rabbit pie day.

So, every Friday that ever comes along,

I get up early and sing this little song:

Run rabbit – run rabbit – Run! Run! Run!

Run rabbit – run rabbit – Run! Run! Run!

Bang! Bang! Bang! Bang!

Goes the farmer's gun.

Run, rabbit, run, rabbit, run.

Run rabbit – run rabbit – Run! Run! Run!

Don't give the farmer his fun! Fun! Fun!

He'll get by

Without his rabbit pie,

So run rabbit – run rabbit – Run! Run! Run!

The story in 'Run Rabbit Run' gets a little silly, but that's what makes it fun. Do you know some other story songs, like 'Billy Boy'? (You can find the words to this song on page 224.)

Sometimes music *without words* can also seem to tell a story. The sounds can almost make you see pictures in your mind. Some music can make you imagine good guys and bad guys, birds singing, a big storm, ships at sea and even brooms marching.

What's that – brooms marching? Yes, that's part of the story told in a famous piece of orchestral music by a French composer named Paul Dukas [doo-KAH]. The music is called *The Sorcerer's Apprentice*.

Do you know what a sorcerer is? He's like a wizard or magician. An apprentice is somebody who is both a helper and a learner. *The Sorcerer's Apprentice* is an old story that

has been told in many ways. The story that Paul Dukas tells in his music is about a young man who helps a sorcerer while he is learning to become a sorcerer himself. One day the sorcerer goes out and leaves the apprentice alone. The apprentice is tired of working, but he still has to carry water in a bucket from the river. 'Oh,' he thinks, 'I would rather do magic than all this work!'

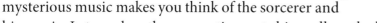

Then the apprentice decides to do something he shouldn't. He takes the sorcerer's magic wand and casts a spell: he makes an old broom come alive! The broom picks up a bucket and fills it with water – it does the apprentice's work for him! When you hear the music for *The Sorcerer's Apprentice*, you can imagine what's happening. Quiet, mysterious music makes you think of the sorcerer and his magic. Later, when the apprentice casts his spell on the broom, the music turns into a kind of funny little march, which helps you imagine how a broom might walk!

But then something goes wrong with the apprentice's spell. He can't make the broom stop! It keeps filling the bucket with water and bringing it back and pouring more and more water on the floor. The apprentice says all the magic words he can think of, but the broom won't stop. So the apprentice grabs an axe and, whack, chops the broom in half. That does it – but no, it doesn't! Each piece gets up, grabs a bucket and gets more and more water, until soon there's water everywhere! When you hear the music, it helps you imagine the apprentice whacking away with his axe, the brooms stomping along and the water swirling into a great flood.

Many recordings of *The Sorcerer's Apprentice* are available, including an excerpt on the Naxos *My First Classical Music Album* (see page 236), which may also be downloaded separately. You can hear the whole thing on *French Symphonic Poems*, conducted by Michel Plasson and played by the Orchestre du Capitole de Toulouse, which is available on iTunes.

You can hear and see the musical story of *The Sorcerer's Apprentice* in the Walt Disney animated film *Fantasia*, with a classic animated sequence in which Mickey Mouse plays the apprentice. The film is available on DVD. If you get a chance to watch the DVD, try this: leave the picture on but turn off the sound. Do you see how important the music is to the story?

Dramas with Music: Opera

Imagine that you wake up one day and find that everybody is singing instead of talking. You're in bed and you hear your mother sing (to the tune of 'On Top of Old Smoky'):

It's time to get up now,

Get ready for school.

Put on your red jumper,

'Cause outside it's cool.

When you get to school, your teacher sings (to the tune of 'Yankee Doodle'):

All right, children, settle down,

It's time to practise writing.

Please make sure your pencil's sharp,

And Billy stop that biting!

When you get home from school, you sing (come on, sing now, to the tune of 'Twinkle, Twinkle Little Star'):

I worked hard at school all day,

Now I'm ready for some play.

Wow! Wouldn't that be weird, but fun, too? It would be like living in an opera.

What is an opera? An opera is like a play in which the words are sung. Have you ever seen a play, or been in one? In a play people put on costumes, then go onstage to act out a story. Now imagine if the actors didn't speak their lines but sang them instead. And imagine that, while they were singing, an orchestra was playing music for them to sing along with.

You've just imagined an opera. Operas tell stories, sometimes funny, sometimes sad. Some operas tell stories you probably know. Two famous operas are called *Cinderella* and *Hansel and Gretel*.

It takes longer to sing words than to speak them, especially if some are repeated. Many operas have well known stories so that they are easier to follow. The language does not matter so much and can be

See page114 to put on your own play

chosen to suit the style and the singers. In the first operas, the singers were often Italian. The opera *Cinderella* is sung in Italian. In Italian it is called *Cenerentola*, which means the same thing. The opera *Hansel and Gretel* is sung in German. Mozart wrote in both languages.

Cinderella and the ugly stepsisters in the Minnesota Opera's production of Cinderella

You can read the story of *Hansel and Gretel* starting on page 51 of this book. *Cinderella* is in the Year 1 book.

Music Can Make You Move

What happens when you hear a fast, happy song you like? Do you clap your hands? Do you tap your toes?

Sometimes music just makes you want to *move*. Dancing is moving to music. People around the world *love* to dance – do you? You can dance just by moving in whatever way the music makes you feel. Or you can do one of many special kinds of dance, such as céilidh [KAY-lee], tap, maypole dancing, morris or ballet.

Maypole dancing

Tap dancers have flat pieces of metal, called taps, on the bottoms of their shoes. They quickly move their feet and legs so that the metal taps make tap-tap-tapping noises as they dance.

Maypole dancing is a beautiful spectacle. Picture a tall pole with coloured ribbons tied to the top and dancers in a circle around it. Each dancer holds a ribbon and as they pass each other, the ribbons form a plait or a web.

Morris Dancers

Morris dancing is so ancient that nobody quite knows how it began. The music often comes from an accordion or concertina. The dancers wear elaborate costumes, with hats and sticks and tied-on bells. A special 'fool' gets to carry a blown-up bladder and dance around the others in his 'side'.

Céilidh [KAY-lee] is a kind of dance for groups, from a celtic word for a gathering. Men and women form circles or lines of couples and perform steps with names like 'threading the needle' or 'stripping the willow'. Sometimes there is an expert 'caller' to remind people of the next step, especially at less traditional events, which are similar to English barn dances. Many céilidh dances involve changing partners, so you may dance with many people in a single evening.

Another kind of dance, called **ballet**, can tell a story. In a ballet there is music, often played by an orchestra, but no one sings or talks. Instead, in many ballets the dancers tell a story through the way they *move*. Some ballets tell stories you may know, like the story of 'Sleeping Beauty'.

Ballet dancers have to practise for years to learn all they need to know. They have to work very hard and grow very strong. They have to work at balancing themselves and controlling their bodies. Sometimes they spin around and around. Sometimes they make high leaps into the air.

Young ballerinas prepare to dance

215

Sometimes the women dance only on the tips of their toes. The men have to be strong enough to lift their partners in the air whilst making it look easy.

Clara dances with the Nutcracker

A popular ballet, performed every year around Christmas, is *The Nutcracker* by the Russian composer Peter Ilyich Tchaikovsky [chy-KOV-ski]. *The Nutcracker* tells a story about a toy nutcracker that magically comes to life and, with a little help from a girl named Clara, battles and defeats a Mouse King. Check your library for books that tell the story of the ballet, such as Alison Jay's *The Nutcracker* (Templar) 2011.

This story is also found within a splendid anthology: *The Orchard Book of Stories from the Ballet* by Geraldine McCaughrean. Other lovely ballet books include James Mayhew's *Ella Bella Ballerina and Cinderella* and *Ella Bella Ballerina and the Sleeping Beauty*, both published by Orchard.

To see some opera or ballet, try these DVDs:

An enjoyable DVD of the Nutcracker ballet is danced by Anthony Dowell, Alina Cojocaru, Miyako Yoshida and others from the Royal Ballet (Opus Arte and BBC) 2001.

Also by the Royal Ballet is *Tales of Beatrix Potter* (Optimum Home), where the dancers have been specially trained to move like animals.

These can be long shows, so you might like to have some small ice cream tubs ready for a half-time interval.

Opera can be even longer than ballet but just as enjoyable. If watching a whole film, be prepared for intervals that break the show into several instalments. Mozart's *Magic Flute* was made into a film by Ingmar Bergman. There are subtitles to follow the story in English. The Metropolitan Opera's show of *Hansel and Gretel*, conducted by Thomas Fulton, takes a traditional approach to the fairy tale. For *Cinderella*, try the film *Cenerentola*, conducted by Claudio Abbado, with the comic singer Claudio Desderi as Don Magnifico. The music is by Rossini and is by turns beautiful and funny. Again, the subtitles are helpful. See more details about these productions on page 235.

Jazz

One kind of music from America is liked by people around the world. This music, called jazz, was invented among communities of former slaves after the American Civil War. It began in New Orleans, a southern city where the Mississippi River flows to the sea. Many people say that jazz is America's most important gift to music. Other styles of music influenced early jazz, such as ragtime, marching bands, blues and the spirituals that were sung on slave plantations.

Jazz band The Zuits

There's one big difference between jazz and most other music. If you sing 'Row, row, row your boat', you don't change the words or the tune. But every time a jazz musician plays a song, it comes out a little different. Particular jazz musicians can play the same songs in different ways. A jazz musician may start with a familiar tune, but then he or she changes the tune while playing it, so that it sounds a little different every time.

When you make something up as you go along, you are improvising. When jazz musicians play, they improvise. Can you imagine how you could improvise on a familiar song? You might start out singing something you know, like this:

Row, row, row your boat,

Gently down the stream.

Merrily, merrily, merrily, merrily,

Life is but a dream.

Now sing it again, but have fun by changing the words and the tune. As you improvise, your words might come out something like this (you'll have to imagine your own tune!):

Row, row, row-ba-doh-ba-doh,

Row my little puddle-paddle boat.

Row so merrily, be-bop-a-bearily,

Down the ice cream peanut-butter dreamy stream!

Ask your local library for these two 'jazzy' books:

Charlie Parker Played Be Bop, written and illustrated by Chris Raschka (Orchard) 1997.

Ben's Trumpet, written and illustrated by Rachel Isadora (Greenwillow) 1979. You can see an animated version of this on YouTube.

One of the first great jazz musicians was Louis Armstrong. Some people called him by a nickname, 'Satchmo', and others called him 'Pops'. When Armstrong was a boy, he lived in New Orleans. He became very good at playing jazz even when he was young. He learned to play the cornet (an instrument like the trumpet) so well that the other musicians in his band would stop playing, or play in the background, and let him play a solo ('solo' means 'alone' in Italian). He played and sang with many different jazz musicians and bands during his life, and he was loved by people all over the world. You can always recognise his warm and gravelly voice.

Louis Armstrong

A song that jazz musicians in New Orleans liked to improvise on is called 'When the Saints Go Marching In'. Let's sing part of it:

Oh, when the saints go marching in,

When the saints go marching in,

I want to be in that number,

When the saints go marching in.

Melody and Harmony

Can you hum? What is your favourite song? Try humming it now. You've just hummed the melody. Sometimes people call the melody of a song the 'tune'. Have you ever played 'Name that tune'? To play the game, you take turns humming a song. Your partner tries to guess the name of the song. You only hum a little of the song at first. If your partner can't guess it, then you hum some more. When he guesses it, then it's his turn to hum and your turn to guess.

Try playing 'Name that tune' with some of your favourite songs and with some of the songs in this book (see pages 222–234).

Have you ever sung in a group or heard a choir sing? If you have, maybe you've heard how a lot of different voices can go together in a way that makes a lovely sound. In music, some sounds go together well. But some don't. It's a bit like clothing: some clothes go together and some don't. If you put on a red-striped shirt with purple-and-green-checked trousers, your clothes don't match. When you put on clothes that match, they go together. Music is like that. When the sounds match, or go together, they make harmony. Instruments can make harmony and voices can make harmony.

Listen to some of your favourite songs to see what instruments are playing at the same time. Listen to a choir sing. If there are men and women singing together, try to hear how the men's low voices and the women's high voices go together.

I've Got Rhythm!

Now that you know what melody and harmony are, let's find out about another important part of music – *rhythm*.

The performers in the stage show Stomp create their own powerful rhythms by using everyday objects like barrels and saucepans. You might like to see one of their performances. You can find out about them here: www.stomponline.com

Rhythm is what makes music move. All music has rhythm. In fact, some kinds of music are mainly rhythm. African drummers play music that is mainly rhythm. Irish music also has a lot of rhythm, sometimes played on a traditional *bodhran*, a type of drum.

A big part of rhythm is called the beat. Some musicians beat a drum or a piece of wood to keep the beat. What does it mean to 'keep the beat' in music? Think about this: have you ever noticed how some music makes you want to clap your hands or tap your feet? When that happens, you don't clap or tap at just any old time. Instead, when you listen to the music, it tells you when to clap in a regular, steady way right in time with the music. That's because you keep hearing the strongest sound in the music, the beat, coming over and over again at the very moment that you expect it to come. If you clap your hands or tap your feet every time you know the strong sound is going to come, then you are 'keeping the beat'. 'Keeping the beat' is also called 'keeping time' to the music.

Here is part of a song you may know, 'Yankee Doodle'. Let's try keeping time to it by clapping our hands on the strong beat every time we know it's going to come. (In the song, the strong beat falls on the underlined parts of the words.)

Yankee <u>Doodle</u> <u>went</u> to <u>town</u>,

A -<u>riding</u> <u>on</u> a <u>po</u>—<u>ny</u>,

<u>Stuck</u> a <u>feather</u> <u>in</u> his <u>cap</u>

And <u>called</u> it <u>macaro</u>—<u>ni</u>.

Reading and Writing Music

PARENTS: Here we introduce your child to some musical notes to convey the idea that music can be written down. Later books in this series will explain more about musical notation.

Have you ever seen music written down on paper? It looks like this:

That's the way you write down the music for 'Twinkle, Twinkle, Little Star'. Reading music is like reading words – it takes time and practice!

When you write words, you use letters. But when you write music, you use notes and other special marks. What the notes look like, where they are and how many of them are together tell the musician what to do on his or her instrument. Here you can see some musical notes and their names.

crotchet   minim   semibreve

When you sing or play a minim, it lasts twice as long as a crotchet. When you sing or play a semibreve, it lasts four times as long as a crotchet.

Music is written down so that anyone who reads music can play it. Two people might live very far away from each other and be very different, but they can play the same music the same way if they can both read music. Writing music down on paper helps people to share the music they like.

A Few Favourite Songs

PARENTS: Here are a few familiar songs to sing with your child. You can find words to more songs earlier in this music section, and we encourage you to sing many other songs with your child as well. Children enjoy listening to and singing along with recordings, too, such as the ones suggested on page 236.

The Grand Old Duke of York

Oh, the grand old Duke of York,

He had ten thousand men;

He marched them up to the top of the hill,

And he marched them down again.

And when they were up, they were up,

And when they were down,
they were down,

And when they were only half-way up,

They were neither up nor down.

Michael Finnigan

There once was a man named
Michael Finnigan,

He grew whiskers on his chinnigan.

The wind came up and blew them in ag'in,

Poor old Michael Finnigan (begin ag'in).

La Cucaracha

La cucaracha, la cucaracha,

Running up and down the house,

La cucaracha, la cucaracha,

Quiet as a little mouse.

He gets in trouble, a lot of trouble,

Snooping here and everywhere,

La cucaracha, la cucaracha,

Always keeps the cupboard bare.

(Many people have made up their own words to this tune.
Try making up some words yourself.)

Billy Boy

Where have you been all the day,
Billy Boy, Billy Boy,
Where have you been
all the day my Billy Boy?
I've been walking all the day,
With my charming Nancy Grey,
And my Nancy
kittled my fancy,
Oh my charming Billy Boy.

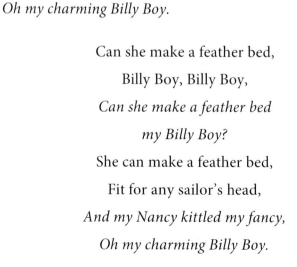

Is she fit to be your wife,
Billy Boy, Billy Boy,
Is she fit to be your
wife my Billy Boy?
She's as fit to be my wife,
As the fork is to the knife,
And my Nancy kittled my fancy,
Oh my charming Billy Boy.

Can she make a feather bed,
Billy Boy, Billy Boy,
Can she make a feather bed
my Billy Boy?
She can make a feather bed,
Fit for any sailor's head,
And my Nancy kittled my fancy,
Oh my charming Billy Boy.

Skip to My Lou

[chorus]

Lou, Lou, skip to my Lou,
Lou, Lou, skip to my Lou,
Lou, Lou, skip to my Lou,
Skip to my Lou, my darling!

[repeat chorus]

Little red wagon, Paint it blue,
Little red wagon, Paint it blue,
Little red wagon, Paint it blue,
Skip to my Lou, my darling!

Lost my partner, what'll I do?
Lost my partner, what'll I do?
Lost my partner, what'll I do?
Skip to my Lou, my darling!

[repeat chorus]

I'll find another one, prettier, too,
I'll find another one, prettier, too,
I'll find another one, prettier, too,
Skip to my Lou, my darling!

[repeat chorus]

Lou, Lou, skip to my Lou,
Lou, Lou, skip to my Lou,
Lou, Lou, skip to my Lou,
Skip to my Lou, my darling!

Frère Jacques / Brother John

(This song is sometimes sung as a 'round', splitting into groups with each group singing the same melody but starting at different times to sing one line after the group before.)

[French]

Frère Jacques, Frère Jacques,

Dormez-vous?
Dormez-vous?

Sonnez les matines!
Sonnez les matines!

Dig, din, don. Dig, din, don.

[English]

Are you sleeping,
Are you sleeping

Brother John, Brother John?

Ring the bell for morning!
Ring the bell for morning!

Ding, dang, dong. Ding, dang, dong.

Dry Bones

Ezekiel cried: 'Them dry bones!'

Ezekiel cried: 'Them dry bones!'

Ezekiel cried: 'Them dry bones!'

Now hear the word of the Lord.

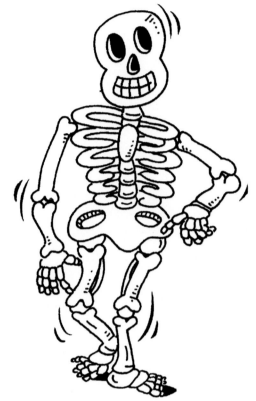

The foot bone connected to the leg bone,
The leg bone connected to the knee bone,
The knee bone connected to the thigh bone,
The thigh bone connected to the hip bone,
The hip bone connected to the back bone,
The back bone connected to the neck bone,
The neck bone connected to the jaw bone,
The jaw bone connected to the head bone,
Now hear the word of the Lord.

Them bones, them bones gonna walk around,
Them bones, them bones gonna walk around,
Them bones, them bones gonna walk around,
Now hear the word of the Lord.

The head bone connected to the jaw bone,
The jaw bone connected to the neck bone,
The neck bone connected to the back bone,
The back bone connected to the hip bone,
The hip bone connected to the thigh bone,
The thigh bone connected to the knee bone,
The knee bone connected to the leg bone,
The leg bone connected to the foot bone,
Now hear the word of the Lord.

You can read more about the skeleton starting on page 302.

There's a Hole in my Bucket

There's a hole in my bucket, dear Liza, dear Liza.
There's a hole in my bucket, dear Liza, a hole.
Well, mend it, dear Henry, dear Henry, dear Henry.
Well, mend it, dear Henry, dear Henry, mend it.

With what shall I mend it? Dear Liza, dear Liza,
With what shall I mend it? Dear Liza, with what?
With straw, dear Henry, dear Henry, dear Henry.
With straw, dear Henry, dear Henry, with straw.

But the straw is too long, dear Liza, dear Liza.
The straw is too long, dear Liza, too long.
Then cut it, dear Henry, dear Henry, dear Henry.
Then cut it, dear Henry, dear Henry, cut it.

With what shall I cut it? Dear Liza, dear Liza,
With what shall I cut it? Dear Liza, with what?
With a knife, dear Henry, dear Henry, dear Henry.
With a knife, dear Henry, dear Henry, a knife.

But the knife is too blunt, dear Liza, dear Liza.
The knife is too blunt, dear Liza, too blunt.
Then sharpen it, dear Henry, dear Henry, dear Henry.
Then sharpen it, dear Henry, dear Henry, sharpen it.

With what shall I sharpen it? Dear Liza, dear Liza,
With what shall I sharpen it? Dear Liza, with what?
With a stone, dear Henry, dear Henry, dear Henry.
With a stone, dear Henry, dear Henry, a stone.

But the stone is too dry, dear Liza, dear Liza.

The stone is too dry, dear Liza, too dry.

Then wet it, dear Henry, dear Henry, dear Henry.

Then wet it, dear Henry, dear Henry, wet it.

With what shall I wet it? Dear Liza, dear Liza,

With what shall I wet it? Dear Liza, with what?

With water, dear Henry, dear Henry, dear Henry.

With water, dear Henry, dear Henry, with water.

In what shall I fetch it? Dear Liza, dear Liza,

In what shall I fetch it? Dear Liza, in what?

In a bucket, dear Henry, dear Henry, dear Henry.

In a bucket, dear Henry, dear Henry, a bucket.

But there's a hole in my bucket, Dear Liza, dear Liza.

There's a hole in my bucket, Dear Liza, a hole.

What Shall We Do With the Drunken Sailor?

What shall we do with the drunken sailor?

What shall we do with the drunken sailor?

What shall we do with the drunken sailor

Early in the morning?

Hooray and up she rises!

Hooray and up she rises!

Hooray and up she rises

Early in the morning!

Put him in the long-boat until he's sober...

Hooray and up she rises...

Pull out the plug and wet him all over...

Hooray and up she rises...

Ten Green Bottles

Ten green bottles, hanging on the wall,

Ten green bottles, hanging on the wall,

And if one green bottle should accidentally fall

There'll be nine green bottles, hanging on the wall.

...

There'll be nine green bottles, hanging on the wall...

...

There'll be one green bottle, hanging on the wall...

There'll be no green bottles hanging on the wall!

For He's a Jolly Good Fellow

For he's a jolly good fellow, [three times]

And so say all of us. [once]

And so say all of us. [twice]

For he's a jolly good fellow, [three times]

And so say all of us. [once]

This song has the same tune as the song 'The Bear Went Over the Mountain' that we sang in Year 1.

Michael, Row the Boat Ashore

Michael, row the boat ashore, Hallelujah,

Michael, row the boat ashore, Hallelujah.

Sister, help to trim the sail, Hallelujah,

Sister, help to trim the sail, Hallelujah.

Jordan's river is chilly and cold, Hallelujah,

Chills the body but not the soul, Hallelujah.

The river is deep and the river is wide, Hallelujah,

Milk and honey on the other side, Hallelujah.

Michael, row the boat ashore, Hallelujah.

Michael, row the boat ashore, Hallelujah.

She'll Be Comin' Round the Mountain

She'll be comin' round the mountain when she comes.

She'll be comin' round the mountain when she comes.

She'll be comin' round the mountain,

She'll be comin' round the mountain,

She'll be comin' round the mountain when she comes.

She'll be drivin' six white horses when she comes, [as above]

Oh, we'll all go out to meet her when she comes, [as above]

She'll be wearing pink pyjamas when she comes, [as above]

She'll be comin' round the mountain when she comes, [as above]

On Top of Old Smoky

On top of Old Smoky,

All covered with snow,

I lost my true lover

For courting too slow.

Well, courting's a pleasure

And parting is grief,

But a false-hearted lover

Is worse than a thief.

On top of Old Smoky,

All covered with snow,

I lost my true lover

For courting too slow.

I Had a Little Nut Tree

I had a little nut tree

Nothing would it bear

But a silver nutmeg

And a golden pear.

The king of Spain's daughter

Came to visit me,

And all for the sake of my little nut tree.

Lavender's Blue

Lavender's blue,
diddle, diddle,
Lavender's green.
When I am king,
diddle, diddle,
You shall be queen.

Call up your men,
diddle, diddle,
Set them to work,
Some to the plough,
diddle, diddle,
Some to the cart.

Some to make hay,
diddle, diddle,
Some to cut corn,
Whilst you and I,
diddle, diddle,
Keep ourselves warm.

Polly Put the Kettle On

Polly, put the kettle on,
Polly, put the kettle on,
Polly, put the kettle on,
We'll all have tea.

Suggested Resources

Books

Penny Dale, *Ten in the Bed* (Walker) 2011

Anna-Marie D'Cruz, *Make and Use Musical Instruments* (Wayland) 2007

Opal Dunn, *Number Rhymes Tens and Teens* (Frances Lincoln) 2009

Grace Hallworth, *Sing Me a Story: Song and Dance Tales from the Caribbean* (Frances Lincoln) 2007

Gerard Hoffnung, *Hoffnung Symphony Orchestra* (Hoffnung Partnership) 2000

Rachel Isadora, *Ben's Trumpet* (Greenwillow) 1979

Alison Jay, *The Nutcracker* (Templar) 2011

Geraldine McCaughrean, *Orchard Book of Stories from the Ballet* (Orchard) 2003

James Mayhew, *Ella Bella Ballerina and Cinderella* (Orchard) 2010

James Mayhew, *Ella Bella Ballerina and the Sleeping Beauty* (Orchard) 2008

Chris Raschka, *Charlie Parker Played Be Bop* (Orchard) 1997

Michael Rosen, *Little Rabbit Foo Foo* (Walker) 1989

DVDs and YouTube

Ben's Trumpet (Tibbetts Productions), available at http://www.youtube.com/watch?v=Hea0leH40j4

Cenerentola conducted by Claudio Abbado (Deutsche Grammophon) 2006

Fantasia including *The Sorcerer's Apprentice* (Walt Disney) 2010

Hansel Und Gretel, conducted by Thomas Fulton and played by the Metropolitan Opera (Deutsche Grammophon) 2010

The Magic Flute, directed by Ingmar Bergman (Gaumont) 1975

The Nutcracker, performed by Anthony Dowell, Alina Cojocaru, and others from the Royal Ballet (Opus Arte and BBC) 2001

Tales of Beatrix Potter, performed by the Royal Ballet (Optimum Home) 2006

Songbooks with CDs

Caroline Hooper, *The Usbourne Nursery Rhyme Songbook* (Usbourne) 2004

Beatrice Harrop and Jane Sebba, *Sing Hey Diddle Diddle* (A & C Black) 2001

Michael Rosen, *Sonsense Nongs* (A & C Black) 2001

Audio Recordings

Composer of the Week series by BBC Radio 3 (90 – 92 FM), available at www.bbc.co.uk/podcasts/series/cotw/all

My First Classical Music Album (Naxos) 2011

Prokofiev: Peter and the Wolf / Britten: Young Person's Guide to the Orchestra (EMI) 2007

The Sorcerer's Apprentice: French Symphonic Poems, directed by Michel Plasson and performed by Orchestre du Capitole de Toulouse, available from www.apple.com/itunes

Mobile Apps

Classical I (Magic Anywhere) app for iPad or iPhone

Musical Flash Cards (Kids Place) app for iPad or iPhone

Music Sparkles (Kids Games Club) app for iPad or iPhone

WI Orchestra (Wallander Instruments) app for iPad or iPhone

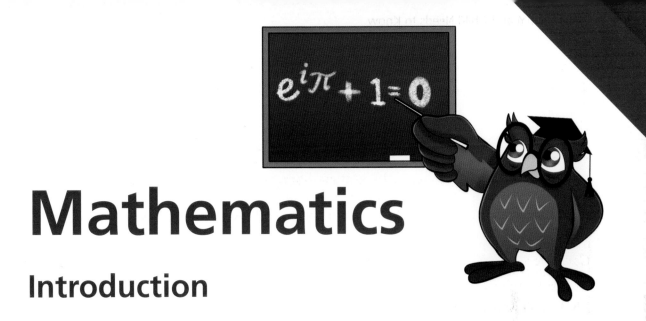

Mathematics

Introduction

In this section we sometimes address your child and sometimes address you as parents, particularly in the directions for activities you can do with your child.

We encourage you to give the topics and activities in this section some special emphasis. In international evaluations of mathematics performance by students in various countries, the performance of pupils in the UK is weak. One reason is that pupils in other countries are building a firmer foundation in mathematics in the earliest years of their schooling, accompanied by more consistent practice and more challenging work.

In primary school, any successful programme for teaching maths to young children follows these three cardinal rules: (1) practise, (2) practise and (3) practise. Not mindless repetition, of course, but thoughtful and varied practice, in which children are given opportunities to approach problems from a variety of angles, and in which, as they proceed to learn new facts and operations, they consistently review and reinforce their earlier learning.

In primary school, Year 2 pupils should practise maths daily, in order to ensure that they can effortlessly and automatically perform the basic operations upon which all problem solving and other sophisticated maths applications depend. Some well-meaning people fear that practice in mathematics – for example, memorising addition and subtraction facts or doing timed worksheets with problems – leads to joyless, soul-killing drudgery. Nothing could be farther from the truth. The destroyer of joy in learning mathematics is not practice but anxiety – the anxiety that comes from feeling that one is mathematically stupid or lacks any 'special talent' for maths.

We adults must be careful not to convey to our children any feelings that we 'don't like maths' or are 'not good at maths' or any other symptoms of what has been called 'maths anxiety'. By engaging our children in the kinds of activities suggested in this section, we can let them know that mathematics is important and interesting to us. Keep in mind, however, *that the activities suggested here are supplementary ways for parents to reinforce their children's learning at home. They are not sufficient for teaching maths in school*, where children need more regular and structured opportunities for practice and review.

Patterns and Classifications

PARENTS: Learning to see similarities, differences and patterns is an essential part of mathematical thinking. A Year 2 child should be able to sort objects according to some specific attributes, such as colour, shape and function; to define a set of items by what the items have in common; to tell which item does not belong in a set; and to recognise patterns and predict how a pattern will continue. To review these skills, see *What Your Year 1 Child Needs to Know.* Your Year 2 child should also learn to recognise similarities and differences in printed symbols. For example, ask your child to look at the following groups of squares and to point to the one in each group that is different. Also, check your local library for resources such as those suggested on page 284.

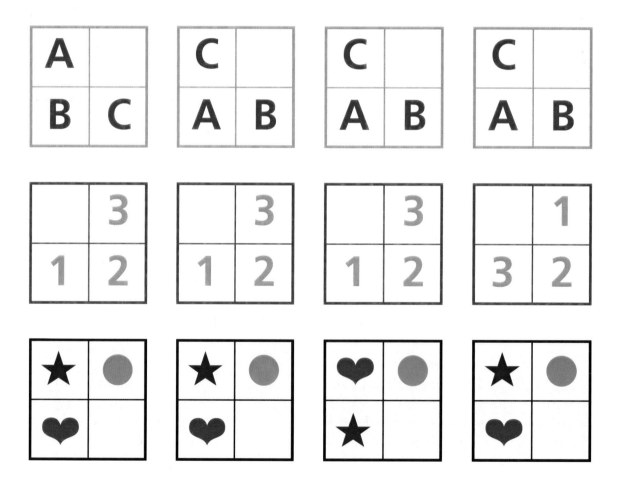

Numbers and Number Sense

PARENTS: By now your Year 2 child has probably had many experiences with numbers and counting. She knows her age and her address and can probably recite her telephone number. She can probably count to 30 or more, and she understands that each number stands for a specific quantity of items. (To review these concepts, see the section on Numbers and Number Sense in *What Your Year 1 Child Needs to Know*.) Now your child is ready to learn that there are different ways of counting. By the end of Year 2 she should know how to count to 100 in ones, twos, fives and tens, both forwards and backwards. She should also learn to write the words for the numbers from one to twenty.

Year 2 children should be learning to compare numbers to see which is greater and which is less, and to have a sense of how big 100 is. They can also begin to understand that a digit in the tens place of a number means something different from a digit in the ones place. In school, your child should also be introduced to number lines, tallies, simple bar graphs and pictorial graphs.

Some Things to Prepare in Advance

It helps to have real things for children to count. If you can gather and prepare these items in advance, you'll have a useful supply of materials to use for activities in this section and the Addition and Subtraction section.

- Keep a ready supply of countable things, such as dried beans, buttons, paper clips or small pasta shapes.

- It's very handy to have a set of number cards numbered from 0 to 100 for all sorts of games and counting activities. You can buy number cards at early learning centres or from many online suppliers, or you can make them out of index cards.

Numbers from 1 to 10

Count out loud from 1 to 10. Afterwards, practise writing the words for the numbers from one to ten.

1	one	★
2	two	★★
3	three	★★★
4	four	★★★★
5	five	★★★★★
6	six	★★★★★★
7	seven	★★★★★★★
8	eight	★★★★★★★★
9	nine	★★★★★★★★★
10	ten	★★★★★★★★★★

Zero is a special number. It tells how many you have when you don't have any. How many elephants do you have in your pocket?

One More and One Less

In counting, the number that comes after another number is always 1 more. For example, 6 is 1 more than 5. If you had 5 star stickers and you got 1 more, you would have 6 star stickers.

★ ★ ★ ★ ★ **+** ★ **=** ★ ★ ★ ★ ★ ★

In counting, the number that comes before another number is always 1 less. For example, 3 is 1 less than 4. If you had 4 pencils and you gave 1 away, you would have 3 pencils left.

To figure out what 1 less is, you can count backward. Learn to count backwards from 10 to 0, like this:

10, 9, 8, 7, 6, 5, 4, 3, 2, 1, 0

Numbers for Things in Order

Here are ten fish. One fish is out of line. Which one? The seventh fish.

When you say 'seventh', you are using a special kind of number called an ordinal number. Ordinal numbers name the number of something in an order. Practise saying and writing the first ten ordinal numbers in order. Except for first, second, and third, ordinal numbers up to twentieth end in 'th'.

Which one of the fish is facing the wrong way?

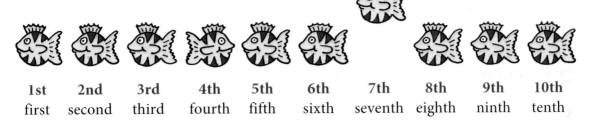

| 1st | 2nd | 3rd | 4th | 5th | 6th | 7th | 8th | 9th | 10th |
| first | second | third | fourth | fifth | sixth | seventh | eighth | ninth | tenth |

Place Value

10 is a number with two digits. A digit is any of the single numbers from 0 to 9. 10 has 2 digits, a 1 and a 0.

In the number 10, we say that the first digit is in the tens place, and the second digit is in the ones place. The 1 in the tens place means 1 group of ten.

The number after 10 is 11. 11 means 1 ten and 1 one.

A group of ten is called a ten. The 0 in the ones place means 0 ones.

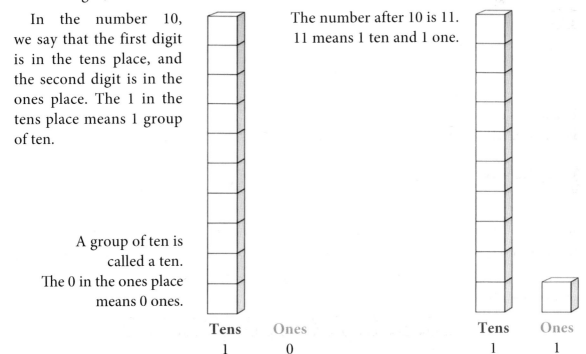

| Tens | Ones | | Tens | Ones |
| 1 | 0 | | 1 | 1 |

The next number is 12, which is 1 ten and 2 ones.

The numbers continue: 13, 14, 15, 16, 17, 18, 19.

19 means 1 ten and 9 ones. After 19 the next number is 20. 20 means 2 tens and 0 ones.

Here are the words for the numbers from 11 to 20:

11	**eleven**	16	**sixteen**
12	**twelve**	17	**seventeen**
13	**thirteen**	18	**eighteen**
14	**fourteen**	19	**nineteen**
15	**fifteen**	20	**twenty**

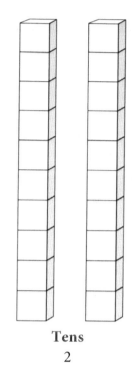

Tens   Ones
2   0

Place Value from 21 to 100

After 20, the numbers continue: 21, 22, 23, 24, 25, 26, 27, 28, 29, 30.

25 means 2 tens and 5 ones.

21	**twenty-one**	26	**twenty-six**
22	**twenty-two**	27	**twenty-seven**
23	**twenty-three**	28	**twenty-eight**
24	**twenty-four**	29	**twenty-nine**
25	**twenty-five**	30	**thirty**

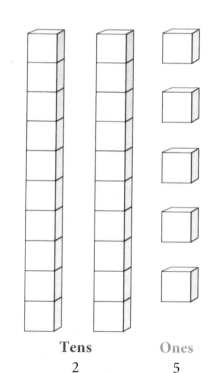

Tens   Ones
2   5

Let's count in tens: 10, 20, 30, 40, 50, 60, 70, 80, 90. The words for these numbers are ten, twenty, thirty, forty, fifty, sixty, seventy, eighty, ninety. 30 means 3 tens and 0 ones. 40 means 4 tens and 0 ones. 67 means 6 tens and 7 ones.

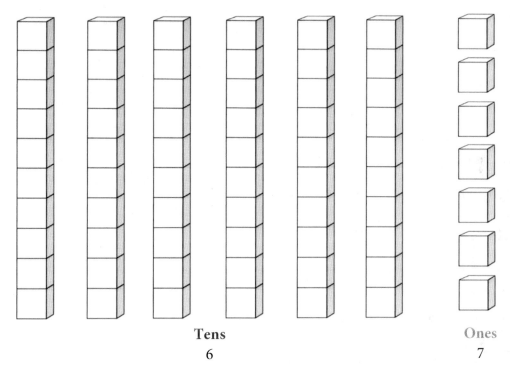

Tens
6

Ones
7

The numbers continue to 99, which is 9 tens and 9 ones. Do you know what comes after 99? The number after 99 is 100, which is written in words as one hundred.

Counting to 100

Practise counting out loud from 1 to 100, so that you can do it easily. Practise counting to 100 in tens: 10, 20, 30, 40, 50, 60, 70, 80, 90, 100. Practise counting to 100 in fives: 5, 10, 15, 20, 25, 30, 35, 40, and so on.

You should also practise counting by tens starting on different numbers, like this: 14, 24, 34, 44, 54, 64, 74, 84, 94. Notice that when you count by tens, the ones place stays the same but the tens place gets 1 number larger each time.

Also practise counting backwards from one ten to another. For example, try counting backwards from 30 to 20, like this: 30, 29, 28, 27, 26, 25, 24, 23, 22, 21, 20. You should also be able to say the name of any number between 0 and 100. For example, when you see 78, you say 'seventy-eight'. You should be able to read any number between 0 and 100 when it is spelt out. For example, eighty-three is 83.

Even and Odd Numbers

Try this. Gather a small pile of coloured pens. Count how many you have. Then arrange them in pairs. After you arrange them in pairs, are there any left over? If there are none left over, then you picked up an even number of pens. If there is one left over, then you picked up an odd number of pens.

There are 11 coloured pens here. 11 is an odd number.

When you start at 0 and count in twos, you are naming the even numbers. The even numbers up to 30 are:

0, 2, 4, 6, 8, 10, 12, 14, 16, 18, 20, 22, 24, 26, 28, 30

When you start at 1 and count by twos, you are naming the odd numbers. The odd numbers up to 30 are:

1, 3, 5, 7, 9, 11, 13, 15, 17, 19, 21, 23, 25, 27, 29

Can you name the next even number after 30? Can you name the next odd number after 29? Now try counting the even and odd numbers up to 100!

Twelve Is a Dozen

When you have 12 of something, you have a dozen. At the supermarket, eggs often come in cartons of a dozen or half-a-dozen.

If you need half-a-dozen eggs to bake a few cakes, how many eggs do you need? (A half-dozen is 6.)

Greater Than and Less Than

Which number is greater, 5 or 4? 5 is greater than 4 because 5 is 1 more than 4. For example, 5 balls are more than 4 balls.

We say 5 is greater than 4, and we write that like this:

$$5 > 4$$

The sign > means 'is greater than'. When you count, 5 comes after 4. Numbers that are greater come after in counting.

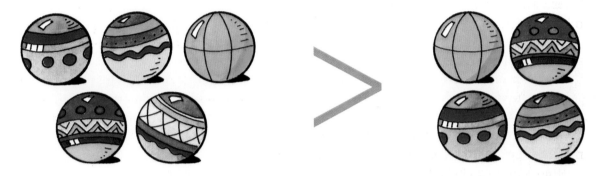

The number 3 is less than the number 4. For example, 3 pennies are less than 4 pennies.

We say 3 is less than 4, and we write that like this:

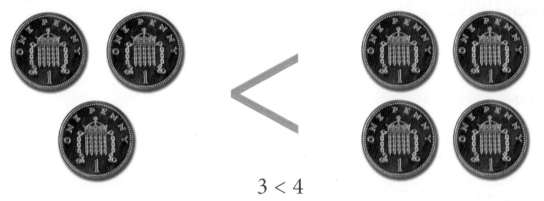

$$3 < 4$$

The sign < means 'is less than'. When you count, 3 comes before 4. Numbers that are less come before in counting.

Learn to compare numbers using the signs > < and =. Remember that = (the equals sign) means 'is the same as'. Notice that the small end of the signs < and > always points to the smaller number. What sign would you put between each pair of numbers here?

$$10 \_ 3 \qquad 6 \_ 8 \qquad 9 \_ 9$$

Activity 1: Before and after

PARENTS: Show your child a book with numbered pages. Try to use a book with at least 100 pages. If your child is not familiar with reading numbers over 100, you may want to try to find a book that has only about 100 pages. Leaf through the book with your child and talk about how the pages are numbered in order.

Have your child open the book to any right-handed page. Ask her to predict the page number that comes right after that page. Then have her turn the page to check her prediction. Close the book then open it again at random. Have her look at the number on a left-handed page, then ask her the number of the page just before. Have her turn back and check. Later you can ask your child to predict the page that comes before page 42, after page 13 and before page 60. Then try a more complicated task that asks her to count backwards, such as predicting, in order, the pages that go from page 63 to page 56. Each time, have her say the numbers first and then check the book.

Activity 2: Number flash card activities

PARENTS: You will need a deck of flash cards with the numbers from 0 to 100. You can make these from index cards, or buy them at many early learning centres or from online suppliers.
Here are some activities you can do quickly and occasionally repeat for practice:

- Hold up a card and have your child say the number on the card.

- Hold up two cards and ask which number is greater.

- Hold up two cards and ask your child to count forwards or backwards from one of the numbers to the other.

- Pick a card without showing it. Have your child guess the number by solving a number clue such as: 'This number is one more than 63', or: 'This number is one less than 35', or: 'This number is between 59 and 61.'

- After you use your 0 to 100 number cards, they'll probably be out of order. Before putting them away, ask your child to rearrange them in the correct order. This will provide an extra chance to practise counting from 0 to 100 in order.

Using Graphs

The children in Ms. Williams's class took a vote on their favourite colour. Different children chose red, blue, green, pink and purple. The teacher counted their votes and put them on a special kind of chart called a graph. Here it is:

red											
blue											
green											
pink											
purple											

Look at the graph and see if you can answer these questions:

- Which colour was chosen as the favourite by the most children?
- Which colour was chosen as the favourite by the fewest children?
- Which two colours were chosen as favourites by the same number of children?
- How many children chose each colour?

The children in Ms. Johnson's class voted on their favourite flavour of ice cream. Seven children voted for chocolate. Five children voted for vanilla. Three children voted for strawberry. Show how the children in Ms. Johnson's class voted by filling in a graph like the one below. Use a different colour for each flavour of ice cream, such as brown for chocolate, yellow for vanilla and pink for strawberry.

chocolate									
vanilla									
strawberry									

247

Fractions

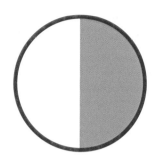

A fraction is a part of something. ½ is a fraction. If something is divided into two equal parts, each part is ½. ½ is written in words as one half.

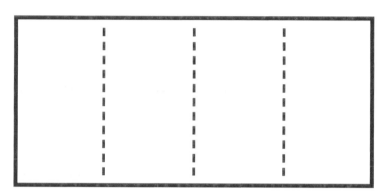

¼ is also a fraction. If something is divided into 4 equal parts, each part is ¼. ¼ is written in words as one quarter.

Each part is ¼ of the rectangle

Learn to recognise the fractions ½, ¼, ³/₄.

Here is a whole apple

³/₄ of an apple

½ of an apple

¼ of an apple

When you divide something into parts, the parts are equal only if they are the same size. For example, the parts of this rectangle are equal. But the parts of this square are not equal.

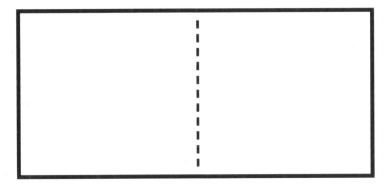

The rectangle has 2 parts.
The parts are equal. Each part is ½.

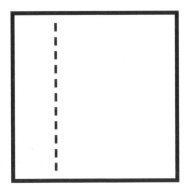

The square has 2 parts.
The parts are not equal.

Learn to recognise the fractions ½, ¼, ¾.

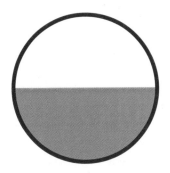 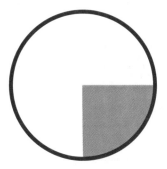 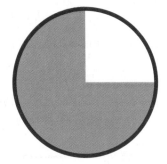

Addition and Subtraction

PARENTS: From Year 1, your child should understand that in a group of up to 10 objects there are ways to change the number of objects by adding to them and taking away from them, and that these changes can be shown in writing: for example, 2 + 2 = 4, or 4 - 3 = 1. In Year 2, your child should learn more about how addition and subtraction work. With repeated and varied practice, he or she should know addition and subtraction facts to 20, as well as learn how to apply these memorised facts when solving problems that ask your child to add or subtract two-digit numbers (without having to carry or borrow). Your child should also gain a firmer grasp of the connection between number sentences and the physical objects they represent.

From Counters to Mental Maths:

As children begin to learn to add and subtract, they may sometimes use countable objects, such as buttons, beans or paper clips. Such objects can help children to make the connection between numbers, which are symbols, and the actual items that are being added or subtracted. The goal in Year 2, however, is for children to become more competent at making calculations in their heads, without using countable objects. While children who are just learning their maths facts should not be discouraged from using objects or counting on their fingers, they should, with repeated practice, make the transition to more 'mental maths'. You can help your child by playing the number games we suggest below, by using addition and subtraction flash cards and, if you have access to a computer or mobile technology, by having your child play the calculation games on websites and apps such as those suggested on page 284.

Learn a Fact a Day:

You can use the charts on pages 251 and 252 to help your child learn one addition or subtraction fact a day. Pick one fact and, beginning in the morning, repeat it aloud together. For example: 'Nine minus seven is two'. Say it over many times. Add a little fun by saying it in different voices (high, low, squeaky, growly), or even sing it! Repeat it often throughout the day. Later, use the charts for review and practice.

Addition Facts from 0 to 12

Sum of 0	Sum of 1	Sum of 2	Sum of 3	Sum of 4
0 + 0 = 0	1 + 0 = 1	2 + 0 = 2	3 + 0 = 3	4 + 0 = 4
	0 + 1 = 1	1 + 1 = 2	2 + 1 = 3	3 + 1 = 4
		0 + 2 = 2	1 + 2 = 3	2 + 2 = 4
			0 + 3 = 3	1 + 3 = 4
				0 + 4 = 4

Sum of 5	Sum of 6	Sum of 7	Sum of 8
5 + 0 = 5	6 + 0 = 6	7 + 0 = 7	8 + 0 = 8
4 + 1 = 5	5 + 1 = 6	6 + 1 = 7	7 + 1 = 8
3 + 2 = 5	4 + 2 = 6	5 + 2 = 7	6 + 2 = 8
2 + 3 = 5	3 + 3 = 6	4 + 3 = 7	5 + 3 = 8
1 + 4 = 5	2 + 4 = 6	3 + 4 = 7	4 + 4 = 8
0 + 5 = 5	1 + 5 = 6	2 + 5 = 7	3 + 5 = 8
	0 + 6 = 6	1 + 6 = 7	2 + 6 = 8
		0 + 7 = 7	1 + 7 = 8
			0 + 8 = 8

Sum of 9	Sum of 10	Sum of 11	Sum of 12
9 + 0 = 9	10 + 0 = 10	11 + 0 = 11	12 + 0 = 12
8 + 1 = 9	9 + 1 = 10	10 + 1 = 11	11 + 1 = 12
7 + 2 = 9	8 + 2 = 10	9 + 2 = 11	10 + 2 = 12
6 + 3 = 9	7 + 3 = 10	8 + 3 = 11	9 + 3 = 12
5 + 4 = 9	6 + 4 = 10	7 + 4 = 11	8 + 4 = 12
4 + 5 = 9	5 + 5 = 10	6 + 5 = 11	7 + 5 = 12
3 + 6 = 9	4 + 6 = 10	5 + 6 = 11	6 + 6 = 12
2 + 7 = 9	3 + 7 = 10	4 + 7 = 11	5 + 7 = 12
1 + 8 = 9	2 + 8 = 10	3 + 8 = 11	4 + 8 = 12
0 + 9 = 9	1 + 9 = 10	2 + 9 = 11	3 + 9 = 12
	0 + 10 = 10	1 + 10 = 11	2 + 10 = 12
		0 + 11 = 11	1 + 11 = 12
			0 + 12 = 12

Subtraction Facts from 0 to 12

From 0

$0 - 0 = 0$

From 1

$1 - 0 = 1$
$1 - 1 = 0$

From 2

$2 - 0 = 2$
$2 - 1 = 1$
$2 - 0 = 0$

From 3

$3 - 0 = 3$
$3 - 1 = 2$
$3 - 2 = 1$
$3 - 3 = 0$

From 4

$4 - 0 = 4$
$4 - 1 = 3$
$4 - 2 = 2$
$4 - 3 = 1$
$4 - 4 = 0$

From 5

$5 - 0 = 5$
$5 - 1 = 4$
$5 - 2 = 3$
$5 - 3 = 2$
$5 - 4 = 1$
$5 - 5 = 0$

From 6

$6 - 0 = 6$
$6 - 1 = 5$
$6 - 2 = 4$
$6 - 3 = 3$
$6 - 4 = 2$
$6 - 5 = 1$
$6 - 6 = 0$

From 7

$7 - 0 = 7$
$7 - 1 = 6$
$7 - 2 = 5$
$7 - 3 = 4$
$7 - 4 = 3$
$7 - 5 = 2$
$7 - 6 = 1$
$7 - 7 = 0$

From 8

$8 - 0 = 8$
$8 - 1 = 7$
$8 - 2 = 6$
$8 - 3 = 5$
$8 - 4 = 4$
$8 - 5 = 3$
$8 - 6 = 2$
$8 - 7 = 1$
$8 - 8 = 0$

From 9

$9 - 0 = 9$
$9 - 1 = 8$
$9 - 2 = 7$
$9 - 3 = 6$
$9 - 4 = 5$
$9 - 5 = 4$
$9 - 6 = 3$
$9 - 7 = 2$
$9 - 8 = 1$
$9 - 9 = 0$

From 10

$10 - 0 = 10$
$10 - 1 = 9$
$10 - 2 = 8$
$10 - 3 = 7$
$10 - 4 = 6$
$10 - 5 = 5$
$10 - 6 = 4$
$10 - 7 = 3$
$10 - 8 = 2$
$10 - 9 = 1$
$10 - 10 = 0$

From 11

$11 - 0 = 11$
$11 - 1 = 10$
$11 - 2 = 9$
$11 - 3 = 8$
$11 - 4 = 7$
$11 - 5 = 6$
$11 - 6 = 5$
$11 - 7 = 4$
$11 - 8 = 3$
$11 - 9 = 2$
$11 - 10 = 1$
$11 - 11 = 0$

From 12

$12 - 0 = 12$
$12 - 1 = 11$
$12 - 2 = 10$
$12 - 3 = 9$
$12 - 4 = 8$
$12 - 5 = 7$
$12 - 6 = 6$
$12 - 7 = 5$
$12 - 8 = 4$
$12 - 9 = 3$
$12 - 10 = 2$
$12 - 11 = 1$
$12 - 12 = 0$

Activity 3: Addition and subtraction facts – try it yourself!

PARENTS: After reviewing the addition and subtraction facts for 0 to 12 with your child, have her review these facts and learn the addition and subtraction facts for 13 to 20 by creating (and decorating) her own tables.

Have you learned the addition and subtraction facts from 0 to 12? Did you see the patterns in the facts listed on the previous pages? Now create your own addition facts table. Grab your favourite pencil and some paper and let's begin. Start by labelling the top of your paper with 'Addition Facts from 13 to 20'. Now write your first heading 'Sum of 13' and write the addition facts for 13 below it, starting with '13 + 0 = 13' and completing all of the other addition facts that make 13. Continue on with the sums for 14 to 20. Now do the same for the subtraction facts. This will help you practise your addition and subtraction facts, and you can decorate your tables so they are pretty to look at. Perhaps you can hang them on the fridge or in your room?

Practise Your Addition

One way to practise addition is with things you can count. For example, if you have 3 keys, and you get 5 more keys, how many will you have?

You start with 3 keys:

You get 5 more keys:

Now count how many keys you have in all.
So, 3 + 5 = 8.

Another way to practise addition is to count forwards. What does 5 + 2 equal? You want the number that is 2 more than 5. So count forwards 2 numbers from 5, like this: 5 → 6 → 7. So, 5 + 2 = 7.

When you know how to add by counting forwards, keep practising your addition facts until you know them by heart, without counting. Practise writing and saying the addition facts a lot. It's important that you learn how to give the sums of addition facts quickly, without making mistakes.

> Do you remember the saying 'practice makes perfect'? Practising your maths will make you good at it!

Addition Facts with the Same Sum

Learn to give all the addition facts that have the same sum. For example, if you were asked for all the addition facts with a sum of 5, you would write:

$5 + 0 = 5$ $3 + 2 = 5$ $1 + 4 = 5$

$4 + 1 = 5$ $2 + 3 = 5$ $0 + 5 = 5$

Try this: can you write all the addition facts with a sum of 6?

Things to Know About Addition

● When you add numbers together, the answer you get is called the sum. The sum of $3 + 2$ is 5. The sum of $3 + 4$ is 7. What is the sum of $5 + 3$?

● When you add zero to a number, you get the same number. That's because zero means 'nothing', so if you add 0, you're adding nothing. For example, $5 + 0$ adds up to 5. What is the sum of $8 + 0$? How much is $27 + 0$?

● It does not matter what order you add numbers in, the sum is still the same. $3 + 4 = 7$ and $4 + 3 = 7$. So, if you know that $2 + 6 = 8$, you also know what $6 + 2$ equals.

● You can write addition problems across or up and down. They both mean the same thing. For example:

$$5 + 3 = 8 \text{ is the same as} \quad \begin{array}{r} 5 \\ + 3 \\ \hline 8 \end{array}$$

Activity 4: Dicey addition

PARENTS: For this activity you will need number cards from 2 to 12, a pencil, paper and two six-sided dice.

Give your child a pencil and a sheet of paper. Ask him to place the number cards face up in order. Now have him roll the dice, then add the two numbers that are rolled. He should say aloud the numbers he has rolled and then write them as an equation on his paper. For example, if he rolls a 6 and a 4, he writes (and reads aloud)

$$6 + 4 = 10.$$

If he needs to, your child can count the dots on the dice to add the numbers. When he finds the correct sum, he turns the number card representing that sum face down. When all the number cards from 2 to 12 have been turned face down, the game is over. (You can also adapt this game to include two or more players.)

Adding Three Numbers

To add three numbers, begin by adding the first two numbers. For example:

$$\begin{array}{r} 4 \\ 2 \\ + 1 \\ \hline \end{array} \qquad \text{First add} \begin{array}{r} 4 \\ + 2 \\ \hline 6 \end{array} \qquad \text{So} \begin{array}{r} 4 \\ 2 \\ + 1 \\ \hline \end{array} \begin{array}{r} 6 \\ + 1 \\ \hline 7 \end{array}$$

Can you solve this problem? Remember, begin by adding the first two numbers.

$$\begin{array}{r} 5 \\ 2 \\ + 3 \\ \hline \end{array}$$

Subtraction: Taking Away Leaves the Difference

Subtraction means taking a number away. Pretend you have five toy robots. You take away 2 toy robots and give them to a friend. How many are left?

There were 5, but you took away 2. 5 take away 2 is 3. Or you can say: 'Five minus two equals three.' And you can write that in two ways:

$$5 - 2 = 3 \qquad \text{is the same as} \qquad \begin{array}{r} 5 \\ -\ 2 \\ \hline 3 \end{array}$$

The number you have left after you subtract is called the difference. So, the difference of 5 - 2 is 3. What is the difference of 7 - 4? The difference is 3.

You can practise subtraction by counting backwards. What does 9 - 4 equal? You want the number that is 4 less than 9, so you can start at 9 and count backwards 4 numbers, like this: 9 → 8 → 7 → 6 → 5. So, 9 − 4 = 5.

Practise your subtraction facts until you know them without having to count backward. Practise writing and saying the subtraction facts up to 12, and do this many times. (See the chart on page 252.) With practice, you will learn them so well that you don't have to stop and work them out.

You know what happens when you add zero to a number. What is 8 + 0? Yes, it's 8. What do you think happens when you subtract zero from a number? When you subtract zero, you take away nothing, so you get the same number.

$$5 - 0 = 5 \qquad\qquad 12 - 0 = \underline{} \qquad\qquad 43 - 0 = \underline{}$$

Comparing Differences and Sums

You know these signs:

$$> \text{ greater than}$$
$$< \text{ less than}$$
$$= \text{ equals}$$

You can use these signs to compare differences and sums. Here are some examples:

$$10 - 2 > 6 \qquad\qquad 6 - 4 < 5 - 1 \qquad\qquad 8 - 4 = 7 - 3$$

What sign belongs in the squares here?

$$5 + 3 \ \square\ 6 + 2 \qquad\qquad 9 - 7 \ \square\ 2 + 6 \qquad 10 - 3 \ \square\ 6 - 1$$

Fact Families

A family is a group of related people. In maths, a fact family is a group of related maths facts. A fact family brings together addition facts with their opposite subtraction facts. For example, here is a fact family:

$$5 + 2 = 7 \qquad\qquad 7 - 2 = 5$$
$$2 + 5 = 7 \qquad\qquad 7 - 5 = 2$$

Here is another fact family:

$$6 + 2 = 8 \qquad\qquad 8 - 2 = 6$$
$$2 + 6 = 8 \qquad\qquad 8 - 6 = 2$$

If you are given $4 + 2 = 6$, can you figure out all facts in the fact family? Here they are:

$$4 + 2 = 6 \qquad\qquad 6 - 2 = 4$$
$$2 + 4 = 6 \qquad\qquad 6 - 4 = 2$$

Practise finding the facts in a fact family. For example, try to figure out the fact family for $3 + 2$. Try to figure out the fact family for $4 + 3$.

Activity 5: Find the mystery number

PARENTS:

Get Ready

You will need:

index cards

marker or crayon

number cards from 0 to 12

countable objects such as buttons, dried beans or pasta shapes

Go

Write a plus sign, a minus sign, an equals sign and a question mark on individual index cards. If you do not have ready-made number cards, make cards for the numbers 0 to 12. Tell your child that you're going to ask him to solve some number problems.

Tell your child this number story. As you tell the story, use the cards to show what's happening. Say: 'I had 5 buttons. I'll use this card with the number 5 to show how many buttons I have. Then I bought some more buttons. I'll use the plus sign to show that some buttons were added. This question mark shows that we don't know how many buttons were added. Now I have 9 buttons. I can show the equals sign and the sum of 9.'

Ask your child to figure out the mystery number. This process is hard for many

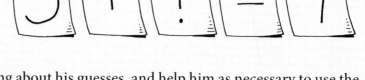

children, so be encouraging about his guesses, and help him as necessary to use the countable objects. Your child might need to set up 5 countable objects and then add one object at a time as he counts onward from 5 to find the mystery number.

When your child gets the correct answer, have him replace the question mark with the appropriate number card, then ask him to read the equation using the correct mathematical language, for example: 'Five plus four equals nine.'

Repeat the process with a subtraction story, such as: 'I had 7 buttons in a box. Then I took away some of those buttons to sew on a jacket. Now I have 2 buttons left in the box. How many buttons did I take away?' Repeat the process using the cards to show the following:

$$7 - ? = 2$$

Have your child find the missing number, using countable objects as necessary, and again have him read the equation using the correct mathematical language. Continue with other addition and subtraction stories that you make up.

As your child becomes more confident with addition and subtraction, encourage him to try working out the missing number without using the countable objects.

Activity 6: Addition and subtraction stories

PARENTS: Make up little stories that ask your child to add and subtract with numbers of 20 or less. Have on hand some countable objects for your child to use as necessary, but encourage her to try to do these problems on paper or in her head.

For your addition and subtraction stories, you can use real-life or imaginary situations. For example:

- 'Pretend you have a box of ten crayons. Two of the crayons roll under the bed and you can't find them. How many crayons are left in the box?'

- 'Once a spaceship from another planet landed on Earth. Out of the ship came 3 space people. Then 8 more space people came out. How many space people came out of the ship in all?' After she has solved that problem, you can continue the same story if you wish. For example: 'That's right, there were 11 space people in all. But four of them got homesick and decided to go back to their own planet. How many stayed on Earth?'

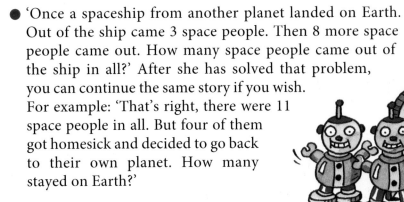

Activity 7: A hundred table

PARENTS: Show your child the 1 to 100 number table on this page. Show your child how the table is laid out by counting with him from 1 to 21, having him point at the numbers as he counts. Then ask questions like these:

● 'What's the largest number in the table?' (100)

● 'What's the same about the number in the first box in each row?' (They all end in 1.)

● 'What's the same about the number in the last box in each row?' (They all end in 0.)

The hundred table highlights number patterns that will help reinforce your child's understanding of place value and adding and subtracting with tens. This is a first step towards being able to compute with two-digit numbers. On the next page there are more questions you can ask:

1	2	3	4	5	6	7	8	9	10
11	12	13	14	15	16	17	18	19	20
21	22	23	24	25	26	27	28	29	30
31	32	33	34	35	36	37	38	39	40
41	42	43	44	45	46	47	48	49	50
51	52	53	54	55	56	57	58	59	60
61	62	63	64	65	66	67	68	69	70
71	72	73	74	75	76	77	78	79	80
81	82	83	84	85	86	87	88	89	90
91	92	93	94	95	96	97	98	99	100

- 'Look at the third row, with the numbers from 21 to 30. Look at the last number in the row: what's in the tens place?' (3 is in the tens place in the number 30.) 'How is that different from all the other numbers in the row?' (All the other numbers have a 2 in the tens place.) 'So, how many tens are in 30?' (3 tens are in 30.) 'How many tens are in 25?' (2 tens are in 25.)

- 'Find the number 53. Count to find 10 more than 53. What number do you get? Look at where 53 and 63 are on the table. What do you see?'

- 'Let's look at the table again, but this time let's not count. What do you think 28 + 10 is? Now count to see if you were right.'

- 'What do you think will happen when you add 17 + 20? How can you figure it out using the number table?' (Look two rows down from 17 to find 37.)

Later you can use the same kind of questions with several cases of subtracting 10 from a number.

Two-Digit Addition

You can use the addition facts you have learned so far to add numbers that have two digits. Let's look at this problem:

$$
\begin{array}{r}
43 \\
+\ 25 \\
\hline
\end{array}
$$

First you add the 3 and the 5 in the ones place:

tens $\quad$ 43 $\quad$ ones

$$
\begin{array}{r}
43 \\
+\ 25 \\
\hline
8
\end{array}
$$

Then add the 4 and 2 in the tens place:

tens $\quad\quad$ 43 $\quad\quad$ ones

$$
\begin{array}{r}
43 \\
+\ 25 \\
\hline
68
\end{array}
$$

So, the sum is 68. Altogether you have 6 tens and 8 ones.

Sometimes one of the numbers you are adding has two digits, but the other has only one digit.

For example, look at this problem:

$$22 \atop {+\ 6}$$

To solve that problem, you begin in the same way. First you add the numbers in the ones place. Then, since there are no tens to add to the 2 in the tens place, you just bring the 2 down into your answer.

add the ones

tens   22   ones
     + 6
    ─────
        8

bring down the 2 into the tens place

tens   22   ones
     + 6
    ─────
       28

So, the sum is 28, which is 2 tens and 8 ones. Don't forget to bring down the 2 tens into your answer!

Two-Digit Subtraction

You can use the subtraction facts you have learned to do subtraction with two-digit numbers.

Find the difference:

$$76 \atop {-\ 34}$$

First you subtract the numbers in the ones place:

tens   76   ones
     − 34
    ─────
         2

Then subtract the numbers in the tens place:

tens   76   ones
     − 34
    ─────
        42

So, the difference is 42, which is 4 tens and 2 ones.

Let's look at another problem:

subtract the ones   bring down the 5 into the tens place

```
   57              57                    57
 -  6            -  6                  -  6
 ____            ____                  ____
                    1                    51
```

In a problem like that, don't forget to bring down the number in the tens place. Practise doing many two-digit addition and subtraction problems, like these:

```
  34        25        52        68        75        49
+ 13      - 12      + 7       - 5       +12       - 27
____      ____      ____      ____      ____      ____
```

Money

PARENTS: Your Year 2 child should already be familiar with the names of the coins and understand that each one has a particular value; if not, see the 'Money' activities in *What Your Year 1 Child Needs to Know*. Once your child is comfortable with different coin values, as well as with some basic addition (see above, Addition and Subtraction), you can do the following activity, which shows that different combinations of coins can equal the same amount of money.

Activity 8: Coin combinations

PARENTS:

Get Ready

You will need:

pencils and several sheets of plain paper

Coins: 1p, 2p, 5p, 10p, 20p, 50p, £1 and £2

Go

Before you start counting coins, make sure your child can name each one and tell you how many pence it is worth. A fun way to review the names of the coins is to make coin rubbings by placing a coin under a sheet of paper and rubbing a pencil lightly over the coin until an impression shows up.

To get started, ask your child to show a combination of coins worth 11p. Then ask her to show another coin combination worth the same amount. Offer help as needed. For example, your child might decide to show a 10p coin and a 1p coin, or eleven 1p coins. Then ask: 'Can you think of any other ways to show 11p? How about starting with two 5p coins? And if you use just one 5p coin, what else do you need to make 11p?'

Now repeat the above steps with a combination of coins of another amount up to 20p.

To focus on the idea that different combinations of coins can be worth the same amount of money, ask questions like the following (have some real coins on hand for your child to use if she needs them to answer the questions):

● 'What coin is worth the same as two 5p coins?'

● 'If I give you two 2p coins and one 1p coin, what coin would you give me that is worth the same amount?'

● 'If I have a 10p coin and a 5p coin, and you have a 10p coin, two 2p coins, and one 1p coin, does one of us have more money?'

When your child is comfortable with combinations up to 20p, try combinations of coins from 21p to £1. Start with 21p, and provide enough coins for your child to make as many possible combinations as you and she can think of.

One pound is 100 pence

Here is the way you write one pound, using numbers and the pound sign:

$$£1.00$$

£1.00 is worth the same as 100 pence.

$$£1.00 = 100p$$

You can write amounts of money using the pence sign or the pound sign.

pence **p**   pound **£**

When you write an amount of money with a pound sign, the numbers to the right of the little dot (called a 'decimal point') are pence. For example, £1.50 is 1 pound and 50 pence. £2.98 is 2 pounds and 98 pence.

You can write amounts less than a pound with a pound sign or a pence sign.

£0.89 = 89p

You read £0.89 and 89p in the same way: 89 pence.

How much does this toy bus cost?

95p

How would you write 95p using a pound sign instead?

Counting in 20p coins

Remember: two 20p coins make 40p, and three 20p coins make 60p, four 20p coins make 80p and five 20p pieces make £1.00. When you count 20p coins, you count in 20s. Practise counting in 20s to 100:

20, 40, 60, 80, 100

Now let's look at some word problems:

Henry wants to buy an orange juice at the school cafeteria. It costs 80p. His mother gives him 20p coins to pay for the orange juice. How many 20p coins does she give him?

Mr. Jones buys a newspaper. It costs 40p. He gives the newsagent a one-pound coin. The man gives him 20p coins for change. How many 20p coins does he give Mr. Jones? (Solve the subtraction problem first: 100p – 40p, then work out how many 20p coins you need to make up your answer to the subtraction problem.)

Counting Money

Let's count this money. Starting with the two £2 coins, you have £4.00. One £1 coin makes £5.00 in all so far. One 50p coin makes £5.50 in total. Now add the 20p coin and the 10p coin that make 30p, which is £5.80 in total. Now add the 5p coin to the 2p and 1p coins to make 8p. So altogether, you have £5.88.

Practise counting money until you can do it quickly without making mistakes.

Notes

Sometimes we need to buy things for a lot more than one pound and it is hard to carry around enough coins to pay for them. To buy more valuable things, we often use notes. Let's learn about these notes:

A five-pound note is worth the same value as five £1 coins:

Here you can see two £5 notes, a £10 note, and a £20 note. A five-pound note is worth the same as five £1 coins. You would need to carry ten £1 coins to equal a ten-pound note. How many £1 coins would you need to equal a twenty-pound note? Yes, 20! Carrying all of these £1 coins would certainly weigh down the pockets of your trousers.

Geometry

Flat and Solid Shapes

Maths having to do with shapes is called geometry. You probably know the names for many flat shapes. A shape with three sides is called a triangle. Here are two triangles. Count the sides on each.

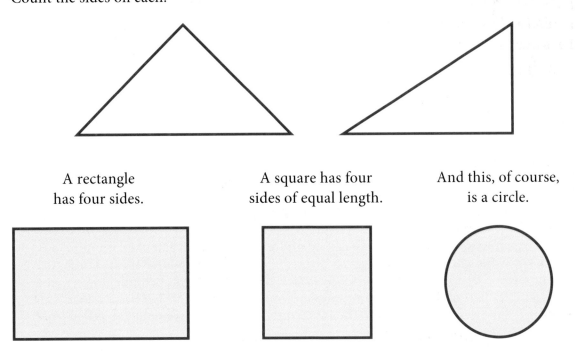

A rectangle
has four sides.

A square has four
sides of equal length.

And this, of course,
is a circle.

267

When two shapes are the same size and shape, we say they are congruent. Two of these triangles are congruent.

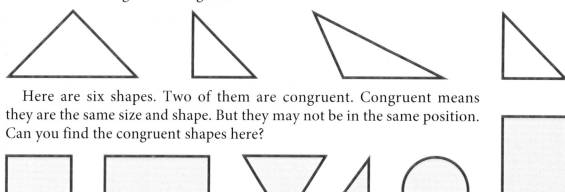

Here are six shapes. Two of them are congruent. Congruent means they are the same size and shape. But they may not be in the same position. Can you find the congruent shapes here?

Learn the names of these solid shapes, and look around your home or school for examples, such as a can of soup (cylinder) or ball (sphere).

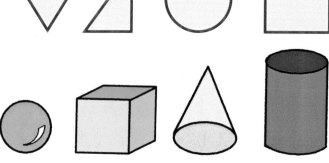

PARENTS: Children often enjoy playing with a tangram, a 7-shape puzzle thought to have been created in China long ago. Check your local library or bookstore for books like: *Magnetic Tangrams: Explore the world of Tangram pictures* by Jon Tremaine (Barron's) 2009.

Activity 9: Simon says

PARENTS: In Year 2, your child should continue to refine her sense of spatial orientation and become more secure using terms of location such as left, right, top, middle and bottom. She should also use terms of relative position such as on, under, over and between. At home, you can adapt the old favourite game of Simon Says so that it helps your child to practise direction words. To practise these words, use commands that incorporate words like over, under, left, right, behind, between and around as part of the game. For example: 'Simon says put your left hand under your chin.' 'Simon says walk around the kitchen table.' 'Simon says hold your right knee between your hands.'

Measurement

PARENTS: By the end of Year 2, children should become more familiar with a few standard measuring tools, as well as units such as centimetres for measuring length; litres, pints, millilitres and tablespoons for volume; kilograms and grams for weight; and degrees Celsius for temperature. To understand measurement, Year 2 children need many opportunities to measure things. Year 2 children also need plenty of practice in measuring time. They need to work with terms and concepts such as before and after, as well as yesterday, today and tomorrow. They should know the days of the week and the months of the year. By the end of Year 2, your child should be able to read a clock face and tell the time to the half hour. You can help him by regularly showing him a calendar and clock as you plan various tasks in your daily lives. Don't rely exclusively on digital clocks or watches; use a clock or watch with hands.

> You will have a go at measuring activities in the Science chapter by answering questions like: How much? How many? How hot?

Calendar Time

There are seven days in a week. Can you name them? (Sunday, Monday, Tuesday, Wednesday, Thursday, Friday, Saturday.) Of those seven days, five are called 'the weekdays' and two days make up 'the weekend'. Can you tell me which two days are the weekend days? (Saturday and Sunday).

There are twelve months in a year. Can you name them, starting with the first month? They are (1) January, (2) February, (3) March, (4) April, (5) May, (6) June, (7) July, (8) August, (9) September, (10) October, (11) November, and (12) December. Make sure you know the names of the months of the year, in order.

What month is it now? In what month is your birthday? In what month is the weather hottest? The twelve months help us describe different times of the year.

You remember ordinal numbers, the numbers that help you put things in order? For the last two months of the year, you can learn two new ordinal numbers: eleventh and twelfth. (Notice the funny spelling of 'twelfth'.) November is the eleventh month, and December is the twelfth month. How many days does November have? What about December?

Do you remember reading the poem 'Thirty Days Hath September' on page 19? Since different months have different numbers of days, this poem can help you remember how many days are in each month.

PARENTS: To strengthen your child's sense of calendar time, display the calendar for the current month and occasionally ask questions like the following:

● 'What day is today?' (Ask for the day of the week and the day, month and year.)

● 'What day of the week was it yesterday?'

● 'What day of the week will tomorrow be?'

● 'Can you show me where yesterday was on the calendar? Can you tell me what the date will be next Sunday?'

Activity 10: Telling the time

PARENTS: What follows is not so much a one-time activity as an explanation you can read aloud to your child, then refer back to on many occasions. Most children need repeated practice and reinforcement before they master the skill of telling the time. In school, your child should get plenty of practice in learning to tell the time. If you want to supplement this, visit your local library for additional resources.

Get Ready

As you read aloud the following section to your child, it will be helpful to have a paper clock face to work with. You can make one from a paper plate, a sheet of coloured paper and a split-pin. To make clock hands, cut two narrow strips of paper from the sheet: one strip should be longer than the other. Then have your child help you turn the paper plate into a clockface by numbering around the rim from 1 to 12. Finally, use the split-pin to attach the ends of both strips of paper to the centre of the clock face. Your child can use this home-made clock face to show different times.

Go

Ask your child to show the times on a home-made clock face as you read aloud the following:

Look at the clock. What time does this clock say it is?

When the long hand is on the 12 and the short hand is on the 8, then the time is 8 o'clock. We can write that in two ways:

8:00 means the same as 8 o'clock

The long hand on a clock is also called the minute hand. The short hand is also called the hour hand. On this clock, the minute hand is on the 12 and the hour hand is on the 4. Can you tell me what time it is?

Look at this clock. Tell me where the minute hand is, and where the hour hand is. Then can you tell me what time it is?

Yes, that clock shows 10 o'clock. Can you show me 10 o'clock on your paper clock?

Your clock could be showing 10:00 in the morning or 10:00 at night. If you want to tell someone to meet you at 10:00, how can you make sure he knows that you mean 10:00 in the morning and not 10:00 at night? One way is to say, 'Meet me at 10 a.m.' A time before noon is called a.m., which is in the morning. Time after noon is called p.m., which is in the afternoon or at night. [Note: You may want to ask your child if he can recognise noon on a clock, and show him if he doesn't know that noon is 12]

Do you eat breakfast closer to 8 a.m. or 8 p.m.? Do you go to bed closer to 8 a.m. or 8 p.m.? Can you think of some things you normally do at about 10 a.m.? What are you normally doing at 10 p.m.?

Now let's look at this clock. What number is the minute hand on? And look at the hour hand — do you see how it's between 7 and 8? This clock is showing half past seven. Another way of saying half past seven is seven-thirty, which we can write like this:

$$7{:}30$$

When we say seven-thirty, we mean that it's 30 minutes after seven o'clock. Seven-thirty is the same as saying 'half past seven' because 30 minutes is half of an hour. A whole hour is 60 minutes. Sixty minutes is how long it takes for the minute hand to go around the clock once, starting at the 12 and coming back to the 12. While the minute hand makes one whole trip around the clock, the hour hand moves from one number to the next.

Can you tell what time it is on this clock?

Some clocks do not have hands. On a digital clock, the time appears in numbers. These two clocks are showing the same time in different ways. Can you tell me what time they are showing?

Here are two more two clocks that are showing the same time in different ways. Can you tell me what time they are showing?

Multiplication and Division

What is Multiplication?

Multiplication is a quick way of adding the same number over and over again. Here's an example. There are five groups of two turtles. How many are there in all?

You could add 2 five times: $2 + 2 + 2 + 2 + 2 = 10.$

You could also say that 5 twos = 10. You can write that as a multiplication problem:

$$5 \times 2 = 10$$

We read that as 'five times two equals ten'. The sign × means 'times', and it shows that you are multiplying. You can also write that problem as

$$\begin{array}{r} 5 \\ \times\, 2 \\ \hline 10 \end{array}$$

The numbers in a multiplication problem have special names. The numbers that are being multiplied are called factors. The answer is called the product. In 2 × 4 = 8, 2 and 4 are **factors**, and 8 is the **product**.

$$\underset{\text{factor}}{2} \quad \times \quad \underset{\text{factor}}{4} \quad = \quad \underset{\text{product}}{8}$$

What are the factors and what is the product in this multiplication problem?

$$5 \times 3 = 15$$

Practising Multiplication

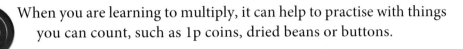

When you are learning to multiply, it can help to practise with things you can count, such as 1p coins, dried beans or buttons.

For example, to figure out 5 × 4, you can make 5 groups of 4, like this:

Count how many you have altogether. You should get 20. So, 5 × 4 = 20.

You can also practise by turning a multiplication problem into an addition problem. For example, what is 2 × 3? You can change that to 2 + 2 + 2, which equals 6.

$$So, 2 \times 3 = 6$$

What is 2 × 5? You can change that to 2 + 2 + 2 + 2 + 2, which equals 10.

$$So, 2 \times 5 = 10$$

Adding 2 over and over again is the same thing as counting in twos: 2, 4, 6, 8, 10.

When you count in twos, you get the products of multiplying by 2, like this:

$$1 \times 2 = 2$$
$$2 \times 2 = 4$$
$$3 \times 2 = 6$$
$$4 \times 2 = 8$$
$$5 \times 2 = 10$$

Practise the multiplication tables for 2, 5 and 10 often. In Year 3 we will learn the rest of the multiplication tables.

Multiplying by 10

Here are five bunches of bananas, with ten bananas in each bunch.

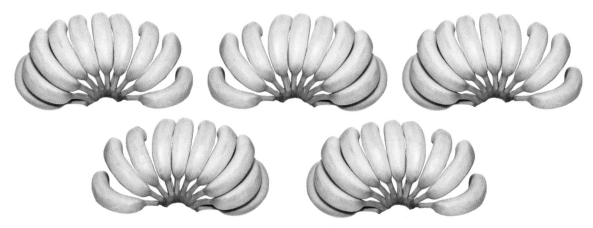

How many bananas are there in all? To find the answer, you could add 10 five times. Or you could count in tens. Try it. Put your finger on each bunch of bananas as you count in tens: 10, 20, 30, 40, 50. There are fifty bananas in all.

So, five groups of ten equals 50. You can also say that as a multiplication problem:

$$5 \times 10 = 50$$

In the picture above, cover one bunch of bananas with your hand. Now how many bananas are in four bunches of ten? You could add 10 four times, or count in tens: 10, 20, 30, 40. Or, the quick way is to multiply.

$$\begin{array}{r} 10 \\ \times\ 4 \\ \hline 40 \end{array}$$

So, four groups of ten equals 40. $4 \times 10 = 40$. And, as you learnt earlier, $5 \times 10 = 50$. Do you see a pattern here? Can you figure out how many are in two groups of ten? And how many are in three groups of ten?

$$\begin{array}{cccccccccc} 10 & 10 & 10 & 10 & 10 & 10 & 10 & 10 & 10 & 10 \\ \times\ 1 & \times\ 2 & \times\ 3 & \times\ 4 & \times\ 5 & \times\ 6 & \times\ 7 & \times\ 8 & \times\ 9 & \times\ 10 \\ \hline \end{array}$$

Multiplication Facts

Practise counting by twos, fives and tens. This will help you learn your multiplication tables for 2, 5 and 10.

Two as a factor	Five as a factor	Ten as a factor
2 × 0 = 0	5 × 0 = 0	10 × 0 = 0
2 × 1 = 2	5 × 1 = 5	10 × 1 = 10
2 × 2 = 4	5 × 2 = 10	10 × 2 = 20
2 × 3 = 6	5 × 3 = 15	10 × 3 = 30
2 × 4 = 8	5 × 4 = 20	10 × 4 = 40
2 × 5 = 10	5 × 5 = 25	10 × 5 = 50
2 × 6 = 12	5 × 6 = 30	10 × 6 = 60
2 × 7 = 14	5 × 7 = 35	10 × 7 = 70
2 × 8 = 16	5 × 8 = 40	10 × 8 = 80
2 × 9 = 18	5 × 9 = 45	10 × 9 = 90
2 × 10 = 20	5 × 10 = 50	10 × 10 = 100

Three rules for multiplication

Rule number 1: no matter what order you multiply numbers in, the product is always the same. For example, look at the groups of oranges in the picture. Two groups of 3 equal the same as three groups of 2.

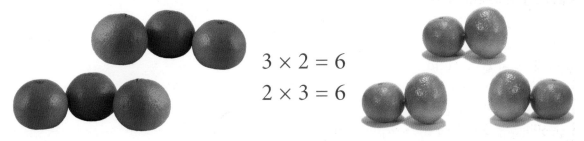

$$3 \times 2 = 6$$
$$2 \times 3 = 6$$

Rule number 2: when you multiply a number by 1, the product is always that number.

$$1 \times 7 = 7 \qquad 5 \times 1 = 5 \qquad 6 \times 1 = 6 \qquad 75 \times 1 = 75$$

Rule number 3: when you multiply a number by 0, the product is always 0.

$$0 \times 9 = 0 \qquad 6 \times 0 = 0 \qquad 0 \times 3 = 0 \qquad 89 \times 0 = 0$$

Word Problems and Missing Factors

You will need to use multiplication to solve some word problems, like this one. Nine children went to the shop. Each child bought 2 markers. How many markers did they buy in all?

You could add 2 nine times, but it's quicker to multiply: $9 \times 2 = 18$. They bought eighteen markers in all.

John baked five trays of muffins. In each tray he has six muffins. How many muffins does he have in all?

John has the same number of muffins in each tray. So, you could add 6 five times, but it's much quicker to multiply. You write: $6 \times 5 = 30$. John has thirty muffins.

Here's another word problem. The librarian asked Robert to help her move books to some new shelves across the room. Robert can carry eight books at a time. He makes five trips across the room. How many books does he carry in all?

Robert carries the same number of books each time. So, you multiply: $8 \times 5 = 40$. Robert carried forty books in all.

Here's a different kind of problem. It gives you the product, but asks you to work out one of the facts.

Mrs. Johnson wants to buy balloons for her class with one for each child. There are sixteen children in the class. The balloons come in packets of four. How many packets does she need to buy?

You can put that in the form of a multiplication problem: $4 \times \_ = 16$. Four times what equals 16? If you know your multiplication tables well, then you know the answer is 4 because $4 \times 4 = 16$. So, Mrs. Johnson needs to buy four packets of balloons.

You can practise your multiplication facts by solving problems with missing factors, like these:

$$3 \times \_ = 15 \quad 5 \times \_ = 35 \quad 4 \times \_ = 20 \quad 2 \times \_ = 14 \quad 3 \times \_ = 30$$

Another way to solve multiplication problems with missing factors is to use division.

Division

Operations

Addition, subtraction and multiplication are called operations. They are three of the four operations of arithmetic. The fourth operation is division.

You already know that subtraction is the inverse of addition. We also say that addition and subtraction are inverse operations. The inverse operation of multiplication is division. Let's see how division works.

An Example of Division

Peter has 20 stamps. He wants to divide them into groups of 5. How many groups will he have?

$$20 \div 5 = 4$$

This is a division problem, because you need to divide the 20 stamps into groups of 5 to solve it. How many groups of 5 are there in 20? There are 4 fives in 20. So Peter will have 4 groups of stamps. We write this division problem: $20 \div 5 = 4$. We read it: 'Twenty divided by five equals four'. The sign $\div$ means 'divided by' and shows that you are dividing.

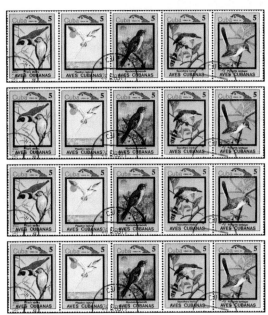

Solving Division Problems

Division and multiplication are inverse operations. Sometimes the easiest way to solve a division problem is to think of a multiplication problem. Here is an example. What is $30 \div 5$? You want to know how many 5s there are in 30. Think: what times 5 equals 30? $6 \times 5 = 30$. So $30 \div 5 = 6$. In the picture below, the 30 pens are divided into 5 groups, with 6 pens in each group.

$$6 \times 5 = 30 \qquad 30 \div 5 = 6$$

Here is another example. What is $50 \div 10$? You want to know how many tens there are in 50. Think: What times ten equals 50? $5 \times 10 = 50$. So $50 \div 10 = 5$.

279

Division Words

The answer to a division problem is called the quotient. The number you are dividing is called the *dividend*. The number you are dividing by is called the divisor.

Learn to use these words to describe the numbers in a division problem. For example, in $35 \div 5 = 7$, 35 is the dividend, 5 is the divisor and 7 is the quotient.

There are two ways to write division. You can write it like this:

$$12 \div 2 = 6 \longleftarrow \text{quotient}$$

dividend   divisor

or like this:

$$\begin{array}{r} 6 \longleftarrow \text{quotient} \\ 2\overline{)12} \longleftarrow \text{dividend} \end{array}$$

divisor $\longrightarrow$

Notice that the answer, the 6, goes over the ones' place. Learn to write division in other ways. For example:

$$8 \div 2 = 4 \quad \text{is the same as} \quad 2\overline{)8}\,^{4}$$

$$10\overline{)60}\,^{6} \quad \text{is the same as} \quad 60 \div 10 = 6$$

Division Facts

Learn the basic division facts. These facts will help you solve division problems. You can use the multiplication facts you already know to find the quotient of each division fact. We'll talk more about this later. Here are the division facts with 2, 5 and 10 as divisors.

2 as a divisor	5 as a divisor	10 as a divisor
$0 \div 2 = 0$	$0 \div 5 = 0$	$0 \div 10 = 0$
$2 \div 2 = 1$	$5 \div 5 = 1$	$10 \div 10 = 1$
$4 \div 2 = 2$	$10 \div 5 = 2$	$20 \div 10 = 2$
$6 \div 2 = 3$	$15 \div 5 = 3$	$30 \div 10 = 3$
$8 \div 2 = 4$	$20 \div 5 = 4$	$40 \div 10 = 4$
$10 \div 2 = 5$	$25 \div 5 = 5$	$50 \div 10 = 5$
$12 \div 2 = 6$	$30 \div 5 = 6$	$60 \div 10 = 6$
$14 \div 2 = 7$	$35 \div 5 = 7$	$70 \div 10 = 7$
$16 \div 2 = 8$	$40 \div 5 = 8$	$80 \div 10 = 8$
$18 \div 2 = 9$	$45 \div 5 = 9$	$90 \div 10 = 9$
$20 \div 2 = 10$	$50 \div 5 = 10$	$100 \div 10 = 10$

Division Rules for 0 and 1

Here are some rules for dividing with 0 and 1.

Rules for 0

1. 0 divided by any number (except 0) equals 0.

$$0 \div 8 = 0 \qquad 0 \div 5 = 0$$

2. You cannot divide by 0.

$5 \div 0$ is an impossible problem. Why? If you have a word problem such as 'How many biscuits does each person have when you give 0 people even numbers of biscuits?' Well, if there are 0 people to give them to, it is impossible for you to give any biscuits away.

Rules for 1

1. Any number (except 0) divided by itself equals 1.

$$8 \div 8 = 1 \qquad 6 \div 6 = 1$$

2. Any number divided by 1 equals that number

$$5 \div 1 = 5 \qquad 7 \div 1 = 7$$

These rules can help you learn the division facts. For example, the last rule makes it easy to learn all the division facts that have 1 as a divisor:

$0 \div 1 = 0$; $1 \div 1 = 1$; $2 \div 1 = 2$; $3 \div 1 = 3$; $4 \div 1 = 4$; $5 \div 1 = 5$; and so on.

Division Word Problems

Here are two kinds of division problems. Let's solve both kinds.

1. Margaret has 35 peppers. She wants to put 5 into each basket. How many baskets does she need?

You want to know how many groups of 5 there are in 35. You write 35 ÷ 5 = 7. She needs 7 baskets. (What other way can you write 35 ÷ 5?)

2. Mrs. Fletcher was given a dozen roses. She wants to divide the twelve roses equally into 2 vases. How many roses should she put into each vase?

You want to know how many will be in each group if you divide 12 into 2 groups. You write 12 ÷ 2 = 6. She should put 6 roses into each vase.

Sometimes you want to know how many groups to have, and sometimes you want to know how many are in each group. You solve both kinds of problems in the same way.

Picturing Multiplication and Division Facts

As you've just read, multiplication and division are inverse operations. For example, the inverse of multiplying by 5 is dividing by 5. The inverse of 8 × 5 = 40 is 40 ÷ 5 = 8. Here is a picture of how this works.

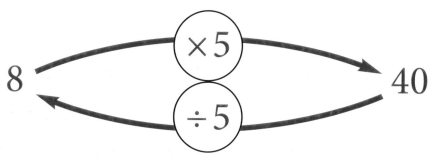

Here is another example. The inverse of 18 ÷ 2 = 9 is 9 × 2 = 18.

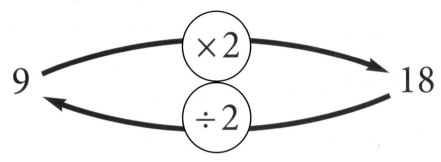

Learn to draw pictures like these to show inverse multiplication and division facts. When you can do this, you can find inverse and multiplication and division facts.

Picturing Multiplication and Division Facts with Blank Spaces

Learn to fill in the blanks in pictures like these:

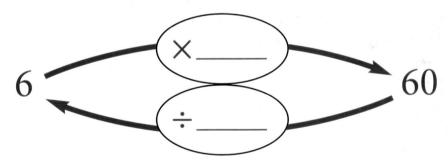

You should also be able to do the same thing with equations that have blank spaces.

$$\underline{\hspace{3em}} \times 5 = 20$$

Think: What times 5 equals 20? 4. So 4 × 5 = 20.

Try these:

1. _____ × 8 = 16   4. 6 × _____ = 30

2. _____ ÷ 10 = 9   5. 3 × _____ = 6

3. 60 ÷ _____ = 6   6. 25 ÷ _____ = 5

Division and Fractions

When something is divided into 2 equal parts, each part is one half, written as a fraction: ½. We previously did this on page 249.

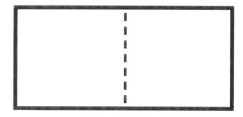

Now if you want to find ½ of 8, you divide it into 2 equal parts. To divide 8 blocks into 2 equal groups, you divide by 2.

$$8 \div 2 = 4$$

Using the division facts, learn to find the fraction ½ of different even numbers.

Suggested Resources

Books

Ken Kimura, *99 Tadpoles Find a Home* by (Gecko) 2011

Vic Parker, *How Long is Long?* (Raintree) 2011

Irina Tyk, *The Butterfly Arithmetic* (Civitas) 2011

Mobile Apps (Free)

Arithmetic Wiz Free (The Rocket Studio) app for iPad and iphone.

Software

Mathletics (3P Learning). For purchase.

TuxMath (Tux4Kids). Free.

Science

Introduction

Children gain knowledge about the world around them in part from observation and experience. To understand animals and their habitats, or human body systems, or electricity, a child needs first-hand experience with many opportunities to observe and experiment. In the words of the Association for Science Education: 'A good primary and early years science education:

- Acknowledges that children come to science education with ideas, observations and questions about the world around them and use these as the foundations for their learning

- Nurtures children's curiosity and inspires them, in a rich learning environment, to discover more and to develop positive attitudes and an appreciation of the nature of science

- Challenges children to develop and use scientific skills; acquire and apply scientific knowledge, understanding and language; investigate through playing, exploring and experimenting; communicate and collaborate effectively with others; challenge scientific evidence

- Enables children to make connections between scientific ideas and to see how they are developed and applied in other disciplines and beyond the classroom.'[1]

While experience counts for much, book learning is also important, for it helps bring coherence and order to a child's scientific knowledge. Only when topics are presented systematically and clearly can children make steady and secure progress in their scientific learning. The child's development of scientific knowledge and understanding is in some ways a very disorderly and complex process, different for each child. But a systematic approach to the exploration of science, one that combines experience with book learning,

---

[1] Association for Science Education Primary Science Committee, 2010: 'ASE Primary and Early Years Science Education Vision Statement'. Available at: http://www.ase.org.uk/documents/primary-vision-statement

can help provide essential building blocks for deeper understanding at a later time. It can also provide the kind of knowledge that one is not likely to gain from observation: consider, for example, how people long believed that the earth stood still while the sun orbited around it, a misconception that 'direct experience' presented as fact.

In this section, we introduce Year 2 children to a variety of topics consistent with the early study of science in countries that have had outstanding results in teaching science at the primary level. The text is meant to be read aloud to your child, and it offers questions for you and your child to discuss, as well as activities for you to do together.

Living Things and Their Habitats

Do you recognise this big furry creature? He's a polar bear. He lives near the North Pole. What's the weather like there? Brrr! Yes, it's cold, cold, cold. Look at what's all around the polar bear: ice, and lots of it.

The polar bear lives where it's cold and icy all the time, but he doesn't seem to mind at all. Look at him again. See his thick, furry coat? With all that thick fur, he stays pretty snug, even near the North Pole.

Now, imagine that the polar bear decides to go on a holiday. (Of course, you and I know that bears don't take holidays, but let's pretend.) He goes on a trip to Spain. How do you think he would like it? What would our big furry friend think of the sunny, sandy beaches of Spain?

Well, if you've ever been to the beach, you might like it, but you can take off your clothes and wear nothing but a swimsuit. The polar bear can't take off his fur!

Poor polar bear! He wouldn't enjoy a trip to warm, sunny Spain. It's a lovely place, but not for him. It's not his habitat.

What's a habitat? For an animal, a habitat is the place where the animal lives, eats, sleeps, makes its home, has babies and gets along (mostly) with other animals. But it's not just any kind of place. An animal's habitat is a special place suited to the animal because the animal is suited to it.

The big furry polar bear isn't suited to the warm beach, but he gets along well in the icy Arctic. A fish that swims in the ocean couldn't possibly survive up a tree, could it? Would a worm that crawls through the moist, rich soil of the forest be happy living in the hot, sandy desert?

Different animals live in different habitats. The way an animal lives has a lot to do with its habitat. Let's explore a few habitats and get to know some animals living in them.

The Woodland Habitat

Imagine you're walking through a beautiful wood. Oak and birch trees stand tall around you. Their highest branches reach upward and form a leafy canopy, which makes it cool and shady for you as you walk along below.

What's that tap-tap-tapping sound? It's a bird called a woodpecker. Woodpeckers peck into the trunks of old trees, looking for insects to eat. The woodpecker lives in this woodland habitat.

A squirrel scampers up a tree. The squirrel also lives in this woodland habitat. Squirrels build nests in the tree branches and gather acorns from the oak trees in the autumn.

What's that large, furry creature darting through the undergrowth? It's a fox! There's also a badger peeping out from behind a tree – look at his black, white and grey fur. He's quite a heavy creature, with short little legs that he uses to dig out his underground home, which is called a badger sett. Badgers eat grubs and worms, as well as mice and even birds. Badgers may look harmless, but don't go near them – they have lots of sharp claws at the end of their stubby little legs, and will attack anyone they think is threatening them. Ooh,

287

what's that sticky stuff on your face? You've walked into the threads of a spider web, strung across your path. Spiders weave their webs where insects fly, hoping to trap some flies for dinner. Yummy!

Down on the woodland floor, the leaves fall and pile up. Beetles and other animals eat the leaves. Along comes a mouse, which eats the beetles, then the mouse gets eaten by a fox – which will eat pretty much anything!

Woodpeckers, squirrels, badgers, spiders, beetles, mice, foxes – all these animals and many, many more live in the woodland habitat. For their homes and food, they depend upon the plants and other animals that live in the wood with them.

What You're Called and What You Eat

Here's a fact you know is true every time your tummy rumbles: animals need to eat. Some animals eat plants. Some animals eat other animals. And some animals eat both. Scientists use special names for animals, depending on whether they eat plants, meat or both. Let's learn these special names: they're big words, so get ready!

Do you eat both plants and meat? Then you're an **omnivore** [OMM-nee-vore]. An omnivore is an animal that eats both plants and animals. Bears are omnivores. They eat berries and they eat small animals like fish. They also use their sharp claws to rip open logs and eat the insects they find there.

Animals that eat only plants are called **herbivores** [HUR-bee-vores]. Some human beings choose to eat only plants and no meat. Many animals, including mice, cows and horses, eat only plants. Even huge elephants eat only leaves, fruits, nuts and grasses.

Some animals would rather eat meat most of all. Can you think of any? Dogs and cats, lions and tigers, sharks and snakes eat meat. They are called **carnivores** [CAR-nee-vores]. A carnivore eats animal flesh, or meat.

What you eat is important, and so is how you eat. You can read a poem about that on page 31.

The Underground Habitat

Imagine that you brought a spade with you on your walk through the forest. Take it out and dig down under the twigs, leaves and mushrooms on the forest floor. What can you see?

A slimy pink earthworm slithers deeper underground. A little white grub curls up in the soil. Soon it will grow into an insect and creep among the woodland ferns and mosses.

The worm and the grub live together in the forest's underground habitat. Even some furry animals, like moles, live underground with them. Moles have long, broad paws just right for digging. They burrow underground and they look for things to eat: things like roots, ants and – sorry, little worm – worms. Actually, moles don't really 'look' for things to eat, since they can't see very well. Instead, moles find their way around underground with a keen sense of smell.

What is this mole eating?

So, moles have big paws for digging, and even though they have weak eyes, they have a strong sense of smell. Do you see how the mole is suited to its underground habitat?

The Desert Habitat

Let's look at the desert, which is a very different habitat from woodlands. Can you think of some differences between woodlands and the desert?

This lizard is returning to her home in the Kalahari Desert of South Africa

A Giant Saguaro cactus

Woodland is often cool. The desert is often hot. Woodland is moist. The desert is dry. Woodland is dark and shady. The desert is bright and sunny.

Sometimes it snows and rains in woodland, but it rarely does in the desert. Compared to woodland, the desert is a very different habitat for plants and animals. So, do you think you'll find the same kind of animals and plants in the desert that you found in the wood?

Lizards live in the hot desert. Their bodies do well in the heat. They like to lie on warm rocks and bask in the blazing sunshine. Cactus plants also grow in the desert. They can grow for a long time without any rain at all. They like heat and a lot of sunshine. Cactus plants and lizards do well in the desert habitat.

But not many animals or plants live in the desert. In fact, the desert is almost deserted – which is how it got its name.

Water Habitats

Can you name some animals that live in water?

Fish live in water, such as ponds, lakes and streams. They eat smaller fish, plants and insects. Think of the ways that a fish is suited to its water habitat. Fish don't have feet, because they don't walk. They live in a water habitat, and so they swim. You can't breathe underwater, but fish can because they have gills. But a fish out of water is in trouble! A fish can't survive outside its water habitat.

This Grey Heron by the Thames in London has a long neck that helps it reach fish under water.

291

Have you ever heard the saying 'like a fish out of water'? Since fish can't breathe out of water, people use this saying to mean that someone is very uncomfortable in a new or unusual situation.

For example, a shy child who is asked to sing a song in front of the whole school might think: 'I don't want to sing in front of all those people. I've never been onstage before. I'd feel like a fish out of water.'

Many other animals do best in a water habitat, too. Some live all their lives underwater, like oysters and starfish. Some live part of their lives underwater and part on land, like frogs and salamanders. Some live on the land near the water, like herons and hermit crabs. All of these animals depend upon the water, the plants and the other animals nearby.

Not all water habitats are the same. Ponds, lakes and rivers are different from oceans. Do you know why? If you've ever played in the waves at the seaside, you know how that water tastes: very salty. Oceans contain salt water. But most ponds, lakes and rivers contain fresh water. What's the difference?

Shark!

Here's an experiment to answer that question. Fill a glass with drinking water. Take a sip. It tastes refreshing. That's the kind of water found in most lakes and rivers.

Now stir in two teaspoonfuls of salt. Take a sip – a very small sip. Yuck! You wouldn't call that refreshing, would you? That glass now contains salt water, like the water in the ocean.

You may not like the taste of salt water, but many plants and animals depend upon it to live. Clams, oysters and jellyfish live in the salty ocean, along with plants such as seaweed. Whales, dolphins, sharks – and all the animals that live in an ocean habitat – need salt water. If you put them into water without salt, they wouldn't survive. And if you put a freshwater fish in salt water, it wouldn't survive. Each water animal and plant needs to be in the kind of water habitat to which it's suited.

The Food Chain

As you've learned about different habitats, you've heard a lot about animals and what they eat. Has it made you hungry? You've got to eat to live. Not just you, but every living thing needs food to survive. Plants make their own food out of sunshine, air, water and nutrients from the soil in which they grow. But animals can't do that. Animals eat other living things, including plants and other animals. Big animals may eat little ones. And when the big animal dies, it may be eaten by little animals. All this eating is called the food chain. Let's see how it works.

Imagine a green plant growing by the side of a river. A caterpillar comes along and chews on the leaves. Later the caterpillar grows into a flying insect. The insect flies across the river, when suddenly, swoosh, a fish leaps out of the water and swallows it.

A food chain

The fish splashes back into the water, feeling full and happy – but not for long. A big bear reaches into the river and grabs the fish in his paw. The bear has caught a tasty supper.

Later that year the bear dies, and through the winter its body rots away. The rotting body turns to nutrients that soak into the soil by the side of the river. When spring comes, the nutrients help green plants grow. One of those green plants grows by the side of the river. A caterpillar comes along and chews on the leaves and...

Do you see? It's a cycle, starting again, and going round and round. It's a cycle of one creature feeding upon another, a cycle of life and death and life again.

People call this cycle the food chain because it seems to link together the plants and animals in nature. Animals eat plants, and these animals are sometimes eaten by other animals. Plants and animals die and rot, which returns nutrients to the soil, which helps more plants grow. It's all a part of the food chain that keeps nature alive, and it all starts with plants growing from sunshine, air, water and nutrients.

Animals and Plants Need Their Habitats, So Be Careful

You've seen that there are many different kinds of habitats and many different kinds of animals and plants in each one. Different plants are suited to different habitats: an oak tree thrives in the forest but could not grow in the desert. Most animals are so well suited to living in one kind of habitat that it would be difficult for them to live in another. They might not be able to find the right kind of food, or the right kind of water, or the materials they need to make a home or nest.

Sometimes people can mess up a habitat. People cut down forests to get trees for timber or to make space for new houses and office buildings. People bring water to the desert so that they can make more farms. People drain ponds so that they can build houses.

The orangutan is endangered

What happens to the animals and plants when their habitat is destroyed? Sometimes they die.

In one habitat, the world's rainforests, many animals and plants are in danger. That's because people are cutting down too many trees in the rainforests. Rainforests are tall, dense green forests that grow in the hottest parts of the world. They are called rainforests because there is always moisture in the air, and it drips off the leaves as if it were always raining. Not many people live in the rainforests, but thousands of different plants and animals do. We need to be careful not to hurt this precious habitat or we will lose even more of the animals and plants that live there.

When a habitat is destroyed, plants and animals die. When something happens that causes all of a certain kind of plant or animal to die off, then we say that kind of plant or animal is extinct, which means it no longer exists anywhere in the world: it has died off, never to be seen again.

You may know about some very famous extinct animals: the dinosaurs. They became extinct millions of years ago. We think this happened when a big rock from space hit the Earth and caused the climate to change suddenly. Dinosaurs, and many other animals, could not survive the change in their habitat. But extinction is not just something that happened millions or thousands or even hundreds

The jaguar is in danger of becoming extinct

of years ago. Today many different kinds of animals and plants are endangered, which means that there are not many of them left in the world and they are in danger of becoming extinct. They are sometimes endangered because of things that people do to hurt their habitats: things like cutting down trees or polluting the land and water.

If people make problems, they can also solve them. Jane Goodall, whose biography you may have read in Year 1, and the youth who are members of her Roots and Shoots programme work to make the world a better place for animals, people and the environment. Many people today understand that it is not a good thing to destroy the habitats of plants and animals. These people are working to make sure that we find ways to protect the different habitats and the living things that depend on them.

Extinct but Still Popular: Dinosaurs

They haven't been around for millions of years, but many people are crazy about them. How about you? Do you like dinosaurs?

Some dinosaurs, like the huge Brachiosaurus [BRAK-ee-uh-SAWR-us], were taller than a house. Like many dinosaurs, the Brachiosaurus was a herbivore (which means it ate only what?). Other dinosaurs were carnivores: they ate animal flesh, including other dinosaurs. One fierce carnivore was the Tyrannosaurus Rex.

Dinosaurs have been extinct for so long that no one has ever seen one. So how do we know they ever lived at all? Because dinosaur bones have been found in the ground all around the world. From these remains, scientists can work out a lot about what dinosaurs looked like and how they lived.

To learn more about dinosaurs, look in your local library for the many good books in the Suggested Resources section on page 337 that will tell you more about these fascinating creatures.

Dinosaur bones at London's Natural History Museum

Oceans and Undersea Life

The Oceans and the Tides

Take a look at a globe or a map of the world and notice how much of its area is covered in water. How much? A lot! Water covers three-quarters of the earth.

Where will you find most of this water? In the big oceans and smaller seas. Look at a globe or world map and see if you can find these big oceans: the Pacific Ocean, the Atlantic Ocean, the Indian Ocean and the Arctic Ocean.

The place where the sea meets the land is called the shore. If you've ever walked along the seashore, you may have noticed that sometimes the water comes high up on the shore, and sometimes it stays farther out.

Low tide. High tide.

Every day, twice a day, in a regular pattern, the level of the sea rises and falls as it meets the shore. These changes are called the tides. If you were to spend a day on the beach (wouldn't that be nice?), you could see how the tide changes from high to low and back again. At high tide, the edge of the sea comes way up, covering the beach, so that, if it is a sandy beach, all you see is a little stretch of sand. At low tide, the water level drops and the edge of the sea moves farther away, leaving a broad sandy beach. At high tide, that beach is covered with water.

Ocean Currents

The water in the oceans moves all the time. The wind moves it and forms the surface into waves. The tides move it, up towards the shore and back down again.

In some parts of the ocean, water moves in great streams, almost like rivers flowing through the ocean. We call these moving streams ocean currents. When ship captains sail the ocean, they pay close attention to currents because a current can carry a ship along with it, just as a river carries a stick or a paper boat downstream.

When ship captains sail across the Atlantic Ocean, they pay special attention to a current called the Gulf Stream. The Gulf Stream runs from the Gulf of Mexico, up the coast of Florida, and then north up the coast of the United States before it crosses the Atlantic Ocean and makes its way towards Europe. The weather in Britain is warmer and wetter because of the Gulf Stream. Use your finger on the map to trace the path of the Gulf Stream.

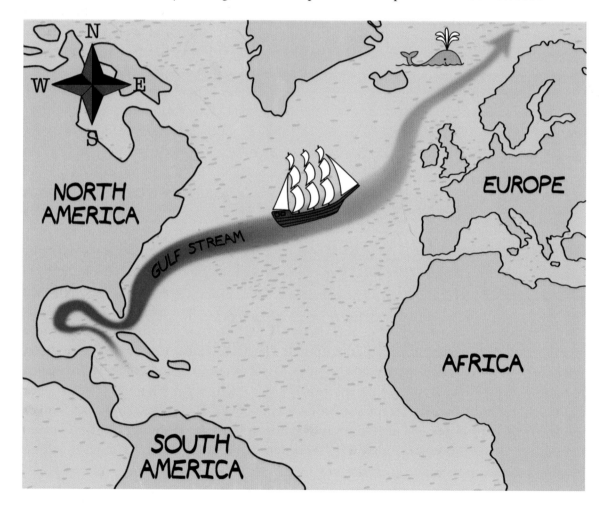

The water in the Gulf Stream is warmer than the ocean it flows through. If a ship sailing out of Florida wants to go due east, the Gulf Stream will push it to the north. So, if you were steering the ship, you would have to know about the strong currents of the Gulf Stream if you planned to get where you wanted to go!

Under the Sea

Let's have a look beneath the surface of the ocean. Put on your scuba-diving gear. Is your mask on tight? Are the air tanks full? Okay, let's jump in!

Look at the ground under the water. The sandy beach continues to slope down. We call the bottom of the sea the sea bed. Where the sea is shallow, the sea bed is close to the water's surface. Sometimes the seabed rises out of the water, and that makes an island. Where the wider ocean is deep, the ocean floor drops a long way down. Long, deep valleys run across it. The deepest valleys are called ocean trenches. You can think of the ocean floor as a landscape of mountains, valleys and trenches, stretching out for thousands of miles underwater.

The ocean floor has hills and valleys just like the dry parts of the earth

So many different animals live in the sea. Can you name some? Did you think of fish, sharks, dolphins, octopuses and others? Did you know that if you scoop up a handful of sea water, you're holding quite a few living creatures? These creatures are so tiny that you can't see them. It would seem as if you were holding just a handful of water, but really the water is full of little living things! There's a special name for all these teeny-tiny animals, along with many teeny-tiny plants, that drift in the sea: they're called plankton.

This is one of many kinds of plankton that live in the sea. This picture was taken with a special camera to make the plankton big enough to see

The sea is home not only to teeny-tiny plankton but also to some of the world's largest creatures. Can you name any of these big ocean-going creatures? Did you think of whales? The Blue Whale, the

How big is a blue whale? Compare it to an elephant.

biggest whale of all, can grow to 30 metres long and weigh almost 180,000 kilograms. It's hard to imagine how big that is! If about thirty children your size were to lie down in a line, head to toe, they might add up to the length of a blue whale. But to add up to the weight of a blue whale, it would take about seven thousand children your size!

There's a food chain for animals and plants in the sea, just as there is for animals and plants on land. One ocean food chain is amazing: some whales eat only plankton. Think about it: some of the biggest ocean animals eat only some of the smallest plants and animals! How would you like to have the same thing every day for breakfast, lunch, dinner and snacks, and never see what you're swallowing?

Humans and the Marine World

People all over the world depend upon the sea. Ships travel on the oceans, moving things from one continent to another. Fishermen catch food in the sea for us to eat. Tuna comes from the ocean. So do prawns. And many people around the world enjoy eating some kinds of seaweed.

The sea helps the world's people. It has many different habitats for many different plants and animals. It helps the planet earth stay healthy. That's why people have to be careful not to do things to harm the sea.

People can harm the sea by putting the wrong things in it, like rubbish and litter. Sometimes people put things in by accident. When an oil tanker leaks oil into the sea, the surface of the water turns black and dingy. An oil slick kills many fish and birds. It also kills plankton, which may be too small to see but is important to the habitat. When an accident like an oil spill happens, people may come quickly to the rescue, but such a big mess is very hard to clean up.

People can also harm the sea by taking too much from it. For example, fishermen can 'overfish' if they catch the same kind of fish for a long time in one small region. Sometimes, if fishermen catch too many of one kind of fish, not enough fish are left behind to have babies, and then that kind of fish can become extinct. When one kind of fish disappears, it can disturb the lives of other animals and plants living in that part of the sea. Today many countries have laws telling people how many fish they are allowed to catch and during what time of the year people can catch them. These laws are one way to keep overfishing from damaging the habitat forever.

This gannet is having a bubble bath to get cleaned up after an oil spill

The Human Body

> **PARENTS:** In this book, we introduce the major body systems. Later books in this series present the body systems in greater detail.

Have you ever thought about what happens inside your body when you breathe? When you eat? When you stand up? When you jump? When you run? Your body can do so many things! Different parts of your body work together to let you breathe, eat, stand up, jump, run and do lots more. Let's find out about what's going on inside. Let's learn about some of the systems of your body.

The Skeletal System

There are more than two hundred bones inside you

Hold up a jacket by the collar. It just falls limp. Now, put the jacket over a coat hanger. The hard coat hanger gives the soft jacket a shape.

Inside your body there's something that gives you a shape. No, not a bundle of coat hangers, but a bundle of bones – more than two hundred of them! These bones make up your skeleton. Your skeleton is the hard part inside your body. It looks something like the drawings you might see around Halloween time.

Squeeze one of your fingers: do you feel the hard bone inside? Now, tap your head with your knuckles – not too hard! The sound you hear is the sound of the bone inside your finger knocking against your skull, which is the bone inside your head.

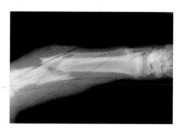

This is an X-ray of a broken arm bone

Bones are hard, but they can break, such as when a person falls badly. Doctors can mend most broken bones. They use a special machine called an X-ray machine.

An X-ray machine takes a picture through your skin and lets the doctor see the broken bone. Often the doctor will wrap the injured part of the body in a hard cast, which will protect the broken bone and keep it straight until it grows back together again.

This girl is getting a cast put on to her broken arm

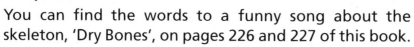

You can find the words to a funny song about the skeleton, 'Dry Bones', on pages 226 and 227 of this book.

302

The Muscular System

Squeeze one of your arms and you can feel the solid bone inside. You feel something firm around it, too, that's a muscle.

Muscles wrap around bones and stretch from one bone to another. Hold one hand under your arm, between your wrist and your elbow. Make a tight fist with the arm that you're holding. Do you feel something tighten up inside? That's your muscle. Muscles make you move. You use your muscles to walk, run, jump, draw, stretch and lift. You even use your muscles to talk, yawn, laugh, wink and sing.

Your muscles help you move

The Circulatory System

Now put your hand on your chest. Do you feel something beating inside? If you don't, run around quickly and then try again. That beating you feel is a very important muscle: it's your heart. Your heart is beating all the time, day and night. When your heart beats, it pumps blood. It pumps blood through tubes that go all around your body and then come back to your heart. By beat-beat-beating, your heart keeps the blood circulating to every part of your body. ('Circulating' means going round and round.)

The Digestive System

Your blood carries good things from the food you eat to all parts of your body. But how did your food get into your blood?

Your circulatory system moves your blood around your body

It got there because your body digested it. Whatever you eat – a burger, a banana, a plate of rice, a jam sandwich, a carrot, a glass of milk, an egg roll – your body has to digest it. Here is how that happens. When you put a piece of food in your mouth, you chew it with your teeth, which break

303

the food into little pieces. There's a watery fluid in your mouth called saliva that also helps break down the food. When you swallow, the food goes down a tube into your stomach. (When you drink something, you just swallow, and the liquid you're drinking goes down the same tube to your stomach.)

After you eat, have you ever heard your stomach make some squishy, gurgling noises? These noises show that your stomach and other body parts are continuing the work of digesting your food.

Once your food is digested, it's broken into very tiny bits. The most valuable parts go into your blood and give you the energy you need to do all the things you like to do. Your body cannot use some parts of the food you eat; you get rid of these when you go to the loo.

Your digestive system breaks your food down so your body can use it

The Nervous System

Tap your head – gently! – with your knuckles one more time. There's your skull. Do you know what's inside it? A very important part of your body: your brain.

Your brain is what you use to think, remember and learn. Your brain tells the rest of your body what to do. Your brain is in charge: it's like the captain of a ship or the pilot of an aeroplane.

Your brain sends messages to all parts of your body and gets messages back. These messages are carried through the nerves, which go from your brain all through your body. The nerves look something like the branches of a tree, but they're much thinner.

Your nervous system carries messages to and from your brain

Your nerves carry messages from your five senses.

Do you remember learning about your five senses in the Year 1 book in this series? Can you name them?

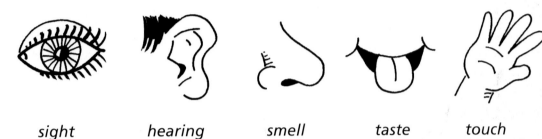

sight   hearing   smell   taste   touch

When you feel an itch on the tip of your nose, nerves are sending a message from your nose to your brain. Then your brain sends a message along the nerves to your fingers. The message says: 'Reach up and scratch that itchy nose.' Ahh, does that feel better? Nerves sent that 'feel-better' message from your nose back to your brain.

In Sickness and in Health

Ah-choo! Wow, that was a big sneeze. Well, that's okay, it was just one and – ah-choo! ah-choo!

Uh-oh. You can't stop sneezing. Your nose is runny. You're starting to feel a little hot. And maybe your tummy aches.

Everybody gets ill now and then. It's no fun. You can feel just terrible.

Some germs can make your body unwell. You can't see germs, but you can certainly feel what the bad ones do to you! When your body gets ill, it fights the germs. Sometimes when your body is working really hard to fight the germs, you have a fever – which means that your body's temperature rises.

Many illnesses, like colds and flu, can be spread from one person to another. If a friend with a cold sneezes right in your face, his cold germs could get into your body through your nose and mouth. Then, in a few days, you might catch that cold, too.

Try not to spread your germs: cover your face when you sneeze or cough. Use tissues when you blow your nose. Wash your hands after using the toilet and before every meal. Your hands can pick up many germs without you even knowing it.

Sometimes when you're ill, you go to a doctor. The doctor may use a thermometer to check your temperature. She may ask you to open your mouth wide and say 'Ah' so that she can look down at your throat. (What's down there? Ask an adult to let you look inside.) The doctor may listen to your heartbeat with a tool called a stethoscope. The doctor may decide that you need medicine to help you get better. Never take any medicine without permission, and only take as much as you are supposed to. Sometimes the doctor may give you an injection. You may not like it, but be brave: the injection helps your body fight the disease.

When you were very young, you probably got a special kind of injection called a vaccination. You didn't get this injection because you were ill. You got a vaccination to help keep you from falling ill with certain bad diseases.

Edward Jenner and Louis Pasteur discovered a lot about how to keep people from falling ill. You can find out more about them on pages 330 to 333.

Vaccination injections might hurt a little, but they help you for a long time.

Take Care of Your Body

It's almost dinner time at Billy's house. Have you ever heard anything like this?

MOTHER: Billy, dinner will be ready in a few minutes. Wash your hands.
BILLY: Okay, just let me finish making this last mud-pie.
MOTHER: Billy, come to the table, dinner's ready.
BILLY [sitting down at table]: Yum, I'm starving, let's eat.
MOTHER: Billy, did you wash your hands?
BILLY: Oh, Mum, come on!

MOTHER: Billy, go and wash your hands before you eat.
BILLY: But Mum, they're clean. I washed them yesterday!

To stay healthy and strong, you've got to do what adults keep telling you to do:

- Wash your hands after using the toilet and before every meal.

- Eat foods that are good for you (and don't overdo the 'junk food').

- Get plenty of exercise.

- Have a regular bath or shower.

- Get a good night's sleep.

Did you hear that, Billy?

Matter: Solid, Liquid and Gas

What do these things have in common: an apple, a river and the air we breathe?

They may seem very different, but they're alike in one way: they are all made of matter.

Matter is the stuff that makes up all the things in the world. Your shoes, a flower, an egg, a dog, a rock, a tyre, a book, a cloud, a goldfish, an aeroplane, a pencil – matter makes up each of these things, and everything else as well. Matter even makes up your body.

Let's go back to our first three examples: an apple, a river and the air we breathe. You can see and touch the matter in an apple. It's solid. Can you think of some other matter that's solid? How about a rock? A football? Your shoes?

You can see and touch the matter in a river, too. It's not solid, though, or hard like a rock. It's liquid. Can you think of some other matter that's liquid? Such as milk? Or the saliva in your mouth?

Now, what about the air we breathe? It's different: it's not a solid or a liquid. You can't see it. You can't reach out and touch it. But sometimes you can feel it, like when the wind blows. When you feel the wind blowing on your face, you are feeling the matter in the air. And think about this: when you blow up a balloon, what goes inside? Some stuff goes into the balloon and makes it bigger. That stuff is air, and air is matter. But air is a different kind of matter: it's not a solid or a liquid. Air is a gas.

Activity 1: Air is matter

Get Ready

You will need:

a cork

a clear plastic drinking cup or a glass

a bowl deeper than the cup

tissues or paper towels

> **PARENTS:** Here are two experiments you can do with your child to see that air is matter.

Go

1. Put water in the bowl but not quite to the top. Ask your child to drop in the cork and describe what happens: it floats. Have your child use her hand to push the cork to the bottom of the bowl, then let it go. What happens? It pops back up and floats again. Now take the clear plastic cup (or glass). Ask your child to lower it over the cork. What happens? The level of the water underneath the cup goes down, while the cork is still floating on the top of the water. Ask your child: 'Why do you think this happens? What is pushing the surface of the water down?' (The air in the cup is pushing the surface of the water down. Air is matter!)

2. Leave the water in the bowl but remove the cork. Dry the cup or glass. Now crumple a few tissues or paper towels (if you use paper towels, first tear them into strips). Stuff the crumpled paper into the bottom of the cup. The paper should stay firmly in the bottom of the cup when you turn it over. Have your child confirm that the paper in the bottom of the cup is dry. Now put the cup (open end first) into the bowl of water. Push it down until the rim of the cup touches the bottom of the bowl. Pull the cup straight out of the water, making sure to keep the open end pointing straight down. Let the water drip off the cup, and then turn it over. Check the paper in the bottom of the cup. It should still be dry. Why? Ask your child: 'What do you think kept the paper from getting wet?' (The air in the cup.)

Far too small to see : Atoms

All matter, everything in the world, is made up of tiny building blocks called atoms and molecules. They are much too small to see until you get many of them together. A molecule is a group of atoms arranged in a pattern. Even simple things like water, sand, air, gas for cooking, sugar and petrol need the atoms to be in a pattern, making a molecule, for you to tell what they are.

The atoms in a fork or the molecules in sugar are held tightly together. That's how you can pick up a fork or a grain of sugar. Even one grain still contains many, many molecules. You need a glass or a bowl holding water to stop it all running away, because water is liquid and the molecules are looser. The molecules in air are much looser still, so you need to tie the neck of a balloon to stop the air gases getting out.

Changing States of Matter

Matter doesn't always stay in the same state. Now, 'state' here doesn't mean a place like the United States of America. This is a different kind of state – the states of matter, which you've just learned the names of: solid, liquid and gas. Matter can change from one state to another. A solid can become a liquid. A liquid can become a gas. Let's see how matter can change states.

We can do this by looking at a cup of water. If you put some water in a cup, what state of matter is the water in? Yes, it's a liquid.

If you put that cup of water into a freezer and leave it overnight, what will be its state of matter? The water freezes and becomes ice. The liquid has turned into a solid.

Now let the cup of frozen water sit for a few hours. What happens? The ice melts: the solid has turned back into a liquid. Now take the cup of water, pour it into a pan, and put it on the stove. Ask an adult to help you heat the pan. Don't get too close, but watch what happens. The water begins to boil. Soon it bubbles as steam. The liquid water has turned to gas. Careful – steam is very hot!

If you boil the water for a long time, eventually all the water will turn to steam and the pan will be empty. Where has the water gone? It has been turned into a gas – steam – and has mixed with the air in the room. Now the water is part of the matter that makes up the air in the room.

Water can be a solid, a liquid, or a gas.
Can you point to and name each of them in this picture?

Units of Measurement

What is this girl measuring?

You know that everything is made of matter. Sometimes we need to know things about matter. We need to know how much of something there is, or how much something weighs, or how big or little something is. To find out all this, we need to take some measurements.

Measuring things is a way to use numbers to say how big or small things are, or how heavy or light, or how hot or cold. Has anyone ever measured how tall you are? Has anyone ever measured how much you weigh?

You know how important measurements are if you've ever helped somebody bake a cake. When you bake a cake, you have to measure out each ingredient carefully. You use a cake tin that's a certain size, and you heat the oven to a certain temperature. Every step of the way, you use numbers and make measurements.

Here's a recipe for chocolate cake. But something is wrong with it.

175 sugar	175 butter
2 eggs	50 cocoa powder
175 flour	1 baking powder
½ salt	1 vanilla extract

Mix the sugar and butter together in a large bowl until soft. Add all other ingredients; then put the mixture in a round cake tin 18 across. Bake at 180 for 45.

Do you see what's wrong with the recipe? Could you mix and bake this cake? You would begin by measuring out 175 – 175 what? – of sugar. 175 teaspoons? 175 kilograms? 175 tonnes?! The cake will taste very different, depending on how much sugar you add.

Is the cake tin 18 centimetres across, or 18 metres? Centimetres and metres are both units for measuring length. Now do you bake the cake for 45 minutes or 45 days or 45 years? Minutes, days and years are all units for measuring time.

Now do you see what's wrong with the recipe? Somebody forgot to write in the units of measurement. Measuring means counting, but you have to know what you're counting. To make sense, every measurement needs a number and a unit.

Let's look at the cake recipe as it should be, with numbers and units of measurement:

175 grams sugar	175 grams butter
2 eggs	50 grams cocoa powder
175 grams flour	1 teaspoon baking powder
½ teaspoon salt	1 teaspoon vanilla extract

Mix the sugar and butter together in a large bowl until soft. Add all other ingredients; then put the mixture in round cake tin 18 centimetres across. Bake at 180 degrees Celsius for 45 minutes.

Now that makes more sense. Sounds yummy, too!

How Long? How Tall?

How tall are you? Look back at the cake recipe: are there any units of measurement in it that will help you answer that question? Are you 100 grams tall? No. Are you three teaspoons tall? No. But what about centimetres? Yes, now we're, talking!

To tell how tall you are, most likely you'll use centimetres or metres. Centimetres and metres measure length. You might also use a different set of units of measurement called inches and feet. Inches and feet measure length, too.

PARENTS: Show your child a metre rule (you can also use a tape measure) and discuss the units of measurement: centimetres and metres (100 centimetres) as well as inches, if the ruler shows them. Give him some different objects or distances to measure. For each one, have him say before measuring whether he thinks centimetres or metres would be a better unit of measurement. Then have him do the actual measuring (he may need some help from you). With each object, be sure that your child lines up the end of each ruler with the object that he's measuring. Here are some suggestions for things to measure:

● The length of your child's shoe (centimetres)

● The distance from one room to another (metres)

● The length of an envelope for a letter (centimetres)

● The height of the front door (metres)

● The height of your child (centimetres and metres)

How Much Space Does it Fill?

Pretend that you're at the supermarket. You need to buy some milk. How much milk do you need to buy? What units of measurement could you use to answer that question?

You remember metres and centimetres are some of the units we use to measure length. But if you want to know how much milk to buy, do you think about how long the milk is? Do you think, 'I need fifteen centimetres of milk'? No: you're not thinking about how long the milk is, but how much space it takes up.

We can use many different units to measure how much space something takes up. For example, when you shop for milk, you can buy a pint bottle. Or you can buy a litre carton. You could buy two pint bottles, but it might be easier to buy a one-litre carton: that's because two pints is about the same as one litre (actually it is a bit more).

Every litre carton holds the same amount of milk. Even if litre containers have different labels and come from different companies, they hold the same amount: one litre. That's why units of measurement work: because we all agree on them.

Tablespoons and Millilitres

Another unit for measuring how much space something takes up is a tablespoon. Because tablespoons are usually a particular size and we all agree on how much one tablespoon is, you can be pretty sure that, if you're baking a cake that calls for a tablespoon of baking powder, the cake will rise by just the right amount if you use exactly a tablespoon. This is because you and the person who wrote the recipe both agree on how much a tablespoon is.

Let's find out how many tablespoons are needed to fill a space of 100 millilitres. A millilitre is another unit for measuring the space something takes. Millilitres are much, much smaller than litres and so are good for measuring small spaces just like tablespoons.

Try this somewhere that you can splash a little water. You will need a large bowl, a litre measuring jug, a tablespoon and an empty 100 millilitre container. Often yoghurts, liquid soaps and shampoos come in 100 millilitre containers. A funnel might also come in handy.

Fill the bowl with water. Now dip the tablespoon into the bowl of water, measure out one tablespoon of water and carefully pour the water into the 100 millilitre container (try not to spill). Do this again and again until the container is full. How many tablespoons of water are in 100 millilitres? Did you count around six or seven tablespoons?

Now use the 100 millilitre container to measure water and empty it into the litre measuring jug. Repeat this until the water reaches up to the 1 litre measure on the jug. How many times did you have to fill the 100 millilitre container to reach 1 litre? Was it 10?

Temperature: How Hot? How Cold?

PARENTS: In this book, we introduce temperature only as measured in degrees Celsius. Later books in this series will introduce your child to both degrees Celsius and Fahrenheit.

Before you get in a bath, you might stick your finger in the water to see whether it's too cold, too hot or just right. When you do this, you're checking the temperature. But fingers aren't really a very good way to measure temperature. Some things, like a hot oven, are too hot to touch. So, when we want to know how hot or cold something is, we use a thermometer. Thermometers help us to measure the temperature in units called degrees.

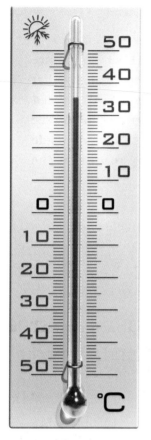

When you go to a doctor's surgery, the doctor or a nurse might use a special kind of thermometer to take your temperature. If you're healthy, your temperature will be 37 degrees, or close to that. If you're ill and have a fever, your temperature might be 38 or 39 degrees.

We use a different kind of thermometer to tell us the temperature of the air around us. Look at the picture of a weather thermometer. A weather thermometer has a tube running up and down its centre, usually with red or silver liquid in it. This liquid goes higher in the tube when the temperature gets warmer. And when the temperature gets cooler, the liquid goes – what do you think? – that's right, lower. To read the thermometer, you find where the liquid has stopped, then you look over to see the number nearest to the top of the liquid. Can you read the temperature on the thermometer in the picture? It's 35 degrees. If the thermometer reaches 35 degrees, you'll be perspiring. That's a very hot day!

Can you find 18 on the thermometer? 18 degrees is a comfortable temperature – for most people, it's not too hot and not too cold. Older people often prefer a slightly warmer room temperature, perhaps around 21. Can you find that on the thermometer? Now, can you find 30?

Can you find 0 (zero)? If you put a glass of water outside on a day on which the temperature is 0 degrees or lower, do you know what will happen to the water? The water will freeze: it will turn to ice. So, if the temperature outside is 0 degrees, wrap up before you go out because it's freezing outside!

Can you find -5 on the thermometer? Only on the really cold days in the winter does it ever get so cold that we have to use those numbers below 0 on the thermometer. Those are the days when we say the temperature is 'below zero'.

Activity 2: Taking the Temperature

PARENTS: In this activity it is fine for your child to read the temperature (with your help) to the nearest degree Celsius. If your thermometer has both Fahrenheit and Celsius scales, you can explain the Fahrenheit scale if you wish, or tell your child that the degrees Fahrenheit are 'different units of measurement that we'll learn about a little later'.

Use a thermometer like the one in the picture on the opposite page. Be very careful with it because some parts may be glass and easy to break. Take the temperature indoors. What is it? Now put the thermometer in a glass of iced water. What happens to the coloured liquid in the thermometer? About how cold is the iced water? Now put the thermometer in a bowl of warm (not hot) water: can you see the liquid rise? About how warm is the water? Next, take the thermometer outside and wait until the coloured liquid stays in one place. Can you read what the temperature is outside?

Electricity:
An Introduction to the Shocking Facts

Look around the room and see how many things you can turn on and off. Is there a light with a light switch? Is there a mobile phone, or a television, or maybe a computer? Is there a toy that uses batteries and moves or makes a noise when you turn it on?

All of these things use electricity. Electricity is the power that makes them work. Electricity makes them shine, beep, show pictures or move around.

Static Electricity

Everything in the world, even your body, carries a little bit of electricity in it. Have you ever combed your hair and noticed the hairs on your head standing up as you pull the comb away? That's electricity. Have you ever rubbed a balloon against your shirt, then pressed it against the wall and watched it stick? That's electricity, too.

There's a special name for this electrical attraction between a comb and your hair, or between the balloon and the wall. It's called static electricity. Maybe you have walked across a room and touched somebody's hand and felt a little zap! That also happens because of static electricity. If it happens in a dark room, you might see a little flash of light. That little zap of static electricity works the same way as a lightning bolt streaking through the sky in a thunderstorm. But the lightning bolt is a lot more powerful!

On and Off

Thanks to electricity, light bulbs shine and mobile phones ring when they receive a call. When you turn on a light at home or at school, you are letting electricity flow through wires all the way to the light bulb. Where does the electricity come from? Probably from a power station miles away, where big machines generate the electricity and send it through wires to your home and school and lots of other places.

A big power station makes the electricity used in this home.

What happens when you turn on a light? Let's find out by looking at a small model. Look at the picture and find these parts: the battery, wire, switch and the light bulb.

Look at the battery in the picture with the zigzag electric bolt on it. The battery is like a little electric power factory. It uses chemicals to make electricity. (Never try to open a battery! The chemicals inside could hurt you.)

Do you see the wire? Use your finger to follow the path of the wire. It goes from one end of the battery to a switch. Then it goes from the switch to a light bulb. Then it goes from the light bulb back to the other end of the battery. The wire has to be connected to both ends of the battery to make the electricity flow.

Let's follow the electricity on its path from one end of the battery to the light bulb. Put your finger on the picture of the battery. The electricity from the battery flows through the wire, rather like water flowing through a hose. Move your finger along the wire until you get to the switch. What happens when the electricity gets to the switch? That depends on whether the switch is turned 'off' or 'on'.

If the switch is 'on' then the electricity can continue along its path to the bulb. But if the switch is 'off', then the path is broken.

Here's a way to imagine what happens when the electricity reaches the switch. Pretend that you are walking along a path. You come to a river, and there you find that there's no bridge: the path is broken, so you can't keep going. But now, pretend there is a bridge: now there's no break in the path, and you can continue on your way.

That's like what happens with electricity: as it travels along the wire, it comes to the switch. If the switch is turned 'off', it's like there's no bridge: the electricity cannot continue along the path to the light bulb. But when the switch is turned 'on', it's like there is a bridge: the electricity can keep right on going from the battery, through the wire, through the turned-on switch, through more wire, and to the bulb. When electricity flows through the light bulb, the bulb lights up. What a bright idea!

Who invented a light bulb and a whole lot more? You can find out about Thomas Edison on page 333.

Conductors

Electricity flows through some materials but not through others. Materials that allow electricity to flow through them are called conductors: they 'conduct' electricity. Copper is a very good conductor of electricity. If you look at a cord running from a lamp or radio, you'll see a plastic covering, but inside that covering is copper wire. (Do not try to take the plastic covering off! It is there to protect you from the electricity in the wires, which can hurt you.)

Activity 3: An experiment: what conducts?

PARENTS: This experiment will require your time and assistance. The components of a simple tabletop electrical system like the one described below are often available at electronics and hobby shops.

Get Ready

You will need:

2 batteries

a double battery holder

a bulb and bulb holder

3 wires

2 crocodile clips

various items, such as: a pencil, a shoelace, a metal spoon, a plastic utensil, a piece of paper, a safety pin, a crayon, a rubber band, a penny, a paper clip

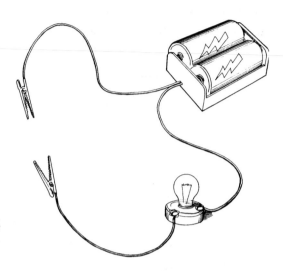

Go

Begin by connecting the batteries, the bulb, the wires and the crocodile clips as shown in the picture.

Next clip the two crocodile clips together. The light bulb should light up. When the crocodile clips touch, you are making a pathway going from the batteries, through the light bulb, and back to the batteries again. Now pull the crocodile clips apart. What happens? Why does the light go out?

You can use this system to test what things are good conductors of electricity. Let's test many things, such as a pencil, a shoelace, a metal spoon, a plastic utensil, a piece of paper, a safety pin, a crayon, a rubber band, a penny and a paper clip.

To test each item, 'bite' one end with one crocodile clip, then attach the other crocodile clip to the other end. If the object you are testing is a good conductor, what do you think will happen? The electricity will flow from the batteries, through the wires, through the object you are testing, to the bulb. If the object conducts electricity, the bulb will light up. You can make a chart of everything you test. Make two columns: on one side, put 'Conductors'. On the other side put items that 'Do Not Conduct'. What do you find? Does plastic conduct electricity? What about paper? Do most things made of metal conduct electricity?

Safety Rules Around Electricity

A little battery puts out a little bit of electricity, so you can use it safely for your experiments. But the electricity that comes through the wires in your house or school is much more powerful, so you need to remember some safety rules.

Inside the walls where you live or go to school, there are big wires that carry electricity. When you plug in a light or radio or other electrical appliance, you are putting the light or radio in the pathway of the electricity. You have heard adults say: 'Don't stick your finger into the socket on the wall!' Now do you know why? If you did, you would become part of the electrical pathway. Your body is a pretty good conductor of electricity. The electrical current coming through the wires to the wall outlet is so strong that it would hurt a lot if you stuck your finger in the socket.

What if you held a piece of metal, like a fork or knife, and stuck it into the socket? Don't do it! Why? Because metals conduct electricity, and you would get a terrible shock!

Another rule you may have heard is: 'Don't touch any electrical appliance when you are wet.' Can you think why? It's because water is a good conductor of electricity. When your hands are wet or when your body is in a bathtub full of water, the electricity could flow right through you and give you an awful shock, or even kill you.

Think: Why should you never put your fingers into the socket where the light bulb screws into a lamp? That's the place where the electricity flows into the light bulb, isn't it? Put your finger in there and it could be you, rather than the light bulb, that becomes part of the electrical pathway. And that would hurt!

Electricity is very useful, but it can be dangerous. Be careful, be safe, be clever. Let electricity help you, not hurt you.

Astronomy:
Our Solar System

Buzz Aldrin walking on the moon

Meet two astronauts. They are some of the many scientists who have flown in powerful rockets to outer space. Helen Sharman was the first British person in outer space. Buzz Aldrin was one of the first people to walk on the moon.

Helen Sharman with her spacesuit

This is how the Earth looked to Buzz when he was on the moon

Far out in space, astronauts can look back and use cameras to take pictures of the Earth. From space, our planet looks like a round ball.

A Star and Nine Planets

Don't you love a sunny day? The sun makes the days bright. The sun may look like a big bright yellow ball. But did you know that the sun is a star? It's like many other stars that you see shining in the sky on a clear night. What makes the sun different from those other stars? The big difference is that the sun is closer to us than any other star. If you could get in a rocket ship and travel far, far out in space, you would see that the sun has planets going around it. Our Earth is only one of those planets. There are eight others: some are closer than we are to the sun, some are farther away. Some are bigger than the Earth, some are smaller. Each planet goes around the sun on its own special path, called an orbit. The sun and the planets that go around it are part of what we call the solar system. Let's take an imaginary rocket ship journey. We'll start near the sun, at the centre of our solar system, and spiral out from there. This really is an imaginary ride, because the sun is so hot you could never fly close to it. The sun is not a solid planet like the Earth. The sun is a huge ball of superhot burning gases. If a rocket really approached the sun, it would melt long before it could land.

Our solar system

As you fly away from the sun, what's the first planet you see? It's the planet Mercury. Mercury is a small planet, and it's the closest planet to the sun.

Next you come to Venus, the second planet from the sun. After that, you see the third planet from the sun – and it looks very familiar! It's Earth, your home planet. Earth is 93 million miles from the sun. That sounds far, but six more planets are even farther away. Better get going!

The fourth planet out from the sun is Mars. Some people nickname Mars 'the red planet' because when you are lucky enough to see it in the night-time sky, it seems to have an orangey, red colour.

Next comes Jupiter, the fifth planet from the sun. Jupiter is the largest planet in our solar system. There's something unusual about Saturn, the sixth planet from the sun. Saturn is surrounded by beautiful rings.

The next two planets, Uranus [YOO-rain-us] and Neptune, are very large compared to Earth. The ninth and last planet, farthest from the sun, is Pluto, the smallest planet in our solar system. Some people call Pluto a dwarf planet because it is so small. Pluto is a super frozen planet, since it's so far from the sun. How far? Three billion miles away – a distance so huge it's hard to imagine!

Hey, you'd better turn that rocket around and head back to Earth at maximum speed! You don't want to be late for dinner!

In Year 3, we will learn more about the Roman gods and goddesses who gave their names to these planets.

The Moon

During your imaginary rocket ship journey, when you passed the Earth, you may have noticed what looked like a ball circling around it. What was that? It's something you know very well: the moon.

The moon that you see in the sky goes around the Earth. You can also say that the moon orbits the Earth, just as the Earth and the other eight planets orbit the sun.

Have you noticed that the moon seems to change shape? Sometimes it's a full moon, with a big round face. Sometimes it's a half-moon, shaped like half of a pizza. Sometimes it's only a thin crescent. Some days, the moon crosses the sky near the sun. We can't see it because the half facing us is much less bright than the sun. When this happens we call it a new moon. We call these different shapes the phases of the moon.

Phases of the moon

The moon only seems to change shape. Really, it's always a big round ball. Sometimes we see the whole ball, and sometimes we only see part of it. We see the part that is lit by the sun. Did you know that the moon itself does not shine? When the moon seems to shine, it's really reflecting light from the sun.

Sometimes when the moon is bright and big in the sky, it might almost seem as if a face is looking down at you. People even jokingly refer to 'the man in the moon'. But there are no people on the moon – no animals or plants either, and no trees, grass or clouds. There is no water or air. Astronauts like Buzz Aldrin who visited the moon had to wear space suits to give them air to breathe. The moon may look lovely but it's not a friendly place to visit.

So far, astronauts have visited the moon, but no astronaut has landed on another planet. Not yet, at least. Who knows what may happen when you grow up? Maybe then astronauts will make a trip to Mars. Maybe you will be one of them!

The Plough

Constellations:
Join-the-Dots Stars

On a clear night, go outside and look up at the stars. For thousands of years, people have enjoyed looking up at the stars. Long ago, people used their imaginations and found pictures among the stars, like big join-the-dots drawings in the sky. They imagined they saw pictures of bears and horses, or a man shooting an arrow. People still look for those join-the-dots pictures today. They are called the constellations.

Here's a constellation you can look for: the Plough. It got that name because it looks like an old-fashioned horse-drawn plough. On a clear night, ask an adult to help point your gaze toward north. In that direction, look for a square of four stars that seem to connect to form the blade of the plough. Then look for three more bright stars that seem to connect to one corner of the blade and form a shaft connecting it to the horse. There are a lot of other stars in the sky near these, but if you just concentrate on the brightest ones, you can see the Plough.

Our Big, Round, Moving Earth

Photographs taken from outer space like the one on page 320 (of the earth rising) show that the earth is a big ball. Then why doesn't it seem round to us? It's because the earth is so large that you don't notice that the ground you're standing on has a curve to it. If the earth were the size of a football, one entire city would be no bigger than a speck of dust. That's why it's hard to get a sense of the vast, curving surface of our earth.

If you could watch a boat sail away from you out into the ocean, where there's nothing but water as far as the eye can see, you could catch a glimpse of the earth's curving surface. As the boat gets farther away, it approaches the place where the sky seems to meet the sea: we call this the horizon. Slowly, the boat seems to sink below the horizon. You see less and less of the boat until finally all you see is the tip of the mast, and then nothing. The boat hasn't sunk or fallen off the earth! It has gone around to part of this big ball of a planet that you can no longer see.

As it sails away, a boat seems to sink below the horizon

Try this: stand up and be as still as you can. It doesn't feel as if the ground beneath your feet is moving, does it? But in fact the earth is spinning around all the time. It spins like a top. And that's not all. As the earth spins around like a top, it is also circling through space in an orbit around the sun. Whoa, we're really moving here!

Hundreds of years ago, people used to believe that the sun went around the earth. It's easy to see why people thought so, because the sun does seem to travel slowly across the sky, from morning to night.

But a man named Nicolaus Copernicus showed people that they had it the wrong way around. The sun doesn't move, said Copernicus; it only looks that way because really the earth is moving, spinning around like a top. To understand Copernicus's idea, try this: look straight ahead of you and spin around very fast. When you do this, things seem to move around you in a circle, but really you are the one doing the moving.

You may hear people talk about the sun rising in the morning and setting in the

The earth spins like a top

evening, which makes it sound as if the sun were moving through our sky. But the sun is not moving. It's the earth that does the moving. The earth spins around one complete turn every day. One complete rotation takes twenty-four hours. The spinning of the earth makes day and night. You can do an experiment to understand how.

We will find out more about Copernicus in Year 4.

Activity 4: An Experiment: What Makes Day and Night?

Get Ready

You will need:

a globe

blue-tack®

a strong light (such as a desk lamp)

Go

Pretend that the globe is the earth.
Take a little piece of blu-tack® and stick it onto the globe. That's you!

Pretend the light is the sun. Shine the light at the middle of the globe. Now make the globe spin slowly. When the sun (the light) shines on you (the blue-tack®), it's daytime. But as the earth continues to spin around, soon the light isn't on you anymore: that's night-time.

What about the people who live on the other side of the earth? Put another piece of blue-tack® on the opposite side of the earth from where you are. Now shine the light on the globe and slowly spin it again. What happens? When it's bright daytime for you, it's night for people on the opposite side of the earth. But when the sun shines on them, you're fast asleep!

Around and around goes the earth, spinning like a top – and that's what makes day and night.

Down to Earth

Let's take a closer look at the third planet from the sun: our home, the earth.

You already know some things about the earth. You know that its surface is covered with land and water. What are the biggest chunks of land called? Yes, the continents. And the biggest bodies of water? Yes, the oceans.

Imagine drawing a line around the middle of the earth, as though you were putting a big belt around it. We call that imaginary line the equator. Many world maps and globes have this imaginary line drawn on them; see if you can find it. The sun always shines strongly at the equator, so the land and oceans near the equator stay warm all year round. Do you remember learning about the warm rainforests? They are all near the earth's equator.

The top and the bottom of the earth are called poles. What's on top? The North Pole, near to where polar bears live. And down on the bottom is the South Pole. The sun never shines as strongly at the poles as it does at the equator. In fact, the water at the poles stays frozen all year round.

If you look at a globe, you might think that people living near the South Pole must feel as if they were standing upside down. But in fact, standing up near the South Pole feels just like standing up in your own neighbourhood – feet down, head up, only colder!

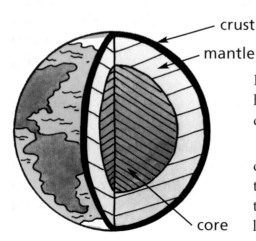

crust

mantle

core

Inside the Earth

Have you ever started digging a hole and wondered how far you could go? What would it be like to dig deep down into the earth?

Scientists have used special equipment to drill deep down into the earth. They have found out that the earth has many layers. If you could slice right through the earth, you would see the different layers, all the way to the centre, like the picture.

The outermost layer is called the crust. That's the surface of the earth, the part we live on. Mountains and valleys, rivers and deserts, oceans and continents make up the earth's crust. The crust is a thin outer coating compared to the other layers inside. Beneath the crust lies a thick layer of hot, melted rock called the mantle. The deeper the mantle, the hotter it gets. At the centre of the earth burns a core of hot melted rock. No one has ever travelled through the earth's mantle to the core. No one would want to! It gets hotter than 5,000 degrees Celsius down there!

Sometimes holes open in the earth's crust. When these holes open, hot gas and liquid can escape from deep down in the earth.

In some places, boiling hot steam explodes out of a hole in the ground, spewing high up into the air. Do you know what we call this? A geyser. In the state of Wyoming in America, at least two hundred geysers shoot up out of the ground. The most famous one shoots 50,000 litres of water – boiling hot, so it's steam – 50 metres up, far above the treetops around it. For a long time, this geyser has seemed to shoot up regularly, nearly once an hour, so people call it 'Old Faithful'.

Do you see how small the people are compared with 'Old Faithful'?

Icelandic volcano Eyjafjallajökull erupting in 2010

At other places, hot, molten, liquid rock bursts out of the ground. What do we call this feature? A volcano. Volcanoes give us an idea of what it's like beneath the earth's crust. We know that the molten rock comes from deep down inside the earth's mantle layer. Then it can spurt out through the top of a mountain. The molten rock, called lava, can travel in fiery streams down the mountainside, burning everything in its path.

Sometimes a volcano can erupt, then remain quiet for many years, and then erupt again. In 2010, a volcano in Iceland that hadn't erupted for almost a hundred years threw so much ash up into the air that aeroplanes couldn't fly in parts of Europe for several days.

The Earth Makes Different Kinds of Rocks

The next time you have a chance, pick up a handful of rocks and look at them. You'll notice how different rocks can be. Some seem all one colour, while others are streaked with different colours. Some are dark, while some are light; some are so light that you can almost see through them, like looking through a foggy glass. Some are so smooth that it almost makes you want to rub them, while others are rough and jagged.

So many different rocks – granite, quartz, coal, shale, limestone and many more. Scientists put each of these different rocks into one of three groups, depending on how the rock was formed. Here are the names that scientists use for the three types of rocks. Like the names of dinosaurs, they're big words, and fun to say aloud. Ready?

Igneous [IG-nee-us]
Sedimentary [sed-ee-MEN-tarr-ee]
Metamorphic [met-ah-MORE-fik]

Granite

Marble

Let's see what those fancy names mean. Igneous means 'made by fire'. Granite is one of the most common igneous rocks. It is made underground, where it's very hot. Some igneous rocks come from volcanoes. Volcanoes have been erupting on earth for millions of years. Whenever lava flowed out, it cooled and hardened into rock. Pumice is an igneous rock that's full of little holes. Pumice is so light that it floats in water!

Sedimentary means 'made by settling down'. Sometimes, often under the sea or in a riverbed, lots of little rocks and sea shells settle down on top of one another. Over thousands and thousands of years, they press down until they form one big rock.

Sandstone is a sedimentary rock. You can see and feel the grains of sand that settled down together to form sandstone.

Metamorphic means 'made through change'. Deep inside the earth, powerful forces and intense heat are squeezing and cooking

Sandstone

the material down there. All this squeezing and cooking can change rocks. For example, look what can happen to limestone, which is a kind of sedimentary rock. Deep in the earth, limestone can get heated and squeezed and changed into a rock called marble. Marble is a metamorphic rock: it was made through change. Some artists like to make statues out of marble. Marble is often used for the walls and stairs of big buildings. People like to build with it because of its beautiful streaks of colour, formed over long periods of time by forces under the earth.

The Great Sphinx that we saw on page 131 was made from sandstone.

The Earth's Important Minerals

Just as it takes different ingredients to bake a cake, lots of different ingredients also go into making rocks. Each of these ingredients is a mineral. Most rocks are made up of more than one kind of mineral.

We can find lots of different minerals in the earth. Gold is a mineral. When you think of gold, maybe you think of jewellery or pirate's treasure. For thousands of years, people have used gold to make the things they consider most valuable, such as coins, rings and crowns. All the gold in the world comes from the earth.

You can see some golden jewellery from the Staffordshire Hoard on page 167.

Uncut diamonds

Diamonds are minerals. Have you ever seen a diamond in a ring or necklace? Just like gold, all the diamonds in the world come from the earth. In the earth they don't look like they do in a ring or necklace: it takes a lot of work to make them so pretty and shiny. People use diamonds for more than jewellery. Diamonds are harder than any other rock or mineral, so people use diamonds to help cut other rocks!

Quartz is a mineral. Quartz is much more common than gold and diamonds. In many places, you can find quartz lying on the ground. Quartz comes in many forms, such as white quartz, rose quartz, amethyst and tiger's eye. Quartz crystals are valuable for keeping clocks and watches accurate.

People have learned how to find minerals in the earth and how to dig them out, or mine them. We mine the mineral called halite, then use it to make salt for our food. We mine the mineral iron ore, then use it to make steel, which goes into cars, refrigerators and bicycles. We mine the mineral copper, then use it to make cooking pots, electrical wiring and pennies.

Quartz

Stories About Scientists

Edward Jenner

Today children around the world receive vaccinations. Do you remember being vaccinated? The injection may have hurt a little, but it helped a lot to keep you safe from serious diseases.

Vaccinations work in a way that might surprise you. Most keep you from getting a disease by actually putting a little bit of the disease germs in you. Your body fights these germs, and from then on your body is ready to keep you from catching the disease.

More than two hundred years ago, before anyone knew about vaccination, many people died of a disease called smallpox. They would get terrible sores on their bodies, and those who managed to survive could end up blind, weak and covered with scars for the rest of their lives. But those who survived knew they would never catch the disease again – just the way you know that after you have had chicken pox, you will never catch it again.

Doctors in those days started thinking that maybe, just maybe, they could figure out a way to make people catch a mild case of smallpox. Then they might get a little poorly, but they would never catch smallpox again. So doctors tried taking a little fluid from a sick person's smallpox sore and putting it into a cut on a well person's arm. Sometimes this worked. The person would get a little sick but soon feel better, and then he would never catch smallpox again. But sometimes the people got very sick, and even died. In those cases, it seemed as if the doctor was spreading the smallpox disease.

The problem concerned Edward Jenner, an English doctor. Once, when he met a woman who worked on a dairy farm, she showed him her hands; they were covered with the marks of old sores. But she told Jenner: 'It can't be the smallpox. I've already had the cowpox. Everybody knows you never get smallpox after you've had cowpox.'

Jenner had seen cattle with the disease called cowpox. The cows got sores on their body, just as humans with smallpox did. Jenner had seen people with cowpox, too. They got a little poorly, and they got a few sores, but then they got better. Jenner began asking questions and studying. He started to think that it might be true: by catching cowpox, a person could keep from catching smallpox.

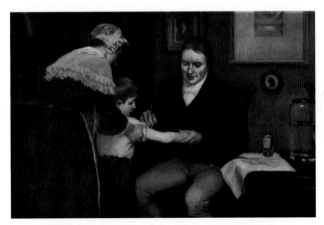

Edward Jenner trying his smallpox experiment with James Phipps

Finally Jenner was ready to try an experiment. On 14 May 1796, he took fluid from a cowpox sore and put it into a cut on the arm of an eight-year-old boy named James Phipps. James caught cowpox. He came down with a fever, headaches and sores, but he soon got better. Now came the important and risky next step: on 1 July, Jenner infected the boy with fluid from a smallpox sore. For days and weeks, Jenner watched and waited. James stayed healthy.

The cowpox kept him from catching smallpox.

Jenner told other doctors about his discovery, but at first they didn't believe him. But Jenner believed in his idea, and he kept giving people cowpox. He believed so much, he even gave his own baby son the cowpox germs. Finally he wrote a book explaining his discovery. He called it 'vaccination', from the Latin word *vacca* for 'cow'.

As Jenner vaccinated more people successfully, his work became well known. King George IV asked to be vaccinated by him and also made Jenner his Physician Extraordinary. Soon it became the fashion to be injected by Jenner!

Other scientists learned from Edward Jenner's ideas, and they worked to make vaccinations even safer and more reliable. Today vaccinations protect us against many serious diseases, such as polio, tuberculosis and measles. Jenner's bold experiments, and the work of the scientists who learned from his ideas, have helped to save many, many lives.

Louis Pasteur

Louis Pasteur

Take a look at the label on almost any carton of milk and you're likely to see the word PASTEURISED [PASS-chuh-rized]. What does that mean? Let's find out by meeting Louis Pasteur [pass-TUR].

Louis Pasteur was born in 1822 in a little town in France. As he grew up, he loved to paint. He loved to look at the world around him. When he went to the university in Paris, he turned his attention to looking through a microscope. A microscope makes things look a lot bigger; it lets you see things you can't see just with your eyes. Looking through a microscope, Pasteur observed a living world in a drop of water. He saw and drew pictures of the tiny living creatures – he called them 'microbes' or 'germs' – that squirmed in the drop of water.

One day a winemaker came into the laboratory, hoping that someone could help him solve a problem. 'Sometimes my wine tastes delicious, but sometimes it turns sour,' he said to Pasteur. 'Can you help me find out why?' Pasteur put some drops of the wine under the microscope. He noticed that the sour wine had some unusual germs. If he could kill these germs, maybe he could keep the wine from turning sour. He experimented with different ways to kill the germs. He tried freezing, then electric shock. But in the end, heating the wine seemed to work best. The winemaker tried it, and every bottle of wine tasted good.

Pasteur's idea worked for other people, too. When dairies heated milk, it didn't go sour so quickly. When breweries heated beer, it tasted better. People called the process 'pasteurisation' – heating a liquid to kill harmful germs. Aren't you glad that the milk you drink has been pasteurised?

Louis Pasteur's good ideas didn't stop there. He also worked on vaccinations, building upon the discoveries of Edward Jenner. He developed a vaccine to treat rabies, a serious disease carried by some dogs, wolves and other wild animals. Rabies made the animals vicious, and if they bit a person, the person would get terribly ill and die. Pasteur was still experimenting with his rabies vaccine when one day a sick little boy named Joseph Meister was brought to Pasteur. Joseph's parents said: 'We know we are taking a risk, letting you experiment on him, but he will die of rabies soon unless you try your medicine.' Joseph Meister was the first person to receive a rabies vaccine and it worked. In a few weeks he was feeling well.

Louis Pasteur's countrymen recognised how important his discoveries were to the health of the world. They honoured him by building a great laboratory, called the Pasteur Institute, where they could continue the work Pasteur had begun. Later, a man came to work at the Institute, taking care of one of the buildings: a man named Joseph Meister, who recognised that he owed his life to the great scientist, Louis Pasteur.

Thomas Edison

Do you like being able to turn on a light when it's dark? Do you like films? Do you enjoy listening to music on an MP3 player? If you like any of these things, you have a reason to say: 'Thanks, Thomas Edison!'

Born in Ohio in the United States in 1847, Thomas Alva Edison had a restless mind. As a child, he was always asking questions that confused many adults. He wanted to know how things worked, and if someone couldn't tell him, well, he would just figure it out for himself. He experimented with chemicals, batteries and wires. Sometimes his experiments got out of hand: he got into trouble when he set things on fire or sent broken glass flying into the air!

Thomas Edison with one of his inventions: the phonograph

As he grew up, Thomas Edison was fascinated by the new science of electricity. He began inventing new machines, such as an electric stock-ticker for printing share prices and a two-way telegraph machine that used electricity to send and receive news in New York City offices. People began to believe in Edison and his inventions. Finally he had enough money to build a science laboratory in Menlo Park, New Jersey, where he and his helpers could work day and night on new inventions.

One day Edison invited his friends into his lab to see a new invention. It looked like a big metal drum with a handle. He turned the handle, and as he did so he said: 'Mary had a little lamb.' He adjusted the machine, then turned the handle again. The machine made a noise, then it played back the words 'Mary had a little lamb'! Edison had invented the first phonograph. Today we download music onto MP3 players, but it all began with the ideas of Thomas Edison. People began calling him 'the Wizard of Menlo Park'.

Next, Edison put his mind to the problem of electric light. For hundreds of years, the only things that people had to light their way in the dark were oil lamps, candles or fire. Using fire for light was not very safe or clean, so people began to try to find a way to use electricity to make light. But so far, no one had found a safe, easy and inexpensive way to do it. Edison asked a glass-blower to make him a round bulb with a long neck. Inside the bulb he placed a thin wire. He connected the wire to a source of electricity. The wire glowed – but then it burned out, very fast. He tried making the other wires out of many different materials. For months everything he tried would not work: all the wires just burned out. People began to wonder if maybe the Wizard of Menlo Park had lost his magic touch. But Edison didn't give up. He kept on trying until he finally got it right.

He sent electricity through a wire in a bulb, and the electricity lit up the wire – and it didn't burn out! He had invented the light bulb. He built a small electric power factory at Menlo Park and put his new light bulbs in lamps all around his laboratories. Soon people from all over the world came to see this wonderful new marvel: electric light – a clean, steady light without flame, without smoke!

Thomas Edison's mind jumped to another project. He thought: 'If I can record sound, perhaps I can record pictures, too.' He invented a machine that moved a strip of film pictures past a light and projected the pictures onto a wall. This was the first film! It wasn't very exciting – it showed a man sneezing – but people were so amazed to see moving pictures that they gladly watched that man sneeze over and over again!

The phonograph, the light bulb and the motion picture are considered Thomas Edison's most important inventions. But they are only a few of the more than a thousand things he invented! What a genius! But as Edison himself said: 'Genius is one percent inspiration and ninety-nine percent perspiration.' In other words, it helps to be clever, but it helps a lot more to work hard.

Rosalind Franklin

Rosalind Franklin was born in London in 1920. Like her father, who taught classes about electricity and magnetism, Rosalind Franklin liked learning about science. She also enjoyed Latin and sports.

Franklin was a pioneering woman scientist. She studied at Newnham College at Cambridge University before women were officially awarded the same degrees that men received. She studied chemistry and, just like you, learned about the atoms and molecules that make up matter.

Rosalind Franklin

Later, Franklin worked at King's College London in a scientific laboratory. She was the only experienced researcher there who had done experiments on deoxyribonucleic [dee-OX-ee-REE-bow-new-CLAY-ic] acid, or DNA. DNA is found inside plant and animal cells and stores the information that controls how we develop.

Franklin began new experiments to learn about the shape and structure of DNA because no one knew exactly how its atoms are linked or what it looks like. She used X-rays together with a special tube and a magnifying camera to take photographs of short pieces of DNA. Another scientist said that Franklin's pictures were 'amongst the most beautiful X-ray photographs of any substance ever taken'.

Franklin was one of several scientists working separately to discover the shape of DNA.

Others were her colleague Maurice Wilkins at King's College London, and James Watson and Francis Crick at Cambridge. When Watson and Crick visited the labs at King's College London, Wilkins showed them some of Franklin's X-ray photos of DNA.

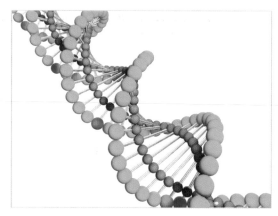

DNA's double-helix shape

From her X-ray photos, Franklin found that DNA has the shape of a double-helix that twists around itself like a braid of plaited hair. Watson and Crick used Franklin's photos to make a model of DNA, which they finished a few days after Franklin had made her discovery. They also concluded that DNA has a double-helix shape.

Watson and Crick published their findings about DNA in an article in *Nature*, a scientific journal, in 1953, but their article only hinted that they made their discovery based on studying Franklin's photos. Many people feel that they did not give Franklin the credit she deserved although she was actually the first to discover the shape of DNA. However, at that time, Watson and Crick were credited with the discovery and became famous for it.

In the mid-1950s, Franklin became very ill with cancer, and she died in 1958. Although Franklin, Wilkins, Watson and Crick separately published their very important discoveries of the shape of DNA in 1953, only Watson, Crick and Wilkins received the Nobel Prize for this discovery in 1962 because Nobel Prizes cannot be given to anyone who has died.

Although Watson, Crick and Wilkins received most of the credit for the discovery of the double-helix structure of DNA, Rosalind Franklin made key contributions. Over time, her work has been recognised and she is now remembered for her important contributions to the discovery of the shape of DNA.

Quentin Blake's illustration showing the discovery of the shape of DNA

Suggested Resources

Living Things and Their Habitats

Vivian French, *Caterpillar Butterfly* (Walker) 2008

Lynn Huggins-Cooper, *Minibeasts* (Franklin Watts) 2008

Claire Llewellyn, *Animal Life* (Franklin Watts) 2012

Caroline Pitcher and Jackie Morris, *Lord of the Forest* (Frances Lincoln) 2004

Patricia Whitehouse, *Flowers* (Raintree) 2009

Dinosaurs

Philip Ardagh, *Henry's House: Dinosaurs* (Scholastic) 2009

Caroline Bingham, *Dinosaur Encyclopedia* (Dorling Kindersley) 2011

Dougal Dixon, *Explorers – Dinosaurs* (Kingfisher) 2010

Annabel Savery, *It's Amazing – Dinosaurs* (Franklin Watts) 2011

Oceans and Undersea Life

Katie Daynes, *1001 Things to Spot in the Sea* (Usborne) 2009

Anna Milbourne, *Under the Sea* (Usborne) 2007

Deborah Underwood, *Hiding in the Oceans* (Raintree) 2011

Human Body

Katie Lennard, *Little Genius: Digestion* (Red Fox) 2009

Sally Morgan, *Taste* (Wayland) 2009

Mandy Suhr, *I Am Growing* (Wayland) 2009

Electricity and Magnetism

Jacqui Bailey, *How Do We Use Electricity* (Franklin Watts) 2010

Jacqui Bailey, *What Does a Magnet Do?* (Franklin Watts) 2010

Terry Jennings, *It's Electricity* (Franklin Watts) 2009

Julian Rowe, *Active Science: Flying High* (Franklin Watts) 2004

Astronomy

Angela Aylmore, *I Like Outer Space* (Raintree) 2008

Mike Goldsmith, *Planet Earth* (Kingfisher) 2010

Chris Oxlade, *The Sun* (Wayland) 2009

Leonie Pratt, *Planet Earth* (Usborne) 2007

Inside the Earth

Jacqui Bailey, *A Drop in the Ocean* (Black) 2003

Jen Green, *Rocks and Soil* (Wayland) 2007

Charlotte Guillain, *Earth* (Raintree) 2010

Helen Orme, *The Weather* (Ticktock) 2003

Illustration and Photo Credits

From The Bridgeman Art Library

Sir Lawrence Alma-Tadema (1836-1912), *The Finding of Moses by Pharaoh's Daughter,* 1904 (oil on canvas). Private Collection / The Bridgeman Art Library: **140**

Albrecht Dürer (1471-1528), *Hare,* 1502 (w/c on paper). Graphische Sammlung Albertina, Vienna, Austria / The Bridgeman Art Library: **190**

Hans Holbein the Younger (1497/8-1543), *Portrait of Edward VI as a Child,* c.1538 (oil on panel). National Gallery of Art, Washington DC, USA / The Bridgeman Art Library: **193 (a)**

Peter Jackson (1922-2003), *When They Were Young: Mozart and his Music,* 1966 / Private Collection / Look and Learn / The Bridgeman Art Library: **206**

Claude Monet (1840-1926), *The Beach at Trouville,* 1870 (oil on canvas). National Gallery, London, UK / The Bridgeman Art Library: **184**

Cott Nero D IV f.27 Incipit page to the Gospel of St. Matthew with decorated letters 'LIB', from the Lindisfarne Gospels, 710–721 (vellum) by English School, (8th century). British Library, London, UK / © British Library Board / The Bridgeman Art Library: **183**

Patrick Nicolle (1907-95), *Compilation of the Domesday Book.* Private Collection / The Bridgeman Art Library: **178**

Pablo Picasso (1881-1973), *Portrait of Sylvette,* 1954 (oil on canvas). Private Collection / Giraudon / © Succession Picasso, DACS, London 2012 / The Bridgeman Art Library: **188 (a)**

Pablo Picasso (1881-1973), *Sylvette, 20th May 1954* (oil on panel). Private Collection / Lefevre Fine Art Ltd., London / © Succession Picasso, DACS, London 2012 / The Bridgeman Art Library: **188 (b)**

Thutmose at Tell el-Amarna. Bust of Queen Nefertiti, front view, Egyptian 18th Dynasty c.1567-1320 BC (painted limestone). Aegyptisches Museum, SMPK, Berlin / The Bridgeman Art Library: **180**

Vincent van Gogh (1853-90), *Self portrait,* 1889 (oil on canvas). Musee d'Orsay, Paris, France / Giraudon / The Bridgeman Art Library: **195**

From other sources:

Diaa Abdelmoneim: **146**

Mark Beech: **17, 18 (a, b), 19 (a, b), 20 (a, b), 21, 22 (a, b), 23 (b), 25, 26 (b), 27 (a, b), 28, 29 (a, b), 31, 32, 33, 34, 35, 36, 37, 45, 48, 50, 51, 52, 55, 57, 66, 67, 68, 69, 71, 76, 79, 82, 85, 93, 95, 97, 99, 101, 102, 103, 105, 118, 119 (a-c), 120 (a-c), 121, 211, 219, 222, 223 (a, b), 224, 226, 229, 232**

Quentin Blake / A P Watt Ltd.: **336 (b)**

Ernest Board (1877-1934), *Dr Jenner Performing His First Vaccination,* 1796 (oil on canvas). Wellcome Library, London: **331**

British Museum Images, Sutton Hoo Shoulder Clasp, 7th century. British Museum, London. © Trustees of the British Museum: **182**

Louisa Buller / Press Association Images: **151 (a)**

Nick Butterworth, 'Pussycat, Pussycat, Where Have You Been?' from *B.B. Blacksheep and Co,* (c) 1981: **26a**

Daniel Buxton, Birmingham Museum and Art Gallery / Portable Antiquities: **167 (b)**

Jon Callas: **167 (c)**

Albert Cesare / Press Association Images: **216**

Paul Collicutt / Gail McIntosh: **288**

Geoff Dallimore: **164 (b)**

Michal Daniel, Minnesota Opera's 2010 Production of *Cinderella*, Minnesota, USA / © Michal Daniel for Minnesota Opera, 2010: **214 (a)**

Fabien Dany: **152 (a)**

Patrick Dugan: **152 (b)**

Theresa Elvin: **215 (a)**

Peter Firmin: **106, 107, 108, 109 (a, b), 110, 111, 112 (a, b), 113**

Charles Folkard: **86 (a), 86 (b), 87, 91, 92**

Charles Folkard / Mary Evans Picture Library: **86 (c), 88 (a, b)**

Sudha Ganapathi: **147**

Steve Henry: **212, 227, 231, 239, 241, 245 (a, b), 246, 256, 259, 269, 271 (a), 287, 304 (b), 305 (a, b), 307 (a), 309, 310 (a), 315, 316 (a), 321, 324 (a, b), 326 (a, b)**

David Hockney, *The Road to York through Sledmere,* 1997 (oil on canvas, 48" x 60"), © David Hockney (photo Richard Schmidt): **189**

Gerard Hoffnung, Hoffnung Partnership: **204 (b)**

William Hogarth (1697-1764), *Self-Portrait at an Easel,* c. 1757 (oil on canvas). National Portrait Gallery, London / © National Portrait Gallery, London: **194**

Luke Jefford: **238, 265 (a), 276**

Dan Kass, ImagesofAnthropology.com: **202 (a)**

Bob Kirchman: **300 (b), 316 (b), 317, 318**

Edward Lear: **24 (a), 24 (b)**

Tanya Lubicz-Nawrocka: **271 (b, c), 272 (a, b), 273 (a, b, d)**

Gail McIntosh: **23 (a), 30, 39, 40, 41, 43, 73, 80, 114, 186, 288, 293, 297, 299, 301, 302 (a), 303 (a, b), 304 (a, c), 311, 322, 325**

Neil Munns / Press Association Images: **320 (a)**

NASA: **319, 320 (b)**

Mark Otton: **127, 148, 153, 156 (a), 159, 162, 166, 170, 176 (a), 298** and owls *passim*

Harold John Phillips: **164 (a)**

Photos.com: **2, 4, 11, 15, 126, 128, 129, 130 (a, b), 131, 132, 134 (a, b), 136 (b, c), 137, 139, 143, 150, 151 (b), 154, 155, 160 (a, b), 161, 163, 164, 165, 168, 173, 175, 181, 200 (a-g), 201 (a-c), 202 (b-f), 203 (a-c), 204 (a), 205, 215 (b), 240, 244 (a, b), 245 (c, d), 248, 253, 255, 263, 264, 265 (b), 266 (a, b), 267, 273 (c, e), 274, 275, 277 (a, b), 278 (a-d), 279 (a, b), 282 (a, b), 284, 286, 289, 290 (a, b), 291 (a, b), 292, 294, 295, 300 (a), 302 (b, c), 307 (b), 310 (b), 312 (a, b), 313, 314, 327 (a, b), 328 (a, b), 329, 330 (a, b), 334 (b), 336 (a)**

Providence Lithograph Company: **141**

Rembrandt van Rijn (1606-1669), *Self-portrait in a Flat Cap,* 1642. The Royal Collection, London. Supplied by Royal Collection Trust / © HM Queen Elizabeth II, 2012: **193 (b)**

Paula Rego (1935), *Crivelli's Garden (The Visitation),* 1990. The National Gallery, London. Supplied by The National Gallery, London / © Paula Rego: **196**

RMN - GP (Agence Photographique de la Réunion des Musées Nationaux et du Grand Palais): **135**

David Rowan / Birmingham Museum and Art Gallery: **167 (a)**

Mario Sánchez: **133**

E. H. Shephard: **59, 60, 62, 65**

Stomp (www.stomponline.com): **220**

Les Stone, International Bird Rescue Research Center (IBRRC): **301 (a)**

Gaspard-Félix Tournachon (1820-1910), *Louis Pasteur,* 1895. Dibner Library of the History of Science and Technology, Washington, DC, USA: **332**

Hamo Thornycroft (1850-1925), *King Alfred the Great,* 1899 (bronze) Winchester: **169**

United States Library of Congress / Wikimedia Commons: **218, 334 (a)**

Vincent van Gogh (1853-1890), *The Good Samaritan,* 1890 (oil on canvas). Kröller-Müller Museum, Otterlo, The Netherlands: **144**

Johannes Vermeer (1632-1675), *The Music Lesson,* 1662-1665 (oil on canvas), The Royal Collection, London. Supplied by Royal Collection Trust / © HM Queen Elizabeth II, 2012: **191**

Leonardo da Vinci (1452-1519), *Mona Lisa,* 1503-1506 (oil on panel) / Louvre, Paris, France: **192**

James A. McNeill Whistler (1834-1903), *Arrangement in Grey and Black No. 1* (also called *Portrait of the Artist's Mother*), 1871 (oil on canvas). Musée d'Orsay, Paris: **185**

Wikimedia Commons: **134 (c), 136 (a), 144, 149, 169, 174, 176 – 177, 214 (b), 296, 335**

Anders Beer Wilse: **157**

The Zuits: **217**

Text Credits and Sources

Poems

'Cats Sleep Anywhere' by Eleanor Farjeon. © The Estate of Eleanor Farjeon. Used with permission of David Higham Associates.

'Hope' from Collected Poems of Langston Hughes (Vintage) by Langston Hughes. © The Estate of Langston Hughes. Used with permission of David Higham Associates.

'I Know All the Sounds That the Animals Make' from *Something Big Has Been Here* by Jack Prelutsky. © Jack Prelutsky. Used with permission of HarperCollins Children's Division.

'Jumbo Jet' by Spike Milligan. © Spike Milligan Productions. Used with permission of Spike Milligan Productions.

'Rope Rhyme' from *Honey, I love and Other Poems* by Eloise Greenfield. © Eloise Greenfield. Used with permission of Eloise Greenfield.

'Scissors' from *Please Mrs. Butler* by Allan Ahlberg. © Penguin Group. Used with permission of Penguin Group.

Stories

'All Stories Are Anansi's', adapted from *The Hat-Shaking Dance and Other Tales from the Gold Coast* by Harold Courlander (Harcourt, Brace & World, Inc.) 1957.

'The Boy at the Dike', adapted from 'The Leak in the Dike' in *Everyday Classics Third Reader* by Franklin Baker and Ashley Thorndike (Macmillan) 1920.

'Brer Rabbit and the Tar Baby', adapted from *Uncle Remus and his Legends of the Old Plantation* by Joel Chandler Harris (David Bogue) 1881.

'The Frog Prince', adapted from *Grimm's Household Tales*, translated and edited by Margret Hunt (George Bell and Sons) 1884.

'Hansel and Gretel', adapted from *Grimm's Household Tales*, translated and edited by Margret Hunt (George Bell and Sons) 1884.

Index